Foreign Trade and U.S. Policy

Leland B. Yeager
David G. Tuerck

Supported in part by the
Center for International Business,
Pepperdine University,
Los Angeles, California

The Praeger Special Studies program—
utilizing the most modern and efficient book
production techniques and a selective
worldwide distribution network—makes
available to the academic, government, and
business communities significant, timely
research in U.S. and international economic, social, and political development.

Foreign Trade and U.S. Policy

The Case for Free International Trade

PRAEGER SPECIAL STUDIES IN INTERNATIONAL BUSINESS, FINANCE, AND TRADE

Praeger Publishers   New York   Washington   London

Library of Congress Cataloging in Publication Data

Yeager, Leland B
    Foreign trade and U.S. policy.

    (Praeger special studies in international business,
finance, and trade)
    Includes bibliographical references and index.
    1. Free trade and protection—Free trade.
2. Free trade and protection. 3. United States—
Commercial policy. I. Tuerck, David G., joint
author. II. Title.
HF1713.Y38   382.7'1'0973   75-19832
ISBN 0-275-56270-0
ISBN 0-275-89510-6 student ed.

PRAEGER PUBLISHERS
111 Fourth Avenue, New York, N.Y. 10003, U.S.A.

Published in the United States of America in 1976
by Praeger Publishers, Inc.

As this book goes to press, the words "trade war" are in the wind. Protectionist agitation for higher U.S. duties on automobiles, steel, and a wide variety of other goods provokes threats of retaliation from the EEC and of counterretaliation from the United States. The Trade Act of 1974, which was supposed to liberalize trade, may have done more to liberalize import relief. As a result, the current Geneva trade talks and the very existence of GATT—which has long been (for better or worse) a symbol of Free World commitment to expanded international trade—are said to be in danger.

This state of affairs seems quite different from the one prevailing when we published our *Trade Policy and the Price System* ten years ago. Then the Trade Expansion Act of 1962 was regarded as a symbol of commitment to the idea of freer trade, and the Kennedy Round of Geneva trade talks was progressing toward a successful conclusion. Then, also, the United States had yet to suffer the disruptions of the war in Vietnam and the sustained period of combined inflation and recession that ensued and from which we have still not fully recovered. While a book on free trade might have seemed to lack urgency then because its principles were generally accepted, events of the first half of the 1970s show that protectionist sentiment is alive and resurgent.

Although incorporating portions of our original work, this book is sufficiently revised to justify—and perhaps require—the new title. Having allowed so many years to pass since our first writing, we found it necessary to expand our coverage to several issues—the multinational corporation, the oil crisis, effective protection—that were not in vogue before but which we could not ignore here. In many respects, however, we have retained our original format. Although the book focuses on the single issue of free trade versus protection, we do not consider that old issue of dominant importance in its own right. Rather, we try to give the reader an understandable exposition of the principles of international trade policy in particular and of the price system in general. Our examples deal mainly with the United States (and we do, on that account, provide a summary of the major elements of U.S. trade policy), but our analysis is general enough in scope to apply widely. Although we have not avoided technicalities of substance and do go well beyond the usual textbook examination of tariff arguments, we still have avoided diagrams and mathematics in favor of plain English. Also, we have found that, over the years, there has been no reduction in the volume of comic relief provided by Congressional hearings and similar sources.

Again we would like to thank Miss V. G. Peterson of the Robert Schalkenbach Foundation for early encouragement and Professor Carl McGuire of the University of Colorado for his helpful comments on a draft of *Trade Policy and the Price System*. For this writing we are indebted to Dr. David R. Reagan, who, as Executive Director of the Center for International Business, gave support and encouragement, and to Mr. Robert Cornell of the U.S. International Trade Commission, who responded to our requests for information. Our special thanks and appreciation go to Gay Tuerck, who typed several drafts, helped with the proofreading, and generally labored with David Tuerck through his share of the work.

CONTENTS

Foreign Trade and U.S. Policy

1

PROTECTIONISM IN THEORY AND PRACTICE

This book examines two competing economic ideologies: free trade and protectionism. It asks whether the authority of economics may legitimately be enlisted in support of free trade. How intellectually respectable is it to advocate free trade nowadays? Is it really true, as a former chairman of the Council of Economic Advisers has said, that "the economic welfare of the producer-consumer is maximized by the freest possible trade, both domestic and international"?[1]

CHOOSING BETWEEN ECONOMIC SYSTEMS

It may be well to issue some warnings about the intellectual climate of the regions we propose to explore. In the first place, it is not fashionable nowadays (except among some "extremists" of right and left) to go around professing an ideology. The prevailing vogue is a "pragmatism" or "eclecticism" that shuns mention of any ideology in connection with economic issues.

Second, we are asking what many people would regard as a rhetorical question. When pressed or inclined to identify themselves with an ideology, such people would say that, in principle, they support free (or freer) trade. Since the initiation of reciprocal trade negotiations over forty years ago, free trade has become a prevailing economic ethic, if not the prevailing economic reality. No one favors protection*ism*, just protection for himself or his constituents.

Third, the question of free trade, particularly free *international* trade, is viewed in some quarters as a dead issue. Despite a trend toward lower tariffs, the growth of nontariff trade barriers and multinational firms is said to have rendered pointless any debate over free trade versus protectionism. The question, according to this point of view, is not *whether* the government should protect people from the exigencies of the marketplace, but *how* it should do so.

As we said, however, this book examines the case for and against free trade. Like it or not, there are economic ideologies to consider in deciding economic issues. In the pages that follow, we shall have occasion to mention the Smoot-Hawley Tariff of 1930 and the Burke-Hartke proposals, around which protectionist sentiment crystalized in the early 1970s. These measures flank a period of tariff liberalization during which protectionism, as an *ism,* grew generally dormant. Yet they so challenged the ethic and the reality of free trade that it is difficult now to predict the course of U.S. trade policy. If the economic ills of the mid-1970s (which have been relatively mild by the standards of the Great Depression) should persist into the latter part of the decade, then Burke-Hartke may presage future, possibly more effective, rounds of protectionist agitation.

We shall be concerned primarily with the case for free international trade, in part because of this prospect and in part because the foreign trade sector has always been especially subject to governmental regulation. However, the issue of free or restricted international trade may be most important as a test of a country's overall economic understanding. In this respect it does not matter that international trade accounts for only a relatively small share of U.S. economic activity. The reasoning used by members of Congress to reach some of their opinions about international trade provides insight to their thinking on domestic policy as well. For these reasons, we shall devote considerable space to the wider domestic and political implications of the free-trade issue.

What is at stake is a choice between economic systems. As we shall argue, it is difficult to protect one economic interest without inviting protection for all. Thus the case for free international trade intertwines with the case for overall economic (and even political) freedom. In a world that abounds with half-baked theories and ill-conceived nostrums, it is timely to reexamine this issue in the light of facts and logic.

WHAT WE MEAN BY "FREE TRADE"

Although the distinction between free trade and protectionism may appear self-evident, we would like to put a few definitions on the record. "Trade" is mutually beneficial exchange between contracting parties. We voluntarily give you something, and you give us something in return. Trade is "free" if it is not regulated by others against the will of the contracting parties. More specifically, free trade means noninterference by government in people's business affairs. For trade that crosses national boundaries, it means reliance on the price-and-profit system and government noninterference in exports, imports, and capital movements.

Free trade is not pure laissez-faire. Persons engaged in trade willingly submit to the laws of contract and therefore to a form of government regulation. But neither is it some eclectic mixture of capitalism and socialism. It is capitalism in which there is minimal participation by government in trade. It does not countenance trade which is inherently immoral (such as murder for hire or sale of government secrets to the enemy), but neither does it presume to protect people from themselves or from the rightful actions of others.

WHAT WE MEAN BY "PROTECTIONISM"

"Protectionism" is the regulation of exchange by noncontracting parties. Generally, it is governmental regulation of the terms or conditions on which one person may trade with another. More narrowly construed, it is the regulation of trade between the residents of different countries for the supposed benefit of certain home-country residents. The methods of regulation are as abundant as the special interests they have been devised to serve.

Tariffs—schedules of duties on imports—are the traditional method. Nowadays, however, and despite much progress toward lower tariffs over the past forty years, many countries impose other barriers to trade.

Among these *nontariff barriers* are certain charges imposed on imports in addition to the normal customs duty. For example, as part of its "Common Agricultural Policy," the European Economic Community imposes a "variable levy" on price-supported farm goods. The levy is set just high enough so that farm goods exported to the EEC do not reduce the prices received by EEC farmers below the levels at which they are officially supported.[2]

Another nontariff charge on imports arises from the U.S. excise tax on distilled spirits, which is levied in such a way that it ordinarily falls more heavily on foreign than on domestic producers. Whereas foreign bottled spirits of 100 proof or less are taxed at a flat rate of $10.50 per gallon, U.S. spirits are taxed at a rate proportional to proof. Thus, for example, a foreign producer would pay the full tax of $10.50 for a gallon of 80 proof bottled whisky while a domestic producer would pay only $8.40 (80 percent of $10.50). Other nontariff charges include the import surcharges that have been imposed by the United States, Denmark, and Britain for balance-of-payments reasons and the requirements in some countries that importers place deposits equaling specified fractions of the value of imported goods in non-interest-bearing accounts for specified terms.[3]

A second, more restrictive kind of nontariff barrier—the *import quota*—directly limits the amount of a commodity that may be imported during a given period of time. The consumer does not enjoy a low price just because a quota rather than a duty restricts the amount of the commodity imported; the spread between the world price and the local price goes to the privileged domestic importers or foreign exporters as a "quota profit" rather than to the government as a tax.

The United States maintains import quotas on peanuts, refined sugar, certain syrups, molasses, cotton, and certain dairy products, including American and cheddar cheese and malted milk. The Meat Import Act of 1964 requires that meat imports be reduced to a "basic limitation" (equal to average imports over the period 1959-1963, adjusted for growth in domestic production), once they exceed that limitation by more than 10 percent. Although no quotas are now in effect under the act, meat imports from Canada have been restricted by Presidential proclamation under the Trade Expansion Act of 1962.

Quantitative restrictions are sometimes placed on *exports* in the name of "national security" or as relief from domestic "shortages." For example, the United States and other countries have maintained an embargo (much relaxed in recent years) on the export of some or all materials to Communist countries. During 1974 the United States temporarily imposed a system of licenses authorizing quotas on the export of soybeans, cottonseed, and related farm products. A contract licensing system for the export of ferrous scrap instituted in 1973 was succeeded the following year by a system of export quotas based on country of destination.

Sometimes exports are restricted as a result of *voluntary agreements* between exporting and importing countries. Such agreements are intended to avoid the even sterner controls explicitly or implicitly threatened by the importing country if "voluntary" restraint is not applied. Thus Australia, New Zealand, and other countries restrained their meat exports to the United States over the period 1968-1971, rather than trigger mandatory quotas under the Meat Import Act.

Japan "voluntarily" restricted its exports of cotton textiles to the United States during the 1950s; but when other countries took advantage of Japan's voluntary restraint by increasing their own exports of cotton textiles, multilateral agreement was deemed necessary. Thus, the United States took the lead in negotiating the Long-Term Arrangement Regarding International Trade in Cotton Textiles (LTA) of 1962, whose signatories were authorized to enter into bilateral agreements for the limitation of exports to one another. Textile-exporting countries not entering into such agreements risked having import quotas, also authorized by the arrangement, unilaterally imposed on their goods by the importing countries. In fact, the United States invoked its authority to impose unilateral restraints many times during the early years of the LTA precisely in order to persuade most of the exporting countries to enter into bilateral agreements, which they did eventually.

As it happened, the LTA proved inadequate to protect the U.S. textile industry from foreign competition, as the reduced trade in cotton textiles was offset in large part by an expanded trade in manmade and wool textiles. Thus the United States negotiated a number of bilateral, multifiber agreements during the early 1970s and continues to negotiate such agreements under the authority of a multilateral, multifiber arrangement that took effect in 1974.

In addition to meat and textiles, "voluntary" restraints have been imposed on a wide variety of other exports to the United States, including steel from Japan and the EEC, strawberries and tomatoes from Mexico, canned mushrooms from Taiwan, and footwear from Korea. By 1971, Japan reportedly imposed voluntary quantitative controls on "several dozen items to a number of countries," including bicycles to the United States, Canada, and Mexico; screws, umbrellas, and umbrella ribs to the United States and Western Europe; and silk fabrics, flatware, and binoculars to almost every country in the world.[4] Subsequently, Japan has relaxed some of its self-imposed export restrictions for balance-of-payments reasons.

"Voluntary" agreements fly in the face of U.S. antitrust policy by forcing foreigners to allocate limited markets in the countries from which their goods are "voluntarily" withheld. "No voluntary export control system can work in the absence of an effective cartel in the exporting country," observed Ambassador Carl Gilbert in testimony before Congress. Commenting on the "voluntary" steel agreements, Gilbert expressed concern "about how our steel industry was going to stand up against a very strong cartel, both one in Europe and one in Japan, which we have helped to create."[5] Nevertheless, the Trade Act of 1974, ostensibly intended to promote freer trade, actually encourages the President to negotiate "orderly marketing agreements" for the restriction of foreign exports to the United States.

U.S. *trademark law* allows private firms to operate a nontariff trade barrier with the assistance of customs officials. If a domestic distributor of a foreign-made good is able to have a trademark registered in the United States under his ownership, other domestic distributors will be barred from importing the same goods bearing the same trademark. Thus, a law originally designed mainly to bar imports of foreign items bearing counterfeit American trademarks is sometimes used to keep Americans from buying genuine foreign-made goods except from authorized U.S. distributors.[6] Returning American tourists have been shocked when their purchases were seized without warning. Keeping track of what may and may not be imported, and in what amounts, is difficult enough for customs officials, and more so for private citizens.

Uncertainties due to *customs procedures* harass importers. The Smoot-Hawley Tariff of 1930, much amended but still in effect, says that every article not specifically listed should be taxed as whatever it most closely resembles. Zealous customs officials classify doubtful articles in whatever way makes the duty the highest. The Solomons and metaphysicians of the Court of Customs and Patent Appeals have had to decide questions like the following:

> Whether strips of paper used to make paper toweling cease to be strips when they are very long and made into rolls.
>
> Whether wire "muselets" for holding corks in champagne bottles are metal bottle caps or are miscellaneous small metal articles. (An earlier decision had ruled muselets to be bottle caps, since they had metal disks to keep the wire from cutting into the corks; but the invention of plastic corks requiring no protective disks resurrected the whole momentous issue.)
>
> Whether HO-gauge miniature railroad equipment is or is not "toys," toys being "chiefly used for the amusement of children."
>
> Whether an iconostasis, "a screen or partition which is erected in the sanctuary of a Greek Orthodox Church upon the same platform upon which the altar table stands," is dutiable as an ordinary wooden item or may enter free as a religious shrine.
>
> Whether children's training seats or potties are "chairs" or "other furniture." (The court found that the items were in fact "chairs" and therefore subject to the higher duty.)
>
> Whether or not a stained-glass window depicting the baptism of the infant George Washington is a work of art (and therefore duty-free).[7]*

The uncertainties illustrated by these cases impose a real burden on importers. Some lawsuits are brought by import-competing American manufacturers who, in an apparent effort to harass importers, maintain

---

*In the Washington window case, both sides called expert witnesses to express opinions on what is or is not art. The most famous case of this kind came up in 1927-28, after customs officials had refused the work-of-art classification to *Bird in Space,* an abstract sculpture by the reputable artist Constantin Brancusi and had assessed a 40 percent duty on it as a mere piece of bronze.

that customs officials do not classify the goods in sufficiently high-duty categories.

One of the most notorious U.S. nontariff trade barriers is the American Selling Price (ASP) system of customs valuation. Most U.S. imports are assessed on their "export value" in the country of origin, but for four product categories—benzenoid chemicals, certain rubber-sole footwear, canned clams, and wool knit gloves—the duty is assessed according to the selling price of competitive U.S. products. Interestingly, the ASP system dates back to the Tariff Act of 1922, when it was first applied to the then infant but now $50 billion coal-tar chemical industry.* Since its very purpose is to protect U.S.-made goods from lower priced foreign-made goods, the ASP system causes the amount of duty collected to exceed the amount that would be collected if ordinary valuation procedures were followed. Furthermore, ASP draws complaints from foreigners for making it difficult to calculate what price they can expect to receive for their goods in the United States.

Buy-American rules have been imposed under a hodgepodge of legislation dating back to the Great Depression. U.S. government agencies must buy their supplies from domestic sources unless any additional cost is "unreasonable." Administrative interpretations, modified from time to time, specify what percentages of price differential can count as reasonable and with what exceptions. Most federal agencies apply a 6 or 12 percent margin, though the Department of Defense has adopted the policy of imposing an additional 50 percent margin.

Many states and localities have similar rules. The U.S.-Japan Trade Council has identified 23 states with "intentional Buy-American policies," four of which—Alabama, Illinois, Mississippi, and Maryland—reported a ban on the use of foreign-made steel in state highway and bridge construction. Other states, by statute or administrative decree, exercise a preference for domestically produced goods in general. Pennsylvania enacted a statute in 1968 that forbids the purchase of aluminum or steel manufactured in foreign countries "which discriminate against suppliers, equipment or materials manufactured in Pennsylvania." State officials are supposed to keep a "foreign registry docket" of nations that discriminate in this fashion and to impose the appropriate "reciprocal restrictions."[8]

---

*Ambassador Carl Gilbert, 1970 HW&M III 660-662, reports that, in the same act, the House would have applied ASP to *all* imports but that this was too much for the Senate, which limited its application to coal-tar products and to those products which might eventually be covered by "flexible" tariffs.

The Buy-American idea shades through many gradations from nation-wide policy to local harassment. Some of the state laws—notably California's, which was among the most restrictive—have been declared unconstitutional as an interference with federal prerogatives in the area of international trade. But in the past, state and local governments were quick to take initiatives of their own against foreign goods believed harmful to local interests. Thus in the early 1960s, Alabama restricted purchases of foreign supplies by *private* road-building contractors,[9] and one Southern state required stores selling Japanese textiles to post conspicuous signs proclaiming the shameful fact. Still other examples occur in the form of slogans such as, "Be American, Buy American; The Job You Save May Be Your Own.".

Some states discriminate against not only foreign but also out-of-state goods and services. In addition to the 23 states with intentional Buy-American policies, the U.S.-Japan Trade Council found five—Alaska, Arizona, Arkansas, New Mexico, and Wyoming—that grant a general 5 percent cost preference to in-state bidders. Other states merely reported a preference of an unspecified nature.

Administrative uncertainties can add to the restrictiveness of tariffs and other nontariff trade barriers. Importers must concern themselves not only with trade barriers imposed by statute but also with those that *might* be imposed administratively, through "escape-clause," "antidumping," or "countervailing duty" actions, for example (see below, pp. 126-30, 260-61). The escape clause, routinely included in past trade "expansion" acts, permitted U.S. import-competing industries to get relief from tariff cuts by convincing the Tariff Commission and the President that such cuts had contributed "in major part" to declining profits and employment. The countervailing duty and antidumping laws have made it possible for the same interests to get higher duties on foreign products by showing the existence of foreign subsidies or injury due to below-fair-value sales of those products in the United States. Whereas nontariff trade barriers have come to be recognized in recent years as posing a greater threat to world trade than tariffs themselves, the Trade Act of 1974 actually increases the scope for administrative uncertainties such as these. U.S. import-competing firms are encouraged more than ever to resist foreign penetration of their markets by appealing to the agencies of government for higher trade barriers (see below, pp. 262-63).

Exchange controls and *multiple exchange rates* can serve as protectionist measures, even when not avowedly introduced for that purpose. The government or its agents rations out foreign exchange, making distinctions between prospective buyers and the foreign goods and services they want to buy. Exchange control is usually associated with fixing the foreign-exchange value of the local currency above what it would be in a free market, with the unwanted result that the country's export earnings and thus its capacity to afford imports are smaller than otherwise. Multiple exchange rates further complicate the system by setting different local-currency prices for foreign exchange earned in various ways and to be spent for various purposes. Typically, the government tries to take account of the different degrees of "essentiality" of various imports. Exchange controls and multiple exchange rates have been extensively employed in Latin America and elsewhere but not in the United States, at least not openly.

Numerous other nontariff barriers to international trade could be mentioned, and, indeed, the International Trade Commission study cited above provides a thick volume of information on the subject. We have described some of the barriers that are most likely to receive attention during future trade negotiations, but others, including labeling and marking requirements, health and sanitary standards, and publicly sanctioned discriminatory ocean freight rates may be equally important. In the case of still others, such as border tax adjustments and certain customs-valuation procedures, there exist reasonable differences of opinion about whether the alleged barriers really do discriminate against foreign trade.

Our list of protective barriers can be lengthened by taking into account barriers that are clearly domestic, rather than international, in character. At all levels of government a wide variety of statutes, though purporting to serve the general interest, actually operate to protect their beneficiaries from competition. "Fair-trade" laws, federal and state price supports for agricultural and dairy products, state and local licensing requirements, state bans on advertising the prices of certain goods such as eyeglasses and prescription drugs, labor-union apprenticeship requirements—these are just a few examples of protectionism as practiced in the domestic sector.

The licensing requirements that apply to many professions have produced some of the most bizarre examples of protectionism at the state level. Florida has a large population of Cuban refugees, some of whom have gone to jail for practicing medicine without a license, although they were recognized as qualified doctors at home and although their failure to obtain a license was largely due to their unfamiliarity with the English language. Even native-born doctors complain about Florida's refusal to honor licenses issued by other states. Yet, the Florida Board of Osteopathic Medical Examiners reportedly withheld action against one of its licensees, about whom it had received numerous complaints, until, after two deaths at his hands, the board heard testimony that he had been aided in his diagnoses by a psychic.[10]

In another Florida case, the state Construction Industry Licensing Board attempted in 1973 to fail every one of the 2,149 license applicants who had taken its general contractor's examination. Only after it had been "besieged with indignant complaints" did it relent and allow a majority of the applicants to pass. Medical boards in several states have urged legislation that would require cosmetic ear piercing to be performed only by licensed physicians. Barbers in Iowa have sued to prevent beauticians from cutting men's hair. In Georgia, a state board attempted unsuccessfully to revoke the licenses of optometrists who had been practicing in discount stores and who were on that account said to be guilty of "unprofessional commercialism."[11] A Nebraska regulation, eventually overturned in court, once required each funeral director to keep a prescribed number and variety of caskets in stock, supposedly to ensure the bereaved a large choice but actually to eliminate some competitors. A Georgia law to license photographers, also overturned in court, required a certificate of negative Wasserman test. The list of occupations that have been subject to licensing from time to time and place to place includes, in addition to these examples, threshing-machine operators, dealers in scrap tobacco, egg graders, guide-dog trainers, pest controllers, yacht salesmen, tree surgeons, well diggers, tile layers, potato growers, hair removers, and chiropodists.[12]

Thus, protectionism flourishes at the state as well as the federal level of government and in domestic as well as international trade. It flourishes because each occupational group wants free enterprise for every other occupational group but not for itself. The people who may find themselves barred from an occupation at some time in the future have little influence when restrictive legislation is passed; they may not yet identify themselves with the occupation or may even not yet have been born. The desire of the "ins" to keep the "outs" out has more political influence than the general public interest in competition.

THE PLAN OF THIS BOOK

Having seen just how thoroughly protectionist regulation has pervaded the economic system, we next consider the workings of that system in the absence of such regulation. In Chapters Two and Three, we consider the workings, successes, and failures of a closed economy. Chapters Four and Five narrow the discussion to a consideration of the gains from international trade, both "allocative" and "nonallocative." Chapter Six summarizes the principles of domestic and international finance. Recent monetary developments are examined for their bearing on the free-trade issue.

The remainder of the book is concerned primarily with the case against free trade. Chapter Seven examines the rhetoric and substance of protectionist doctrine. Chapters 8 through 14 develop some protectionist arguments that may be viewed for the most part as sophisticated, if impractical, and Chapter 15 offers some advice to modern free traders for dealing with the case against free trade.

NOTES

1. Gardner Ackley in U.S. Congress, House, *Tariff and Trade Proposals,* Hearings before the Committee on Ways and Means, 91st Cong., 2d Sess., 1970, Part 3, p. 922. (Hereafter, references to these hearings will be abbreviated as in the following example: 1970 HW&M III 922.)

2. U.S. Tariff Commission (now U.S. International Trade Commission), *Trade Barriers* (Washington, D.C.: Government Printing Office, 1974), Chapter VII, pp. 11-18.

3. Ibid., pp. 89, 101-2, 106.

4. Ibid., pp. 241-62.

5. 1970 HW&M 1, p. 146. See also the eloquent condemnation by Charles P. Kindleberger on p. 87 in *Foreign Trade Policy* (papers collected for a subcommittee of the House Ways and Means Committee in 1957; Washington: Government Printing Office, 1958; hereafter cited as *Foreign Trade Policy* (1958). Kindleberger mentions the case in which "we both asked the Swiss to limit exports to this market and prosecuted them for violation of the antitrust laws on the allegation that they had done so."

6. Edward C. Vandenburgh, *Trademark Law and Procedure* (2d ed.; New York: Bobbs-Merrill, 1968), pp. 254-56.

7. *Reports* of the Court of Customs and Patent Appeals, volumes 46ff.

8. "State Barriers to World Trade" (Washington: United States-Japan Trade Council, March, 1973), reprinted in *Trade Reform,* Hearings before the Committee on Ways and Means on the Trade Reform Act of 1973, 93d Cong., 1st Sess., 1973, Part 3, pp. 1051-63. (Hereafter references to these hearings will be abbreviated as in the following example: 1973 HW&M III, 1051-63.)

9. According to testimony of counsel for steel importers in Hearings before the House Ways and Means Committee on the Trade Expansion Act of 1962, Part 6, p. 3598. (Hereafter, references to these hearings will be abbreviated as in 1962 HW&M VI 3598.)

10. "Closed Societies?" *Wall Street Journal,* January 8, 1975, p. 1.

11. Ibid.

12. Walter Gellhorn, *Individual Freedom and Governmental Restraints* (Baton Rouge: Louisiana State University Press, 1956), Chapter 3.

2

THE IDEA OF AN
ECONOMIC SYSTEM

"Practical" men and even some intellectuals like to tease economists for their inability to agree on sweeping issues. While others may make a profession of disagreeing over minutiae, economists are chided for not agreeing on a cure for unemployment, high interest rates, inflation, and declining productivity. Motives may vary: practical men fear having their practical knowledge rendered obsolete and their practical motives exposed, and some intellectuals just have a knack for dispensing economic nihilism and unctuous prose. Nevertheless, such persons commonly hold that economics lacks a scientific core and that, in the end, economic policy is just a matter of personal experience and judgment.

VALUE JUDGMENTS AND POLICY

To appraise such claims, we must make a distinction that may seem abstract but is vital, namely the distinction between "positive propositions" (or "positive analysis") and "value judgments." Both bear on policy recommendations.

Though economics cannot scientifically prove any policy correct or best, neither can any other branch of knowledge. Like physics or medical science, economics explores how different facts and events fit together; it can help predict the effects of a given action. Factual and logical propositions about how things affect each other are the scope of "positive analysis." But again like physics or medical science, economics cannot decree what *ought* to be done. What ought to be done depends not only on what positive analysis tells about the probable effects of various measures but also on how strongly people desire or deplore the various effects (side effects as well as main ones, remote effects as well as immediate ones). Some examples from medicine are obvious: X-rays are advisable for a woman patient, but she happens to be pregnant and the radiation may harm her unborn child; a drug may relieve pain but threaten addiction; an operation will prolong the life of a patient who prefers to die now.

Makers of economic policy also face hard choices. Monetary expansion may help relieve unemployment and high interest rates now but contribute to inflation and still higher interest rates later on (a situation familiar in the mid-1970s). Even when a measure would produce an overwhelmingly desired result, positive analysis alone could not recommend the measure; the judgment about desirability is also necessary. Suppose a marvelous invention enabled the government to abolish earthquakes at negligible cost. Should it do so? Some people would then lose income or face the trouble of switching to other work—seismologists, builders, construction workers, and even some of the present generation of undertakers. Neither geology nor economics can prove scientifically that the harm done to these few people should count less heavily than the benefit to the great majority. Nor can science prove that earthquakes ought to be abolished only if the gainers pay compensation that the losers consider adequate, or, on the other hand, that they ought to be abolished regardless of compensation. In fact, even if *no one* would feel any economic loss from the abolition of earthquakes, someone could still maintain, immune from purely scientific rebuttal, that abolishing them would wickedly interfere with divine punishment.

In short, any policy decision rests in part on nonscientific attitudes about what results are desirable, including attitudes about benefiting some people at others' expense and, in general, about what a "good society" is. These judgments about desirability are called "value judgments" or "values." Disagreement on policy sometimes seems to hinge on values rather than on fact or logic. Anti-intellectuals seize on this disagreement as an excuse for undermining any application of fact or logic.

Since they must enter into policy advice along with positive propositions, do not value judgments unavoidably contaminate scientific work?[1] A researcher who considers a certain state of affairs undesirable might be biased toward seeing facts or reasoning suggesting that it is also unattainable. One who strongly desires the main or intended effects of a certain policy might be biased against seeing any danger of undesirable side effects. Even apart from policy issues, people often have an intellectual vested interest in whatever they have long believed and said. Doesn't bias therefore leave any supposed distinction between value judgments and positive propositions empty after all? No; the distinction stands. In influencing the choice of research projects or in motivating work to test others' results or fill in gaps, bias may be harmless or even useful. As for greater alertness to facts and logic that support rather than undermine one's preconceived notions, this attitude is by no means confined to economics; in the natural sciences, it apparently has a lot to do with disagreement about the effects of aerosol sprays, or DDT, or eating saturated fats. Yet mentioning the possible bias of someone who states a positive proposition is irrelevant to whether the proposition is right or wrong. Knowing a man's biases and motives may give useful hunches about which of his statements most need checking, but the test of any statement is whether it is logically flawless and fits the facts. If it is correct, it is correct regardless of how extreme the man's bias or how low his motives; if it is wrong, pointing out its logical or factual flaws suffices to dispose of it.

It is therefore not true that everything bearing on policy is a matter of taste or judgment. The idea is dangerous that "one man's opinion is as good as another's"; if the respectability of disagreement on values and policy extends to positive propositions as well, it undermines standards of scientific objectivity. When policy disagreements trace to uncertainties on matters of fact and logic, it is anti-intellectual to chalk the disagreements up to differences of equally respectable opinion, since further investigation and discussion might bring agreement closer.

Even when disagreement does seem to hinge on what results people desire, investigation and discussion are not useless. Reasoning combined with positive analysis may reveal hierarchies among value judgments. They may show that some fit together neatly and that others clash, forcing people to choose specific values more in line with their fundamental values. Wanting to eat one's cake is respectable; wanting to save it is respectable; but insisting on both is not. Positive analysis may be able to show that full employment, price-level stability, and strong unions are not compatible with one another (except by extreme and unreliable coincidence), or that free trade, independent national monetary policies, and fixed exchange rates are not compatible. If the analysis of these clashes is correct—a question of fact and logic—then the policy-maker must choose which of the three desirable conditions in each set he values least. In short, neither value judgments nor positive propositions are outside the scope of rational investigation and discussion. Economics may help to systematize value judgments, weeding out both repetitions and contradictions.

This is not the same as deciding which sets of consistent values are right and which are wrong. An irreducible element of nonscientific personal preference remains. Fortunately, discussion will often reveal broadly based consensus on fundamental values. The following propositions seem to underlie the case for free trade: (1) The well-being of individual people, as they themselves see it, is supremely desirable. (Most consider the opportunity for high and rising material standards of living an important, though not necessarily dominant, element in their well-being.) (2) People should have as much freedom to run their own lives as is compatible with the freedom and well-being of others; hence, the ideal in devising political and economic institutions is to minimize possible clashes. (3) Merely being connected with a particular occupation or industry does not give anyone a perpetual right to special favor from the government at the expense of the general public.

While economics cannot decide scientifically between free trade and protection, it can explore how each connects with broader lines of policy and trace how well the probable results of each harmonize with the values that their supporters avow. It cannot settle policy issues but can clarify them by inspecting policy arguments for flaws in fact and logic.

OPPORTUNITY COSTS AND PRICES

The economic case for free trade is the same as the case for technological progress: both increase the yield of useful goods and services from available labor and other resources. "The general case for freedom in international exchange is like the case against putting sand in the gears of a machine."[2] Like improved transportation in particular, interregional and international trade increase the yield of resources by promoting geographical specialization.

Everyone understands how wasteful it would be if the people of each state in the Union tried to make everything that they could locally. Everyone understands the benefits of interregional specialization. Trade among countries is the same. It gets special attention only because migration is more restricted between than within countries, because more detailed statistics are often available about international than about domestic trade, because understanding the use of different currencies requires special study, and because controversies center on government interferences with international trade. These differences are minor. International trade merely extends the principles of interregional trade; they do not lapse at political boundaries.

In a free-market economy, people are informed by prices and disciplined by competition (as well as by ordinary ethical precepts). The logic of a price system leaves people free, with only fringe exceptions, to produce, exchange, and consume goods of whatever kinds, by whatever methods, and in whatever places they think best. Money incomes, costs, and prices are the most obvious elements of advantage (though not the only ones). Buying abroad, just as from other regions at home, obtains products and satisfactions more cheaply than by local production only. If we can get shoes of a certain quality more cheaply by buying them abroad than by making them ourselves, we gain, just as we gain by producing whatever we do produce in the cheapest way we can. Also, if we consumers are indifferent between another $100 worth of local apples and another $80 worth of foreign bananas, we get our satisfaction more cheaply by choosing the bananas.

Just what it means to say that some sources or methods are "cheaper" than others is a question to consider at length later on. Actually, "cheapness" in ordinary money cost or price corresponds to cheapness in a more fundamental sense as well. Exports pay for imports, sooner or later. Under free-market conditions, their total money values tend to stay roughly equal over the long run, as Chapter Six explains. Importing some foreign product for $1 (including transportation and other charges, all translated from foreign currency into dollars at the appropriate exchange rate) fundamentally costs us $1 worth of export products. Producing these exports, like any $1 worth of our goods, keeps us from being able to produce $1 worth of other goods. Ideally, under competition, money cost or price measures this "opportunity cost."

Opportunity cost is one of the most basic ideas in economics: ultimately, the cost of additional units of any particular thing is the sacrifice of other things or benefits that might have been chosen instead. Productive resources are *scarce*. Not even the wealthiest country can produce all the goods and services that everybody would like to have. Given the size, skills, experience, and traditions of the labor force existing at any time, as well as the natural resources, the state of technical knowledge, the accumulated stock of industrial plant and equipment, dams, highways, and other capital goods, and the effectiveness of coordination among parts of the economy, it is simply not possible to produce more of some things without sacrificing some production of other things. Apparent exceptions are not genuine and important. More goods to satisfy wants in the short run could be produced by neglecting maintenance and conservation of capital equipment and natural resources, but this would cut down on production in the future. People could produce more goods by working harder and longer, but at the sacrifice of leisure, which is itself a kind of consumer good. The problem of involuntary leisure, or unemployment, is considered in later chapters. Some of it is unavoidably connected with workers' shifts among jobs in a changing world. Occasional large-scale unemployment shows imperfect economic coordination that better monetary policy might perhaps remedy. With coordination at any given state of effectiveness, however, as with technology at any given level of advancement, the principles of scarcity and opportunity cost hold true; and no conceivable improvement could abolish them entirely. In comparison with production possibilities, human wants are insatiable. People unavoidably must choose what to have and what to pass up. To choose wisely, they need to know how much each thing costs in others sacrificed.

Money costs and prices, against a background of limited money incomes, indicate these sacrifices. People see that when they buy some things, they cannot afford others. Ideally, prices indicate the real production alternatives posed by technology and by availability of resources. However "planned" or "unplanned," an economic system cannot perform efficiently unless money prices and costs take account of physical realities.

Beyond some point, as a rule, further and further increases in the output of some particular good become more and more costly in amounts of other products sacrificed. With given resource and technological endowments, the amount of a good produced depends on individual tastes, which are shaped by ideology and advertising as well as by basic drives and cultural heritage. An efficient economic system will cause money prices and costs to reflect these tastes. If more of a good is wanted, for whatever reason, then its price will rise to reflect the increasing opportunity cost of its production.

The case for prices based on opportunity costs stands unaltered by considerations of economic ideology and organization. For any configuration of tastes and output, money prices should ideally reflect real production alternatives. The rule applies universally to all value systems that count man's material pleasures positively and to all institutions, public and private, through which such pleasures are pursued.

FREE TRADE IN A COMPETITIVE ECONOMY

We must understand how prices signal the real terms of choice in a competitive economy before we can fully grasp the logic of letting people respond to price incentives in international trade. The explanation that follows describes how competitive forces ideally *tend* to work; of course, they do not work this way exactly, everywhere, always, and at once. Except that it would sound awkward and tiresome, the word "tend" or "tendency" belongs in almost every sentence; the reader should supply it mentally. On this understanding, then, we may say that the price of any particular product equals the money cost of producing one more unit of it. This cost, in turn, equals the sum of the prices times quantities of the additional ingredients or resources used in producing the additional unit. If the product's price exceeded its cost, businessmen would profitably produce more, which would bring its price down through competition (and perhaps also raise the cost as additional production became physically more difficult or as prices of ingredients were bid up). A price below cost would motivate businessmen to make less of the product, making it scarcer and higher in price (and perhaps also lowering its cost, partly through less eager bidding for its ingredients). But if price just barely equals cost, what incentive do businessmen have to keep on operating? Part of the answer is that the cost in question is the addition to total cost of producing one more unit of the product; the average cost of all units may be lower. Another part of the answer lies in what the product's "ingredients" are. They include not only such obvious ones as labor and materials but also the wear and tear on plant and equipment due to additional production. They even include the risk-bearing and the alertness to new opportunities for which investors and businessmen expect to receive a so-called "normal profit." These services, too, are among the scarce resources that somehow have to be rationed among different lines of production.

Each ingredient or resource bears a price measuring how much it contributes to the value of output in its various uses. Suppose that one more unit of some ingredient could add more than its own price to the value of output of some industry. Businessmen there would buy more of the ingredient, bidding its price up while lowering the productive contribution of the "last" unit of it. If the ingredient were contributing less than its price, on the other hand, less eager bidding for it would make its price fall. The result is that an additional unit of the ingredient contributes the same amount to the value of output in all its uses, an amount equal to its competitive market price. Contributions to the physical output of various products are valued at the prices consumers pay for them. Of course, not all products are final consumer goods; many are such things as machinery and fertilizer and office supplies. But the prices that businessmen are prepared to pay for them depend on how much these producer goods can contribute to making final consumer goods and on what consumers are prepared to pay. Ultimately, then, different types of *consumption* are in rivalry for the use of resources.

Let us restate this reasoning, remembering that we are still describing ideal competitive tendencies. The price of a product equals the sum of the prices times quantities of ingredients needed to make an additional unit of it. This sum indicates how much more worth of other things could be produced if the ingredients were used for them instead. If the total price of ten electric frying pans equals the price of one television set, this ideally means not only that the ten pans and one TV have the same value to consumers but also that they have the same cost in ingredients-in-general and so in other-production-in-general forgone. If prices are "correct" in the ideal competitive sense, they tell consumers not only how much of some things they personally must sacrifice to be able to buy others instead but also how much production of some things must be sacrificed to free resources for producing other things. Prices transmit information about physical realities in abbreviated form. They let consumers choose as if they directly knew about physical possibilities and alternatives in production.

THE RATIONING FUNCTION OF PRICES

Two sets of choices are really the same: how much of different things to produce and how to parcel out, or "allocate," scarce resources among different lines of production. How should a definite plot of city land be used: as a wheat field, a parking lot, the site of a swimming pool or motel or office building, or what? According to the logic of the price system, the resource will go under the control of whoever will pay the most. In bidding for its use, businessmen estimate how much it can contribute, however indirectly, to producing goods and services that consumers want and will pay for. How much value it can contribute depends not only on physical facts of production but also on the selling price of the final product; and this, in turn, depends partly on the costs of producing the product in other ways. Wheat grown on cheaper land elsewhere would keep anyone who wanted to use city land for a wheat field from affording to be the highest bidder for it. Various resources—not only natural resources but also capital, labor, and business ability—thus move into lines of production where they contribute most to satisfying consumer needs and wants. This is true, though, only so far as satisfactions are measured by the money that consumers will pay to get them; more must be said about this qualification later on.

Explaining how prices allocate resources among rival uses is simplest if we suppose that only a fixed total amount of each resource exists. For some, like sheer land space, this is nearly true. For others, like electrical engineers, the amount will respond to the price or wage. But this responsiveness does not upset the basic fact of scarcity. Behind the flexible quantities or particular resources are still more ultimate scarcities. Increasing the number of electrical engineers cuts into supplies of other kinds of labor. As for labor as a whole, it must share with leisure the limited total of human time and energies. Leisure, like products, is a way of obtaining satisfactions or avoiding dissatisfactions; so, even though the total labor supply is variable, having more of some satisfactions still costs having less of others.

Scarcity and opportunity cost are such basic ideas and so important in understanding the gains from trade that they deserve further emphasis. Rival bidding for a plot of land is a very simple example. A more difficult one considers some imaginary resource technically suitable for only one definite type of production. Still, its available supply must be rationed out among the different companies in the industry. The ones bidding highest for it are presumably those that can use it most effectively. A still more difficult and extreme case would seem to leave no room for rationing. Imagine a river gorge or canyon whose physical features and remote location make it quite useless except as the site of a hydroelectric dam; it can either help produce electricity or do nothing. To rule out any question of which power company is to use the gorge, we suppose that the federal government itself will operate the hydroelectric plant. To further sharpen the issue, we suppose that the government is determined not to use any monopoly advantage. It wants to sell electricity at a price just barely covering the full additional cost of delivering one more kilowatt hour to a customer. The price should correctly tell the customer how much sacrifice in other directions his taking the electricity imposes.

What costs should go into this ideal price? Labor and materials for maintaining the dam, operating the installations, and transmitting power obviously should count as well as an allowance for interest on the investment. But what about the use of the river gorge itself? It was not built by any human effort or at any actual expense; it was just "there," a sheer gift of nature. Yet a price excluding any cost of the gorge might be so low, compared with the price of electricity from other sources, that customers would demand more electricity than the government installation could supply. Because of a not-charged-for opportunity cost, a rationing problem would still exist. Supplying the bargain electricity to some would-be users forecloses the opportunity of supplying it to others.

Again we see what cost basically is: not so much exertions made or materials used as, rather, other opportunities sacrificed in meeting some particular want. Use of the river gorge, "embodied" in electricity, is too scarce to satisfy all demands for it at a price of zero. Giving it to some people means denying it to others. The logic of a price system calls for recognizing this opportunity cost by including it in a price of electricity set high enough to keep the amount demanded in line with the supply.

Though rationing by price is appropriate even for scarce resources given "free" by nature, this in itself says nothing about who ought to receive the price, whether private owners or the government. The purpose of price is not necessarily to provide incentive to supply the resource; obviously that is not its purpose for nature-given and non-producible resources. (It would be stretching the language to say that exploring and so forth can "produce" a natural resource. The expenses involved are the expenses of using *other* resources; the bare natural resource itself is simply "there.") Price serves to ration the resource and keep units of it from meeting less intense demands to the frustration of more intense demands.

The question seldom arises of using a resource all in one way or all in another. Competition parcels out a divisible resource among different lines of production so that no reallocation of it could still further increase its contribution to the total value of all outputs. If this were not so, companies in which units of the resource could contribute more would bid some of it away from companies in which units of it were contributing less.

Most factors of production do not simply exist free; instead, they are produced from still more ultimate resources at a cost even in the ordinary sense of the word. A price must be paid to make people supply as much of such a resource as they do. This is true of labor in general and especially of specific kinds of labor. For some kinds, though, the amount supplied might hardly shrink at all in the face of a price or salary cut; examples are the work of famous sports figures, actors, and singers. In this respect, though less completely, their labor resembles the hydroelectric site. By imposing a discriminatorily heavy income tax, the government might cut itself in on the high salaries that some entertainers receive without much reducing the work they do, especially if they have no attractive second-best uses for their time and energy. Mentioning this special tax is not a proposal to impose it. (Administrative, political, and ethical difficulties stand in the way.) It simply emphasizes that resource prices have a rationing function as basic as their incentive function and sometimes far overshadowing it. The high pay of some entertainers serves mainly to ration out their scarce talent among competing audiences.

Let us summarize what we have said about allocating resources. Each consumer decides how much of each good to buy in the light of his needs and preferences, his income, the price of the good itself, and the prices of other goods. Choosing in the light of prevailing prices, he ideally leaves no opportunity unexploited to increase his total satisfaction by diverting any dollar from one purchase to another. The price of each product measures the total of the prices of the additional resources necessary to supply an additional unit of that product, and these resource prices measure the values of other outputs sacrificed by not using the resources for them instead. Prices therefore tell the consumer how much production of other things has to be forgone in order to supply him with each particular product. With physically real alternatives brought to their attention in this way, consumers choose the pattern of production and resource-use that they prefer. Their bidding sees to it that no unit of a resource goes to meet a less intense effective demand to the denial of a more intense one. Ideally, no opportunity remains to increase the total value of things produced by transferring a unit of any resource from one use to another. Technological progress and changing consumer preferences always keep creating such opportunities afresh, but the profit motive keeps prodding businessmen to ferret them out.

CONSUMER SOVEREIGNTY

Correct price signals make consumer sovereignty possible. To determine how resources are allocated to producing what things in what quantities, consumers need more than mere freedom to spend their incomes as they wish, unregimented by nonprice rationing. They must also be able to choose at unrigged prices reflecting true production alternatives. In centrally planned economies, such as Soviet Russia, the authorities could leave consumers free to spend their money as they wished and yet largely override their desires about production. To choke off demand and restrict production of officially disfavored products, the authorities could impose special taxes to raise their prices above cost. To spur consumption of officially favored products, they could set prices below cost, covering the subsidy from the taxes on the disfavored products or from general tax revenues. These rigged prices would overstate the sacrifices physically necessary to have some goods and understate the sacrifices necessary to have others. This misinformation would keep consumers from choosing as satisfying a pattern of production as they could otherwise have chosen. Admittedly, a central authority may sometimes have reasons for overriding consumer sovereignty; but we should understand the role of rigged prices in doing this.

Actually, the term "consumer sovereignty" is a bit narrow. So far as their abilities permit, people can bring their preferences among occupations as well as among consumer goods to bear upon the pattern of production.* Suppose, for example, that many people craved being actors strongly enough to accept wages below those paid in other jobs requiring similar amounts of training and native ability. This willingness would help keep down the cost of producing plays. Cheap tickets would draw audiences and help maintain job opportunities in the theater. Suppose, in contrast, that practically everybody hated to mine coal. The comparatively high wages needed to attract workers would enter into the production cost and price of coal, signaling power companies to build hydroelectric or other non-coal-burning plants and signaling consumers to employ other fuels or live in warmer climates or smaller houses than they would if coal were cheaper. These responses would keep down the number of distasteful coal-mining jobs to be filled. The few workers who still did this work would be those whose dislike for it was relatively mild and capable of being assuaged by high wages.

There is no profound distinction between workers' sovereignty and consumers' sovereignty or between getting satisfactions or avoiding dissatisfactions in choosing what work to do and in choosing what goods to consume. (Consumer goods are not ends in themselves but just means of getting satisfactions or avoiding dissatisfactions.) People make their

---

*In fact, investors' preferences (including ideas about the glamor of different industries) also have some influence, and we might speak of "investors' sovereignty" as well. The interested reader can find enough clues in the text to think out this refinement for himself.

individual tastes count by their behavior on the markets for goods and labor alike. Whether consumer sovereignty is a good thing, even in this broadened sense, depends on a nonscientific value judgment that individuals' tastes ought to prevail, perhaps even over the opinions of experts. Furthermore, consumer sovereignty is not the same as sovereignty of the whole person or citizen, since a person has some wants that can hardly be expressed on the market alone and must find expression through other channels.

A broadened concept of consumer sovereignty by no means upsets the idea of opportunity cost. We only have to recognize that people choose not simply among commodities but rather among *packages* of satisfactions and dissatisfactions. The choice between additional amounts of A and B is really a choice between the satisfactions gained and dissatisfactions avoided by people as consumers and producers of A and the satisfactions gained and dissatisfactions avoided by people as consumers and producers of B. Choosing package A *costs* the forgoing of package B. Ideally, the prices of products A and B indicate the terms of exchange, so to speak, between the entire combinations of satisfactions gained and dissatisfactions avoided in connection with the two products. Prices reflect realities embracing the psychological as well as physical or technological conditions of production. If we usually mention only how price reflects the physical or technological substitutabilities among goods in production, we do so only to avoid wordiness. Readers should always mentally add a note about the psychological conditions as well. We do not assert that different persons' feelings about goods and about jobs can be accurately measured and compared in terms of price alone or in any other way. People's feelings do exert influence in the marketplace, however; a change in them does affect the pattern of production in a way that makes some sense.

UNPLANNED COORDINATION

A competitive market economy lacks any central control. Government intervenes, but only at the fringes: it promotes some activities and discourages others but provides no overall coordination. Coordination is spontaneous. Types of production proceeding at too high a rate in relation to other production and to physical possibilities and people's wants would be unprofitable. (Consider what would happen if tire production rose far out of line with automobile and gasoline production.) Types of production taking place at relatively too low a rate would be especially profitable. The prod of loss and lure of profit lead businessmen continuously to adjust the kinds and quantities of things they produce. In this way the pattern of production and resource use responds to human preferences and the realities of nature and technology.

Decision-making is decentralized among millions of consumers and businessmen. It must be, if much important knowledge is not to go to waste. Professor F. A. Hayek has called this the "knowledge of the particular circumstances of time and place."[3] Examples are knowledge of empty cargo space in a ship soon to sail, of a machine often idle, of an employee whose abilities are being wasted on inferior tasks, of unusual tastes or shopping habits of consumers in a particular town, of supplementary sources of materials in case regular supplies are interrupted, of whom to see about buying or selling second-hand equipment, of how to get a damaged boiler repaired fast in an emergency, of a temporary glut of some commodity in one place at the same time as a temporary shortage elsewhere, and, of course, individuals' knowledge about their own needs and preferences as consumers and workers. Because it concerns temporary, local conditions, such knowledge cannot be codified in scientific textbooks or assembled for the use of central planners; and even if it somehow could be centralized and continuously kept up to date, its sheer mass would keep the planners from grasping and effectively using it. Only the individual "men on the spot" can use it. But if their millions of separate decisions every day are to add up to more than chaos, these individuals must take account not only of what they know in their own little sphere but also of conditions in the rest of the economic system. Prices give them this further information and the incentive to use it. In abbreviated, symbolic form, prices transmit information about how intense the demands for various products are, relative to supplies. They tell how scarce various materials and resources are in view of rival uses and of possibilities of using substitutes. As an example, Hayek cites either an interruption of usual tin supplies or development of a new use. Significantly, most users of tin need not know which has happened. All they need know is that relative to competing demands for it, tin has become scarcer than before. A price increase tells users to look for ways to economize on tin, as by using less of it in alloys, by switching to aluminum instead of tin-coated cans, or by selling more food frozen or in glass jars. Price changes also tell consumers to buy less canned and more fresh food. The prices and quantities that respond are those not only of tin itself and of products containing tin and of their substitutes but also of materials used along with tin, substitutes for tin, products containing these materials and their substitutes, and so forth. Some users cannot conveniently make adjustments and may keep on using as much tin as before; users that do adjust will be ones that can adjust readily in the light of possibilities of using substitute materials, in the light of the types of products they are producing or consuming, and so forth. All sorts of remote interrelations get taken into account, without any central calculation or central directives, in repatterning uses of tin and related materials and products.

Adjustments to a minor economic change, as in the tin example, would be diffused and inconspicuous, especially since many other economic changes happening at the same time would swamp them. Most people responding to one particular change probably could not even identify their response and motives. But the example does emphasize how prices transmit information to each decision-maker about all sorts of changing natural, technological, and mental conditions and interrelations. The price system works like a giant computer, continually programming itself with the latest data, even of the most localized, fleeting, and subtle kinds.

The foregoing description admittedly idealizes the price system; but insofar as it works at all, it works along the lines described. Understanding this ideal operation, as well as the defects considered next, is essential to understanding the arguments for and against letting the price system work even in the international trade sector of the economy. Incidentally, probably the strongest part of the case for the price system is something that would take us too far afield here—namely, how the system helps preserve individual freedom by largely dispersing economic power and limiting its links with political power.

NOTES

1. On what follows, cf. Peter T. Bauer, "International Economic Development," *Economic Journal,* March 1959, pp. 106-7.

2. C. Lowell Harriss, *The American Economy* (Homewood, Ill.: Richard D. Irwin, 1953), p. 826.

3. F. A. Hayek, "The Use of Knowledge in Society," *American Economic Review,* September 1945, pp. 519-30.

3

IMPERFECTIONS IN
THE MARKET ECONOMY

Having explored the logic of free markets, we now consider ways in which such markets can fail to satisfy generally accepted norms of economic performance. Here we take up three possible imperfections in the market economy—monopoly, externality, and inequality—leaving a fourth, centering on monetary policy, for Chapter Six. We shall observe in the chapters ahead that the case for free international trade rests in part on the assumption that domestic markets perform effectively, in the sense that the problems to be discussed here do not call for pervasive government intervention. Also, we recall that neither free trade nor protectionism (nor any other ism) exists as an end in itself. Each must be evaluated according to how close it comes to working with prices that accurately reflect and implement personal tastes and physical realities.

MONOPOLY AND THE ALLOCATION OF RESOURCES

Monopoly is one example of how the price system may give incorrect signals about the true terms of choice. An extreme example will point up the contrast with the competition we have assumed until now. One single company controlling the world's entire coffee supply might increase its total profit by destroying some of the inventory already on hand and selling the rest at a price in line with the new artificial scarcity. More realistically, the monopoly might plan for scarcity and high price in the first place. It would hold production down to a level that would leave any additional coffee still worth more to consumers than supplying it would cost. (This is not the same as saying that the addition to the monopolist's total sales revenue would still exceed its additional costs; for selling the additional coffee would require a lower price, even on what would have been sold anyway.) The interests of the monopolist and of consumers obviously clash if some coffee is destroyed outright. The clash is just as real, if less obvious, when the monopolist holds production down in the first place; for the increase in total cost of additional coffee measures what the added resources could contribute to the production of other things, valued at prices consumers are prepared to pay for them. Now, since consumers would value additional coffee more highly than the other things forgone, failure to shift resources from these other things into coffee production represents a wasted opportunity to use resources for satisfying relatively more intense consumer demands. Consumers do not bid on the market for the additional coffee production that they prefer to other things because prices give them false information. Because the monopolist prices coffee out of line with its cost, the quantity of other things that consumers would have to forgo to buy additional coffee instead is greater than the quantity of other things whose production must be forgone by physical necessity. The prices guiding consumer choices misrepresent the true costs of some things in terms of others.

Monopoly power explains why prices are wrong. The monopolist can choose between selling many pounds of coffee at only a small markup per pound over cost or few pounds at a large markup over cost or an intermediate number of pounds at an intermediate markup—whichever yields the greatest total profit. But if coffee were not monopolized and instead were grown and sold by hundreds or thousands of independent producers, no one of them, alone, could have appreciable market power. No one would fear beating down the price of coffee by increasing his own production. Each would regard the price as something beyond his control and would simply adjust his coffee-growing to it. As long as supplying an additional pound of coffee would raise costs by less than this price, he would supply more; if cutting back production would save more than this price from his cost, he would cut back. Competitive producers would thus have an incentive to adjust their production to the ideal level at which one more or less pound of coffee would have the same value to consumers as the amount of other things that it would be physically possible to supply them with instead. Decisions that are in the interests of individual producers and of the general public thus coincide under competition but clash under monopoly.

Economists center their complaints about monopoly on this clash of interests associated with false price signals confronting buyers and with "too little" allocation of resources into producing monopolized goods (and therefore "too much" into producing competitively sold goods).

On the other hand, even a monopolist in the literal sense of the word may have only slight scope to raise his profit by restricting production and by holding price greatly above cost. His ability to hold price above cost is limited by the price sensitivity of consumers, connected with generalized competition for the consumer's dollar among all kinds of goods and services.

In some cases, a market may not be large enough for more than one or two companies to produce on an efficiently large scale, so that even an unregulated monopoly might serve consumers better and cheaper than small producers under artificially enforced competition. Below we shall consider in greater detail how companies launching new products, trying new and cheaper production methods, or entering new markets suggest another exception to the standard complaints against monopoly. Far from being something sinister, an unusually large markup of price over cost—or the hope of being able to collect it—is then part of the incentive to shoulder the risk of innovation. Also, competition tends to appear sooner or later and shrink the abnormal markups of innovators. Unless artificially protected, important monopoly power tends to weaken in time. Monopoly seems really sinister only when it rests on coercion to keep out would-be competitors. Ironically enough, it is often government that applies such coercion in open or concealed ways.

Published attempts to estimate the allocative harm done by monopoly have shown that harm to be a very small fraction of national income, usually less than one percent.[1] However rough, these calculations tend to reassure us that the price system is workably competitive after all. It is not our purpose, anyway, to explore all the pros and cons of monopoly.* We mention it for two reasons: to avoid one-sided praise in describing the logic of a competitive price system, and to illustrate again the role of prices as signals of opportunity cost and the harm done by false signals.

Several other conditions can cause similar falsification and similar harm. Higher rates of excise tax on group-A goods than on group-B goods will make it appear to consumers that having additional A-goods costs more in B-goods forgone than is true, considering physical production opportunities. The falsified prices cause consumers to choose fewer A-goods relative to B-goods than they would do in the light of correct signals about the true

*Nor does this chapter pretend to catalogue all suggested defects of an uncontrolled price system. It concentrates on those that seem most relevant to laying a background for later consideration of tariff arguments. It ignores, for example, familiar contentions that an uncontrolled price system has a bias toward too much saving or (less implausibly, we think) toward too little saving. Least of all do we suggest that an uncontrolled price system tends to provide maximum attainable human satisfaction. One reason why we do not is the essential meaninglessness of such a "maximum."

terms of choice in production. Such distortion generally means inefficiency in the process of converting available resources into human satisfactions. The same principle applies when of the two goods in question, one is an import and one a competing domestic good.

"NONALLOCATIVE" EFFECTS OF MONOPOLY

Instead of stressing the already discussed allocative effects of monopoly, some economists focus attention on certain "nonallocative" consequences of the pursuit of *nonprofit* goals by firms with monopoly power. Pursuing them supposedly further contradicts the logic of the price system. Here we shall consider how these nonallocative consequences relate to each other and to the effects described in the preceding section.

1. *Sales versus Profits:* One argument begins on the premise that neither pure competition (with "many" firms producing a good) nor pure monopoly (with only one producer) is the dominant form of economic organization. Rather, the mature capitalistic economy is dominated by a core of capital-intensive, technically oriented industries (automobiles, petroleum, steel), in which production is concentrated in a few large firms. These firms collude implicitly, if not explicitly, to fix price. But, instead of fixing price to maximize profits, they fix price to maximize sales (or the growth of sales) and to guarantee the security of long-term investment. In contrast to the allocative argument against monopoly, this argument holds that production, if anything, is likely to be *too great* for the social good. There is no contrived scarcity. Management is inclined not to withhold sales in the interest of maximizing profits but to maximize sales subject only to the minimal demands of the stockholders.[2]

The corporation maximizes sales rather than profits because management prefers sales and because the stockholders have little or no control. The preference for sales derives from the need for a system of rewards and penalties within the managerial ranks. It is easier to determine whether an individual manager deserves a raise or promotion by observing his sales record than by trying to measure his contribution to profits. Stockholders have lost control over management because of the diffusion of ownership among them and the increasingly technical nature of business.

The corporation not only escapes monitoring by its stockholders but also controls other significant elements of its environment: its consumers through advertising, its suppliers through intimidation, and the government and universities through seduction. The tendency to produce "too much" (rather than "too little," as in the case of our coffee grower) may be traced to the exercise of this control, particularly advertising. The effect is to vitiate the price system:

> Prices are no longer of unique importance in telling how resources are distributed. What counts is the whole deployment of power—over prices, costs, consumers, suppliers, the government. Prices may be less important than the energy, guile or resourcefulness with which the firm persuades the consumer or government to want what it produces or by which it eliminates the possibility of choice.[3]

2. *X-inefficiency:* A separate but related argument holds that firms with monopoly power pursue certain nonmonetary benefits even at the expense of profits or sales. These benefits may take the form of leisure, thick rugs, pretty-but-incompetent secretaries, and corporate jets. Management takes them even though their elimination would lower costs and raise profits. This failure to use resources as efficiently as possible and so to minimize costs is something distinct from monopolistic misallocation of resources. Harvey Leibenstein has called it "X-inefficiency."[4] It stems largely from a lack of motivation on the part of management to work as hard as it could and the tendency to fall into slothful habits.

In the preceding chapter we examined a state of affairs in which resources were allocated efficiently between different uses. There we implicitly assumed the existence of "pure competition," under which, it is generally conceded, firms are motivated to maximize profits. However, we cannot infer, on that account, that either pure competition or the pursuit of maximum profits is necessary for economic efficiency.

A policy of maximizing the revenue from sales or of tolerating some X-inefficiencies is not necessarily inconsistent with the pursuit of maximum profits on an enduring basis. A pure monopolist, if insulated from the threats of competition and government regulation, maximizes profits by holding sales down to the level at which the "last" unit produced adds no more to total costs than to total revenues. On the other hand, pure monopoly is rare; and even in concentrated markets, firms do suffer competition or the threat of competition from each other. Government is sometimes described as an integral part of the industry, taking the form of an important customer or an actual or potential regulator.

Profitability may be more enduring if the firm does *not* minimize the total cost of producing every given amount of some good and does incur some apparent X-inefficiencies. It may *not* be wise to eliminate from production every unit of a good which adds more to total cost than to total revenue in the short run. The reason is the way that competitors and the government might react to the resulting additional profits. Conspicuously large profits might attract keener competition or governmental regulation.[5] (Consider the price controls and threats of nationalization and antitrust action recently confronting the oil industry.) Better to settle for less-than-pure-monopoly profits than to run these risks.

Maximizing sales revenue may be viewed as a firm's best approach to long-run profit maximization. The firm might well set production below and price above the levels of pure competition, while setting production above and price below the levels of pure monopoly. If so, sales maximization would be consistent with both profit-maximizing behavior on the part of the firm and the hypothesis that production and prices tend to approach the competitive ideal as markets become less concentrated. A pure monopolist would not maximize profits by maximizing sales, but a firm in a two- or three-firm industry might, particularly if its competitors followed suit.

Still, a conflict may arise between sales and profit maximization in a large corporation where ownership and control are separated. We may grant that management prefers sales as such to profits and that the stockholders tolerate its practice of expanding sales revenue at the expense of profits. They may tolerate certain X-inefficiencies as well. Regardless of the firm's monopoly power in the product market, relatively free and competitive securities markets would tend to place ownership in the hands of the stockholders most willing and able to exercise control.[6] Even these stockholders may, however, discover that it is rational not to exercise such tight control as to eliminate every unexploited opportunity to increase profit.

Control over management, like every other activity, has costs with which its benefits must be compared. There is, first of all, a limit to the demands that can be made on management. Certain nonpecuniary benefits (such as vacation time and pleasant business trips) are cheaper to provide than the additional salaries otherwise necessary to recruit and retain managers. Second, stockholders have only limited time and energy of their own for overseeing the activities of management. Beyond a certain point, the additional resources necessary for tighter control (through learning the business, attending stockholders' meetings, fighting proxy battles, and so forth) are worth more than what they might add to profits. Besides, each individual stockholder, being just one of many, hardly has an incentive to put forth the required effort.

As we have seen, one strand of the sales-maximization argument holds that monopolists cause consumers to buy too much, rather than too little, of their goods. On this argument, advertising may lure consumers into buying goods which they don't really "need," sidetracking resources from producing more of what they do need. Even apart from advertising, businessmen might be criticized for accommodating frivolous tastes rather than genuine human "needs." The single word "tailfins" was once popular as a label for what the critics object to. Advertising, it is argued, exploits the basic ignorance and impressionability of consumers, who respond irrationally to pressures to keep up with the Joneses.

To appraise this argument, we must consider, on the other hand, the asserted importance of advertising to product development. Firms will not develop new products unless they have a medium through which to inform and persuade potential buyers. A firm might well produce too little of some old good which is, by common consent, "needed" (housing, medical care, and nutritious food are favorite examples) and set about creating and advertising some new good (such as a portable television set or pocket calculator) which was, by assumption, not in existence before and therefore not "needed" by anyone. The firm may require a degree or an interval of shelter from competition if it is to absorb the capital and advertising costs of product development. From the consumer's point of view, however, such development imposes another kind of cost: there is "too much" of the new good—or so one might argue—in the sense that it causes "too little" of the old good to be produced.

We shall not pursue this argument much further, for it depends on value judgments about which goods are needed and which are not. (Considerations of product safety and of income distribution have more to do with the "externalities" and the "distributive" problems discussed below.) However, we may offer a few observations about how the market economy economizes on such value judgments.

The costs of developing a new product are reflected in its price. If the consumer buys the product, then he signals the producer that he prefers having it to more of the other products from which its development has diverted resources. He informs the producer that the costs of advertising and the other activities that went into developing the new product are not as large, from his point of view, as the costs of doing without that product. It is in this way that the marketplace economizes on the value judgments connected with product development: the costs of making those judgments fall directly on the person most interested in holding them down—the consumer.

Advertising, salesmanship, the examples of the Joneses, and other pressures impinging on the consumer serve to convey information, promote experimentation, and hasten adoption of improved standards of health and comfort. Businessmen employ advertising and other marketing techniques not only to persuade the consumer but also to learn from him. Second, people suffer genuine frustration if they are kept from satisfying their tastes, however subject they may have been to business and societal influences. Third, it is difficult, if not pointless, to separate from all other tastes those with which the individual may be biologically, psychologically, or culturally endowed.

However "genuine" such tastes may appear from one person's point of view, they may appear equally frivolous from another's. Furthermore, there is hardly any taste with which a person might in some sense be endowed that is not also influenced by his environment. On the same account, if people really do have certain endowed wants that are distinct from the materialistic forces around them, then they would seem capable of resisting any brainwashing by advertisers, salesmen, or neighbors. (Deception and physical or mental coercion are to be condemned as such and not to be appraised only as supposedly inherent features of the whole business system.) Reformers who argue that regrettable tastes dominate the market act more in the spirit of a free society when they try to educate consumers than when they seek puritanical legislation. The idea of governmental remedies for the influence of lowbrow tastes raises questions about personal freedom and about what if anything would make people act more intelligently as voters than as consumers. Conceivably people might really want the government to impose consumption standards on everybody that they would be unwilling to impose on themselves individually because they could not count on most other people to do the same, but this abstract possibility would seem a flimsy basis for criticizing the existing system.

Finally, the market concentration supposedly responsible for both misallocation and X-inefficiency is itself easily exaggerated. A popular argument holds that the market economy is now dominated by a core of concentrated industries, having evolved from a more or less purely competitive state:

> By the nineteen-thirties the assumption of competition—by many firms, by necessity small, participating in each market—had become untenable. Since late in the previous century the giant corporation had become an increasingly obtrusive feature of the business landscape. Its importance was assumed everywhere except in the economics textbooks.[7]

In fact, however, the theory of increasing concentration is open to considerable doubt. Warren Nutter and Henry Einhorn found that "the fraction of national income originating in privately organized monopolistic industries" actually fell by some 1.5 to 5.9 percentage points over the period 1899 to 1958.[8] Using different methods, J. Fred Weston and Stanley Ornstein found that "there has been little or no change in intra-industry concentration from 1947 to 1967."[9] It is hard to say whether these facts have much to do with the antitrust laws; anyway the prophets of increasing concentration consider those laws ineffective.[10]

MONOPOLY, INFLATION, AND UNEMPLOYMENT

We turn next to a somewhat different argument involving monopoly. Since the late 1960s, the United States and other countries have suffered persistent, simultaneous inflation and unemployment. Whereas the capitalist system once seemed vulnerable to alternative periods of contraction and expansion, it now seems to combine the worst features of both. An increasingly popular explanation points to monopoly—in business and labor—as the culprit. This explanation, which is sometimes linked to the sales-maximization hypothesis explored above, claims that the "old theories" no longer work and that government has no recourse but to impose wage and price controls; inflation is "cost-push" or "price-led" (rather than "demand-pull") in origin. Since the big corporations and unions, insulated from the discipline of the competition, fix (or "administer") prices and wages anyway, the government might as well *refix* them in the public interest.[11] Such reasoning is related to the idea that free trade is now everywhere extinct and that the relevant question nowadays is not *whether* but *how* to protect people from private-sector economic abuses, as through wage-price controls, tariffs, import quotas, or what have you.

One rebuttal to this argument as it pertains to monopoly holds that if government has indeed permitted or caused competition to become so weak as to generate chronic inflation, then it hardly follows that still further controls are desirable. Labor and business monopolies are largely creatures of government. Unions derive their powers from government restrictions on competition for jobs. Business is encouraged to fix prices by import duties and quotas, publicly-erected barriers to entry, and other restraints on competition.

With this in mind, it is difficult to imagine how wage-price controls would deter cost-push inflation. As monopolists, management and labor would still want to fix prices and wages at inflationary levels. Forced by government to refix them at lower levels, labor could strike, and management could reduce service and product quality, actions for which there is ample precedent. In the end the same irrepressible forces that cause inflation in the marketplace would operate in a controlled economy. To control effectively, the controllers would have to eliminate the monopoly power which supposedly lies at the root of the problem. Once that power was eliminated, however, the need for controls would disappear.

This reasoning is not meant to imply that cost-push effects are the principal cause of inflation or even that such effects exist. Inflation, as we shall see, is a monetary phenomenon. Without inflation, the pressure by unions for higher money wages would cause real wages (that is, money wages deflated by consumer prices) to rise above market-clearing levels. The workers still employed would be better off, but some workers would lose their jobs. Price inflation would cancel out the real wage increases that otherwise lead to unemployment. But a sufficiently restrictive monetary policy, applied during periods of heavy pressure from unions for higher money wages, would so restrict demand that management could not profitably respond with higher prices. If sufficient unemployment resulted, some unions and workers might even agree to scale down their wage demands—an action which would alleviate unemployment but which union leaders view as beneath contempt.

We conclude that the cost-pushes on which wage-price controls are predicated do not cause inflation. Rather, they force the monetary authorities to choose between unemployment and inflation. Under wage-price controls, this choice is complicated by the need to ratify or undo the controllers' choices between the same unpleasant alternatives. But the dilemma is not dispelled by the mere presence and wishes of the controllers nor by make-work schemes to broaden the governmental payroll. Assuming that monopoly is in fact as widespread as the cost-push theory requires, then big business and labor are not likely to be subdued by the appointment of another set of regulators.

We also see that there is nothing mysterious about simultaneous unemployment and inflation (see below, pp. 109-10). If cost-push effects are at work in the economy, then government (through its authorities, monetary and otherwise) is likely to opt for some compromise between inflation and unemployment, that is, some combination of both. Conceivably, we could avoid having to make such a compromise by eliminating the monopoly power from which the damaging cost-push effects originate. Though advisable in its own right, however, that step would not eliminate the demand-pull effects on prices and wages, for which the monetary authorities would continue to be responsible.

EXTERNALITIES

So-called externalities enter into further arguments for government intervention, as we shall show later on. External diseconomies and economies are costs and benefits, respectively, that some people inflict or confer on others, who do not, however, ordinarily receive or pay compensation. Both types may occur in either production or consumption. Standard examples mention the damage that a factory does by spewing smoke from its chimneys or dumping wastes into a river. Advertising that promotes dangerous goods may be viewed as causing an external diseconomy. A man may cause his neighbors agony by playing a saxophone or arouse feelings of envy and inferiority in them by driving an expensive new car. An apple grower may illustrate external economies by unintentionally providing nectar for his neighbor's bees. A company's research on its own products may yield widely applicable knowledge to the benefit of all future generations; or one man's care of his lawn may give his neighbors a better neighborhood.

In such cases, the price system transmits inaccurate signals. A person deciding on an activity that incidentally harms others will probably carry the activity "too far" (to the point where additions to the losses of all affected persons outweigh additions to their benefit), since not all the true costs come to his attention as money that he must pay. A person deciding on an activity that incidentally benefits others will probably cut it "too short" (at a point where additions to the benefit of all affected persons would still outweigh additions to total costs), since not all the benefits come to his attention as ones that he receives. Market prices misrepresent the true terms of choice between complete packages of net satisfactions.

This misrepresentation is the main difficulty, not that culprits go unpunished and victims uncompensated. In examples of external harm, it is not even inherently clear who are culprits and who are victims; nor is it always even clear whether an example is of harm or benefit after all. If a factory installed expensive equipment to eliminate smoke, one might say that it was conferring an unrewarded benefit. Preventing an economical production process that incidentally caused river pollution might raise costs by more than all the fish and amenities saved were worth. If a company polluting air or water had to pay a special tax based on the total harm done to all other affected parties, then every person newly moving into the affected territory would victimize the company. The pollution would not deter new residents because they would receive compensation, either in cash or in the lowness of their own property taxes; and in their decisions, they would not take full account of the heavier expenses they were imposing on the company and ultimately on its customers. The viewpoint of private decision-makers and an overall social viewpoint of total benefits and costs would still diverge.

As Professor Ronald Coase has explained,[12] the trouble in this and similar cases lies not in the very nature of a price system but in the vagueness of legal property in rights to do certain things. If it were perfectly clear in the first place who owned the air, or the right to decide whether or not it should be filled with smoke, smells, or noise, the affected parties could buy and sell such rights, in whole or in part; and their prices would bring all costs and benefits to the attention of people making decisions.*

---

*Many cases of supposedly inadequate private incentive for conservation of natural resources trace back to essentially this same difficulty, namely,

Putting such a solution into effect would be hopelessly impractical, of course, for more reasons than we want to devote space to. In our example of research activities, it is out of the question even to identify the ultimate present and future beneficiaries, let alone define property rights clearly enough for them to strike bargains for more research than the company would otherwise do. Remedying all the little externalities of life is still further out of the question. Many have nothing to do with the consumption of goods. A man's fouling the air with cigarette smoke may harm others less than an unkind word. A man deciding whether or not to attend a party might not pay as much attention to the other guests' pleasure or dismay at his being there as a zealous welfare economist might think he should. On philosophical grounds, perhaps, certain effects of one man's actions on other people *ought not* to be brought into his calculations even if they could—for example, others' envy of his success in some undertaking. Similarly, arrangements to let people buy and sell gratification of desires to be meddlesome or sadistic might be philosophically unacceptable even if technically feasible. Seeing externalities in consumption as basically an economic problem is a ponderous joke.

Nevertheless, many types of externality—consider the example of research—are plausible candidates for corrective action. The idea is to supplement the free market when it cannot function in full accord with its own logic. For an economic theorist, it is a routine exercise to cite externalities as an argument, formally valid on a certain level of abstraction, for almost any sort of government intervention plausible enough to command some political support. The practical policy-maker must judge which relatively few of the innumerable conceivable cases really are major enough to be taken seriously. Excessive zeal in trying to correct for all sorts of externalities could cause changes in our whole political and economic system far more harmful than the supposed corrections were worth. We shall return to this point in appraising several externality arguments for tariffs.

----

imprecise specification of property rights. A man may pump oil at a wastefully rapid rate because he is racing with his neighbor to get it out of a single pool under both their fields. Fishing crews of different companies or nations may scramble so fast for fish that they impair breeding. The trouble is that the technologically relevant unit of the resource—the entire oil pool or fishing bank—is not under single ownership. A single owner *would* have incentive to consider the future in the way he used the resource or leased out carefully specified rights to its use.

"DISTRIBUTIVE" PROBLEMS

The rich dowager's pampered cat eats cream while the poor widow's baby lacks milk—so goes another familiar example of how spending fails to indicate genuine needs. Rich people cast more "dollar votes" than the poor and have more influence on the pattern of production and resource use. This fact is no separate and distinct shortcoming of the market economy but just an aspect of differences in incomes and wealth. It would be pointless for some people to have more money than others unless they could spend it and so make their desires count more strongly in determining what things get produced. In responding only to demands backed up with money, the price system is not perverse; it is taking account of people's desires and all the other relevant circumstances, inequality included. Inequality is largely explained (which is not to say justified) by the pattern of consumer demands and the special advantages that fortunate people have in satisfying these demands. A big businessman or fashionable entertainer earns as much as he does largely because of what he contributes to supplying goods and services that consumers value; other people have low incomes because they can or do contribute so little to serving consumers. (As social philosophers, some of us may consider the consumers boorish in appraising certain "cultural" contributions as meagerly as they do; but the remarks on p. 32 are relevant here.)

One point deserves special emphasis. Purely as economists, rather than as citizens or philosophers, economists neither justify nor condemn the fact that people receive big or small incomes according to whether they and their property contribute much or little to producing what consumers want. Questions of fairness belong to the realm of philosophy or ethics. It may be a meaningful question, though not a question in economics, to ask how fair it is that some people should inherit (or derive from their early environment) stronger or more attractive bodies than others, or keener minds, or greater ambition, or more property, or more influential contacts than most people have. It is meaningful to ask how fair it is that other people should be handicapped by inferior bodies or minds or unfortunate childhoods. It is meaningful to ask whether and how the government should try partially to make up for these inequalities, including unequal inheritance of property. Economics has much, though not everything, to say about how equalizing measures of various types and degrees are likely to work. Anyway, inequality is more a consequence of biology and human nature and social relations generally than of a market economy in particular. The problem, if it is a problem, is this, and not that producers respond only to market demands backed up with spending power.

NOTES

1. See Arnold Harberger, "Using the Resources at Hand More Effectively," *American Economic Review,* May 1959, pp. 134-46; Harberger, "Monopoly and Resource Association," *American Economic Review,* May 1954, pp. 77-87; David Schwartzman, "The Effect of Monopoly on Price," *Journal of Political Economy,* August 1959, pp. 352-62 (cf. the same journal, October 1961, p. 494); Albert Fishlow and Paul David, "Optimal Resource Allocation in an Imperfect Market Setting," *Journal of Political Economy,* December 1961, pp. 529-46; and Dean A. Worcester, "New Estimates of the Welfare Loss to Monopoly, United States: 1956-1969," *Southern Economic Journal,* October 1973, pp. 234-45.

2. See two studies by John Kenneth Galbraith, *Economics and the Public Purpose* (Boston: Houghton Mifflin, 1973), and *The New Industrial State* (2d ed., Boston: Houghton Mifflin, 1971).

3. Galbraith, *Economics and the Public Purpose,* op. cit., p. 111.

4. Harvey Leibenstein, "Allocative Efficiency vs. 'X-Efficiency,' " *American Economic Review,* June 1966, pp. 392-413.

5. A similar point about governments is made by Armen A. Alchian and Reben A. Kessel, "Competition, Monopoly, and the Pursuit of Pecuniary Gain," in *Aspects of Labor Economics* (Princeton: Princeton University Press, 1962), pp. 161-63.

6. See Alchian and Kessel, op. cit., p. 160.

7. Galbraith, *Economics and the Public Purpose,* op. cit., p. 15.

8. G. Warren Nutter and Henry Adler Einhorn, *Enterprise Monopoly in the United States, 1899-1958* (New York: Columbia University Press, 1969), pp. 82-83.

9. J. Fred Weston and Stanley I. Ornstein, "Trends and Causes of Concentration—A Survey," in *The Impact of Large Firms on the U.S. Economy,* J. Fred Weston and Stanley I. Ornstein, eds., (Lexington, Massachusetts: Lexington Books, 1973), p. 12.

10. See, for example, Galbraith, op. cit., p. 121.

11. Ibid., p. 315.

12. Ronald Coase, "The Problem of Social Cost," *Journal of Law and Economics,* October 1960, pp. 1-44. Coase argues that to speak of diverging viewpoints is misleading; yet we must retain this terminology in order to deal with tariff arguments that use it.

TAKING ADVANTAGE OF FOREIGN PRICES

International trade seems clearly beneficial when it brings us goods otherwise unavailable. But the gain from cheaper foreign supplies of things we could well make ourselves requires more discussion. The preceding chapter has already paved the way. Ideally, price ratios indicate opportunity costs, or how much each product costs in other production sacrificed.

Suppose that we could either make widgets ourselves for $3 each or buy them abroad for $1. Any of several reasons could explain the lower foreign price—an abundance overseas of resources especially important in making widgets, perhaps including many workers skilled in that line of work; mass production of widgets there to serve a large home market; or a climate favorable to widget-making. Perhaps foreign wages are low, or perhaps the foreign government prices its currency artificially low or subsidizes the widget industry. Widgets might grow wild on bushes and cost little to gather. Whatever the reason, the lower money price of foreign widgets is also a lower opportunity cost for us: to import a widget we must give up only $1 worth of other goods, but if we make it ourselves, the other goods sacrificed are worth $3.

The gains from international trade arise from the real opportunities that low foreign prices give us. These opportunities are genuine regardless of what makes foreign prices lower than our own. How could it matter *why* the foreign widgets are so cheap? If prices *in our own country* did not correctly indicate the quantities of various products whose production is interchangeable in view of technology and the scarcity of resources, that distortion might be relevant to policy. But the opportunity that foreigners offer us is genuine from our point of view, regardless of any distortions in the foreign price system that might explain the low prices of foreign goods. Refusing this opportunity or restricting access to it is the same as refusing or restricting any other kind of opportunity for making or getting goods cheaply.

We have already noted that foreign trade and machinery are alike in increasing the number of ways to choose from in getting wanted goods. Price ratios on the world market different from what would prevail in our own country without trade give us an opportunity, just as a machine does, to transform things we have into other things that we would rather have instead. Suppose that in our country wheat costs two dollars a bushel and wine four dollars a gallon. In an ideal competitive price system, as we know, this indicates that the production of two bushels of wheat and the production of one gallon of wine are indirectly interchangeable with or substitutable for each other; consumers will adjust their consumption of wheat and wine so that they are just barely willing to give up two additional bushels of wheat in exchange for an additional gallon of wine (or, in other words, until they are just barely willing to accept a half gallon of wine in exchange for a bushel of wheat). Wheat producers will adjust their production of wheat until they are just barely willing to accept an additional half gallon of wine in exchange for the production of an additional bushel of wheat. Wine producers will adjust their production of wine until they are just barely willing to accept an additional two bushels of wheat in exchange for the production of an additional gallon of wine.

Now imagine that a machine descends from heaven and somehow gives out one gallon of wine for every one—not two—bushels of wheat put into it. Two kinds of gain, one in consumption and the other in production, become possible. Consumers, previously willing to give up as many as two bushels of wheat for an additional gallon of wine, now have to give up only one bushel. Given the assumed properties of our machine, they can exchange as much as they please of previously consumed wheat for wine at the 1:1 ratio. They carry on this exchange until an additional gallon of wine no longer affords them more satisfaction than a single bushel of wheat.

The consumption gain just described occurs even if domestic wheat and wine production are rigidly fixed. Taking *full* advantage of the opportunity the machine offers requires also exploiting the gain from possible rearrangement of production. Ordinarily, the assumed pretrade domestic prices would indicate the possibility of producing at least somewhat more wheat and less wine (or making the opposite shift) at opportunity costs of one unit of wine for two units of wheat. Conceivably, the machine's appearance might shut the wine industry down completely, freeing all of its resources for wheat production. The additional wheat would then buy our country twice as much wine as we had stopped producing. Or, if we preferred, we could take *half* of our additional wheat and exchange it for the same quantity of wine as we had stopped producing, leaving consumers with as much wine as before and more wheat. Or we could straddle these two responses to our opportunity by having some more of both wine and wheat. We might even prefer using the opportunity to have somewhat less of one product but much more of the other. In any case, the production gain due to transfer of resources from wine to wheat would add to the total gains from trade.

It is also conceivable that not all (or even not any) of the resources used to produce wine would move into wheat, which would limit (or eliminate) the scope for a production gain. Trade with our heaven-sent machine might pull the relative costs of wheat and wine into the 1:1 ratio before wine production reached zero. As wheat production expands, the cost per bushel is likely to rise, while wine production becomes less costly as it shrinks. This could happen partly because factors of production were "immobile," that is, poorly suited for transfer between industries. Perhaps wine workers either hate becoming wheat workers or do not know enough about the opportunity. Shifts of land and capital might also be sluggish. Recognizing this is not to find fault with factor immobility as such. If some wine workers really did not want to move into wheat, they might accept lower wages to gratify their strong job preferences, while wheat producers were raising wages to attract workers. Wage flexibility, if it exists, provides a partial answer to the criticism that free trade causes unemployment in import-competing industries. (See below, pp. 259-60.) These wage changes contribute to increasing the domestic cost and price of wheat relative to wine. As the discrepancy between the home market's and the machine's price ratios narrows, so does the scope for further production gains from trade. The changed relative prices correctly signal consumers not to expand their consumption of wheat too far.

Other reasons besides factor immobility could account for the increasing domestic cost of wheat in terms of wine forgone.* In any case, our example, involving two goods only, exaggerates the difficulty of reaping gain by

---

*For example, as the adjustment process goes on, the additional re-sources transferred might increasingly be ones of relatively low effectiveness in wheat production but relatively high effectiveness in wine. Any resources remaining in wine are likely to be ones relatively effective there but less effective in wheat. Also, the two lines of production probably employ re-sources in different, and differently changeable, proportions. Fortunately, it is not really necessary to understand these technical points to understand the gains from trade.

transferring resources. It ignores all the indirect transfers possible among the thousands of industries of the real world (see below, p. 254).

Intuition suggests that the machine in our example is a "good thing" for the country as a whole. It doesn't shut off any old production or consumption opportunities but just adds new ones. Even if only a slight repatterning of production suffices to pull the relative costs of wheat and wine into line with the 1:1 ratio of the machine, consumption gains still accrue from trading at that ratio. Since protectionists often put great stress on what amounts to the factor-immobility argument (see, for example, below, pp. 210-11), it is important to remember that mobility is only helpful, not necessary, for gain from trade. Although we have used the example of a mythical machine to make our point, there is nothing mythical about the distinction between two kinds of gain. That the one kind can exist without the other has been illustrated in prisoner-of-war camps where the inmates swapped the contents of their Red Cross packages among themselves to get additional satisfaction from these goods in view of their own differing tastes. Exchange can offer gains even when hardly any scope exists for gain from productive specialization.

The opportunity to capture the gains illustrated in our example does not depend on the reason why the machine's trading ratio is different from our pre-trade ratio or on which product the machine supplies more cheaply than we do. All that matters is that the machine's trading ratio is different. Indeed, the opportunity will be greater the *more* different the machine's ratio is from our own.* The more slots it has—the greater the variety of goods we can get out of it—and the cheaper its goods are in terms of the quantities of ours we must insert, the more we gain.

The analogy is apt because of the similarity of any useful machine to a world market price system. Since exports pay for imports, money prices determined on the world market indicate the underlying realities of how much of each import product can be had by "inserting" each export product into the machine-like world. The import product may be a final good like wine or an intermediate good like steel, which, embodied in final consumption, is indistinguishable from goods produced at home. "The production of one good to exchange for another is an *alternative method*

---

*It can be shown, with qualifications, that the more the world market prices deviate from a country's own prices in the absence of trade, the more the country can gain. (See Murray C. Kemp, "The Gain from International Trade," *Economic Journal,* December 1962, p. 808; or Kemp, *The Pure Theory of International Trade* (Englewood Cliffs, New Jersey: Prentice-Hall, 1964), pp. 163-65.)

of producing the second commodity. Under competitive conditions, productive resources will not be used in this indirect process of production unless the yield is greater than that obtained by the use of the direct method."[1] To build a bridge we may produce steel or wheat—steel, if we forgo less wheat by producing the steel ourselves than by having foreigners produce it for us, but wheat for export if the reverse is true. Rather than a choice between production and trade, the choice between steel and wheat offers, in a sense, two different ways of "producing" the bridge.

We do not wish to carry the analogy too far. On the one hand, "trade really adds yet another 'technological' process of transforming exportables into importables..." On the other hand, the question remains whether "free trade *will* in fact enable the economy to exploit the trade opportunity most effectively and thus operate efficiently..." It matters how the domestic price system works.[2] The reader may well ask whether a policy of free trade is the best possible way for a country to capture the gains made possible through the existence of a world-market price system. It is to this question that we turn next.

GAINS, LOSSES, AND TOTAL REAL INCOME

A related question is whether free trade increases a country's "real income." Free trade with the machine of our example could initially make some people worse off—wheat-lovers paying a higher price and wine-workers receiving a lower wage or put to the trouble of changing jobs. Still, the overall gain from using the machine could be distributed so as to give each wheat-lover and wine-worker a bundle of goods that he preferred to what he had before. Even if unanimous consent were required to keep rather than destroy the machine, the promachine people could afford to buy the consent of the antimachine people: buying consent would cost the gainers less than the full amount of their gain.

In reality, a majority strong enough to adopt free trade would not bother negotiating consent. Some wheat-lovers and wine-workers would end up losing, no matter how much other people gained. In fact, practically *all* economic change harms some people at least temporarily; this is true even of generally beneficial changes such as inventions, new machinery, and better or cheaper transportation, as well as the opening of trade. The reader may remember how comically Alec Guinness's movie "The Man in the White Suit" portrayed efforts to scuttle the invention of an absolutely indestructible cloth that threatened the replacement business of the textile and clothing industries. A successful policy of preventing business depressions and recessions by better exercise (not expansion) of government functions would raise real national income and be a "good thing" in almost everyone's judgment. Yet some people would lose, such as receivers of fixed pensions, who could no longer hope for bargain prices in depressions; perhaps pawnbrokers; probably bankruptcy lawyers and some economists.

Because some people always lose, it is never possible to say, rigorously, that a particular change of any kind raises the "real income of the country as a whole." Since "real income" implies something about well-being, we could be absolutely certain that it had increased only if *no* persons considered themselves worse off than before and at least some considered themselves better off. Otherwise, saying anything about "real income" must involve an open or hidden judgment about how heavily some persons' gain should weigh against others' losses. We may feel that it makes sense to count gains and losses equally per dollar's worth, but this is a fuzzy idea and a matter of hesitant intuition rather than of proof. (A dollar's worth of gain or loss may mean more to a poor man than to a rich man, or more to a loser than to a gainer.) All this helps explain why cautious economists shy from endorsing free trade without qualification. They can often pass judgment on whether particular policy arguments are logical or illogical or on whether particular alleged facts are true or false, but this is not the same as rendering a verdict on the policy itself.

Still, too much caution can be stultifying. "An increase in total real income" is a convenient and traditional shorthand description of the gains from trade.[3] It harmonizes with familiar ways of describing the long-run consequences of growth in population, capital stock, technology, and productivity. Even though economists realize that these changes harm some people, they still say that they raise total real income; and some even make tables and charts intended to show by how much it has risen over time.

THE CAUSES OF TRADE

Except for discrepancies preserved by differences in qualities of goods, transportation and trading costs, tariffs and other trade barriers, and the like, each good tends to have the same price everywhere. This happens because businessmen buy things where they are cheap for resale where they are dear. The reader may wonder what incentive for trade remains, once prices have become everywhere the same except for transportation costs and the like. The answer is the remaining profit opportunities that price differences *would* offer if the flow of trade per time period were any smaller than the price-equalizing flow. Price equalization destroys not trade but the incentive to expand it any further or faster (among growing economies, trade keeps expanding because of the price differentials that would otherwise emerge). What motivates trade is not international price differences actually persisting so much as *virtual* differences, those that would exist if the flow of trade were any smaller. The gain, also, depends on these virtual differences.

Trade offers a country worthwhile opportunities regardless of why world market prices differ (actually or virtually) from its own. Intellectual curiosity, though, invites trying to explain the different price patterns. Actually, no simple answer could do justice to the great variety of causes. For one thing, different countries possess different resources in different relative amounts. One country may have much land in relation to labor; another may be short on land but long on labor. Also, resources typically enter in quite different proportions into making different products; to produce wheat requires much land relative to skilled labor, while the reverse is true of watches. In relation to other goods, wheat will probably be cheap in the country with abundant land, and watches cheap in the country with abundant skilled labor.

Even this part of the explanation is not clear-cut. One reason is that the various resources—labor of various types, capital goods, and even land made suitable for particular uses—do not just exist in rigidly fixed amounts. Instead, their amounts respond to demands for them, which in turn are affected by international trade. Trade also affects consumers' incomes and tastes; and these affect the scarcity of resources relative to the demands for them, which is what counts. More vagueness lurks in the notion that the different proportions of resources used in making different products depend on the nature of the products themselves. Businessmen use resources in the light of their prices. Of two products, A might be the more labor-intensive and B the more land-intensive at one ratio of labor and land prices; yet B might be the more labor-intensive and A the more land-intensive at another price ratio.

We could go on at length listing reasons why neither differences in supplies of resources nor any other simple explanation can fully account for the international price differences that lead to beneficial trade. Ultimately we can do little more than take different price patterns for granted, mentioning innumerable differences among countries in soil, mineral resources, population densities, human abilities and skills, accumulations of capital equipment, consumer tastes, and physical and political and even social and ideological "climates." These differences are by no means entirely nature-given and fixed; they not only cause trade but in turn are very much affected by it.

Even one of the most prominent American protectionists begins to understand what opportunities these differences present:

> The theory of free trade is extremely simple and attractive.
> Each country should expend its productive energies in those fields

for which it is best suited by soil, climate, resources, manpower, skill, etc., and buy from other countries the goods in the production of which they, in turn, enjoy particular advantages. In this way presumably all productive energies everywhere would be employed to the highest advantage. A maximum of international trade would thus spring up, to the maximum advantage of all people.

But then the protectionist shows that his understanding is incomplete:

It is perhaps unkind to ask just how countries or areas that enjoy no outstanding advantages, such as do exist in the world, would fare under such conditions of trade. To whom, for example, would they sell? How could their producers survive competition from those countries or areas that are economically favored and well developed?[4]

COMPARATIVE ADVANTAGE

The answer lies in the Principle of Comparative Advantage. Trade can benefit both one country and the rest of the world even if the country does not have an absolute advantage over the outside world in producing some goods and an absolute disadvantage in producing others. *Even in the extreme case* where the country was absolutely less efficient than the outside world in producing everything, trade could still benefit both. Conversely, even if the country were absolutely more efficient than the outside world in producing all goods, it still could gain from trade. As long as its degree of inferior (or superior) efficiency were greater for some goods than for others, the country would benefit by importing the goods in which its efficiency was most inferior (or least superior) and exporting the goods in which its efficiency was least inferior (or most superior).

The Principle of Comparative Advantage, which shows all this, is an "even-if" proposition. Suppose we are comparing production of watches in two countries. In general, terms like "absolute advantage," "absolute disadvantage," and superior and inferior absolute "efficiency" have no precise meaning. For the terms to apply precisely, producing a watch in one country would have to require a smaller amount of *each* ingredient or resource than producing a watch in the other country—less land, less use of machinery, less labor, less business ability, less of everything. Only then could we say that the first country produced a watch at a lower "real" cost or "more efficiently" or with an "absolute advantage." In reality, such a clear-cut comparison is seldom if ever possible. Productive resources

combine in at least slightly different ways in the two countries (each
resource is not perfectly identical in the two countries, anyway), and
producing a watch requires more of at least one narrowly defined resource
in the first country than in the second. If so, neither country makes a watch
at an unambiguously lower real cost than the other, since its package of
resources used is not smaller in every detail.

The Principle of Comparative Advantage does not quibble over these
realistic difficulties. It considers the extreme case of a meaningful real-cost
comparison. For the sake of argument, let us suppose that one country is
more efficient in "real" terms in producing *all* products. Two are enough to
focus the issue. No proof of the gains from trade depends on as simple an
example as the one that follows. Its unrealistic simplifications serve merely
to illustrate the gains *even* under the extreme conditions that might seem
most embarrassing for the free-trade case. In fact, we might as well simplify
all the way and suppose only one single factor of production, adopting the
traditional example from the English classical economist David Ricardo.
Substituting the names "Superia" and "Inferia" for Ricardo's "Portugal"
and "England," though, will emphasize the real-efficiency comparison. The
numbers in the table show how many man-years of labor are required to
produce definite amounts of cloth and wine in the two countries.

	1 Unit of Cloth	1 Unit of Wine
Superia	90 man-years	80 man-years
Inferia	100 man-years	120 man-years

Superia has an *absolute advantage* in both products; it can produce each
with fewer resources than Inferia. But Superia has a *comparative* advantage
only in wine; it can produce wine at two-thirds of Inferia's real cost but
cloth at nine-tenths of Inferia's real cost. Another way of making the
comparison shows the same thing. By shifting labor between industries,
Superia could produce one more unit of cloth at the sacrifice of one and
one-eighth units of wine; Inferia could produce one more unit of cloth at
the sacrifice of only five-sixths of a unit of wine. Superia could produce one
more unit of wine at the cost of only eight-ninths of a unit of cloth sacrificed;
Inferia would have to sacrifice one and one-fifth units of cloth to produce
one more wine. While Inferia's real cost is higher than Superia's for both
products, its cost of cloth in terms of wine sacrificed—its opportunity cost—is
lower than Superia's. Despite its lower efficiency in all production, Inferia
has a *comparative* advantage (and Superia a *comparative disadvantage)* in
cloth. Both countries can gain from trade if each country specializes in its
comparatively more advantageous product. Superia can gain if it can sell a

unit of wine for anything more than eight-ninths of a unit of cloth; Inferia can gain if it can buy wine for anything less than 1 and one-fifth of a unit of cloth. For voluntary trade to take place, the "terms of trade" between cloth and wine must fall somewhere between these two extremes (just where depends on supply and demand, which thereby also determine how the two countries share the total gain). Consider an exchange at any intermediate ratio, say of one unit of Superia's wine for one unit of Inferia's cloth. Superia then "produces" this imported unit of cloth for itself indirectly at a cost of 80 rather than directly at a cost of 90 man-years and saves 10 man-years for making more of either product. Inferia indirectly "produces" its imported wine at a saving of 20 man-years over direct production. Superia, with the additional output of wine gained by transferring labor out of cloth production, can buy more than enough cloth to make up for the cutback in its own production. Inferia, with the additional output of cloth gained by transferring labor out of wine production, can buy more than enough wine to make up for the cutback in its own production. If the consumers so desire, each country can have more of each product.

Under the assumed conditions, trade would expand far beyond an exchange of one wine for one cloth. As long as the costs of each product in terms of the other sacrificed remain apart in the two countries and as long as neither country is yet making only one product and none of the other, further specialization yields further gain. In reality, the two countries' opportunity costs might well pull together as specialization proceeded, which would prevent complete specialization (see footnote, p. 42). Transportation costs, like tariffs, would also narrow the opportunity for specialization and trade.

To clinch an understanding of comparative advantage, textbooks have traditionally offered the examples of the surgeon who can wash instruments even more efficiently than his assistant or the lawyer who can type even more rapidly than his secretary. A better example avoids any distracting thoughts about the wages of different kinds of labor. Jones and Smith are marooned on a desert island. In an hour of work, Jones could pick nine coconuts *or* catch three fish, while Smith could pick four coconuts *or* catch two fish. Jones is superior in producing both goods. He is more superior in coconut-picking, though, since in an hour he can pick 125 percent more coconuts than Smith but catch only 50 percent more fish. Smith has a *comparative advantage* in fishing, his less inferior work. Both men obviously gain if each specializes in his own comparatively advantageous work and if they trade coconuts for fish on terms somewhere between Jones's 3:1 ratio and Smith's 2:1 ratio of coconut-production capacity to fish-production capacity. Of course, if the men strongly preferred coconuts and wanted only a few fish, Smith might pick some coconuts as well as catch all of the few fish desired. If preferences were the reverse of this, Jones might catch some fish as well as pick the few coconuts desired. But given the two men's 3:1 and 2:1 production-possibility ratios, reaping the maximum gain would involve having at least one man specialize completely on a single product. (In an example like this one, a desire for variety in work would be an irrelevant complication.)

The example makes one more noteworthy point. The principle of comparative advantage does *not* call for having each task done by the man who can do it most efficiently. That would mean having Jones divide his time between fishing and coconut-picking, with Smith doing nothing. The gain comes, instead, from each man's concentrating on the work in which he is more superior or less inferior.

The same point carries over to international trade. The principle of comparative advantage does *not* say that every product should be made wherever it can be made most efficiently or cheaply in the real-cost sense. Instead, the principle shows the gain from letting each country specialize in whatever product or products it makes *relatively* most cheaply, in terms of other production sacrificed. Under competitive conditions, ordinary money costs indicate cheapness in this fundamental opportunity-cost sense.

This reminds us that practical businessmen and consumers care about differences in money prices, not about comparative advantage as such. When they can buy goods more cheaply from foreigners than at home, they enjoy a real saving. But this saving may be lost if the country restricts trade or resists a shift of resources from import-competing industries merely out of concern for *why* the foreign goods are so cheap. Whatever its cause, that cheapness is what makes it possible for people to reap the benefits explained by the principle of comparative advantage.

If our mythical Superia were to tax imports for some reason such as Inferia's "cheap labor" or "unfairly depreciated exchange rate," it would throw away benefits for both countries. Low wages and other low incomes ("low" as made comparable by the exchange rate) had allowed Inferia to sell goods in which it is least disadvantaged cheaply enough to compete with the same goods made in Superia. These low costs reflect Inferia's unfortunate position, but Inferia becomes even worse off if it loses its opportunity to export some goods in exchange for those in which it is most disadvantaged. Superia too would suffer from its own tariff. Low wages and other low costs permit a disadvantaged country to offer savings to the rest of the world; they do not make those savings any less genuine.

COMPARISONS OF "EFFICIENCY"

All this prepares us to appraise a familiar contention of free traders, that industries able to beat foreign competition without tariff protection are "efficient" ones, entitled to flourish on the free market, while industries dependent on protection are inefficient and ought to shrivel up. Actually, this contention is a loose one. As an attempt to persuade, it can boomerang. There is scarcely any presumption at all that a hard-pressed domestic industry is less efficient than its foreign competitors in any technological, engineering sense.

An example of how efficiency comparisons can boomerang appears in an exchange that took place between Congressman Sam Gibbons and Mr. Eugene L. Stewart of the Ad Hoc Committee on U.S. Dyestuff Producers during testimony in support of the American Selling Price system of valuing benzenoid chemicals. Under questioning by Congressman Gibbons, Stewart had described the U.S. dyestuff industry as one which employs a relatively "high amount of technical labor" but which nevertheless consists of only a few firms and about 5000 people.

> *Mr. Gibbons.* Are you telling me that to protect those small, and you admit, somewhat inefficient and labor intensive industries we ought to get into a worldwide trade war over the American Selling Price; industries where we have 5,000 workers versus the welfare of 209 million people?
>
> *Mr. Stewart.* Congressman Gibbons, you are the one who introduced the word "inefficient" in the dialog.
>
> *Mr. Gibbons.* It seemed to me the word was applicable here.
>
> *Mr. Stewart.* If having labor costs that are a function of our standard of living in comparison to the rest of the world is equal to inefficiency, so be it. That is not my test of inefficiency.
>
> *Mr. Gibbons.* We could manufacture cloth by hand if we wanted to. That would be plenty labor intensive.
>
> *Mr. Stewart.* We manufacture dyes with the same technology and production methods that are used in Germany, in Switzerland and England and Japan. Our production methods and the units of labor per unit of output are equal to theirs. But our workers receive wages several times higher than theirs, and I would not have it otherwise.[5]

The congressman let his witness outmaneuver him when he permitted the question of relative efficiency to be debated according to irrelevant real-cost comparisons. In the first place, it is impossible in most cases to make such comparisons unambiguously. The witness claims that U.S. dye production requires exactly as much labor for each unit of outputs as foreign dye production. But for U.S. dye production to be equally efficient, it would have to use as much of *each* resource—land and capital, as well as labor—for every unit of output. More importantly, even in the extreme case where we could agree with the dyestuff spokesman that the foreign industry was no more efficient in a technical or engineering sense, buying abroad would still not spell a distortion away from some kind of economic ideal. The foreign industry might even be less efficient than ours in a real-cost sense, yet, as we have seen, it might be more efficient in a comparative-cost sense. Finally, suppose that the foreign industry has neither an absolute advantage nor even a genuine comparative advantage: it has an advantage in mere money cost and price due to some sort of distortion in foreign wages and prices away from the competitive ideal. How does that matter? The cheapness of the foreign product still offers a genuine opportunity *to us;* producing exports to pay for the import costs us a smaller sacrifice of other goods than making the import-type product ourselves.

In short, the question whether a foreign industry is more or less efficient than the corresponding home industry usually lacks precise meaning and in any case is a red herring. What counts for us is whether the foreigners offer us the goods more cheaply than we could make them ourselves. It is not only bad economics but also quite literally adds insult to injury to accuse home producers troubled with import competition of being inefficient.

Efficiency comparisons are perhaps a bit less fallacious if made among different industries *within the home country.* Competition at home in employing resources is at least as important as competition with foreigners in selling products. Consider a home industry that complains about import competition. The squeeze on its profits has two sides—not merely the low product prices dictated by import competition but also the high resource prices dictated by the competition of other home employers in the market for resources. A less intense demand for resources in other uses would have left the import-competing industry in a less uncomfortable cost-price squeeze. As Chapter Two explained, the price system tends to channel resources into the lines where they can contribute most to meeting consumer demands. If the import-competing industry is having trouble avoiding losses while paying its resources their competitive prices, this indicates that at least some of its resources could contribute more to the value of output elsewhere. In this sense the import-competing industry is using resources in a relatively "unproductive" or "inefficient" way.

Protectionists may object to evaluating the productivity of resources in the import-competing industry at a product price kept as low as it is only by import competition. With import competition less intense and the price of its product higher, the industry might compare favorably indeed with other home industries in transforming resources into valuable output. Still, the objection would miss the point. The availability of foreign widgets at bargain prices makes domestic widgets less important or valuable than they otherwise would be, just as truly as the availability of wheat makes corn less important or valuable than otherwise, or just as truly as a warm climate makes furnaces or fuel oil less important or valuable. In economics, everything does depend on everything else. How much a product of a particular kind or from a particular source is worth to consumers depends partly on supplies of other kinds or from other sources. The values of using a plot of land as a parking lot or as a wheat field depend on the availability of other resources for providing parking space and for growing wheat. The function of the price system is to apportion resources among rival uses in the light of circumstances as they really are (or show prospects of becoming), not in the light of imaginary different circumstances. One of the actual circumstances affecting how important it is to use resources in one line of production is what other ways are available to satisfy consumer demands. The availability of foreign bargains is a genuine fact and counts just as appropriately in determining the pattern of production and resource allocation as do climate or technology or consumer tastes.

The logic of a competitive price system does, then, justify saying that the industries which can most profitably bid for resources are likely, in a sense, to be the most productive ones, the ones most efficient in converting resources into things consumers value. (Strictly speaking, the relevant comparison is a marginal one, between segments of industries or segments of production, and not a global comparison of entire industries.) The industries hardest put to cover their costs are likely to be relatively inefficient in converting resources into value for consumers. But note how limited an interpretation this puts on the words "efficient" and "inefficient"! To say that profitable industry A uses resources more efficiently than industry B, suffering from import competition, is not to say that A has keener management, more modern equipment, better human relations, more skilled and experienced and dedicated workers, or anything of the sort. Nor is it to say that B has dull management, stupid and slothful workers, and outmoded production methods. On the contrary, the import-competing industry may be a very model of alert managers and workers and of modern technology. (But if businessmen cling indefinitely to a hopeless situation, doubts do arise about their alertness.) Praiseworthy management and technology are not the same as economic (allocative) efficiency, which concerns how effectively resources are being used to meet the demands that prevail in the light of alternatives open to consumers. In this last respect, an unprofitable import-competing industry is "inefficient." But the word "inefficiency," used in this narrow sense, invites misunderstanding.

The typical free-trader is off the track, then, in sneering at the inefficiency of industries dependent on tariff protection. He rubs salt in the wounds of worthy people who are in enough business trouble anyway. Furthermore, a misdirected charge of inefficiency is open to easy rebuttal; import-competing producers can often truthfully point to their hard work, dedication, alertness to new ideas, and other virtues. Such answers, though pretty much irrelevant, *seem* relevant if the free-trade argument was misstated in the first place. The true issue is not how efficient particular producers are but how efficient, or how economic, the overall patterns of production and resource use is.

THE ALLOCATIVE HARM DONE BY TARIFFS

So far we have focused attention on the gains from using productive resources to take advantage of trading opportunities. Another approach is to see how trade barriers throw some of these gains away.

A tariff drives a wedge between the price received by foreign suppliers and the price paid by home consumers. At the tariff-distorted price, the amount of other goods that must be given up to obtain the taxed import is larger for individual consumers than for the country as a whole. The trouble is not so much that consumers pay increased prices for what they continue importing, since the additional money goes to their own government rather than to the foreign suppliers. (In fact, the government may collect *more* than the price increase that consumers pay, but we neglect this possibility of partly shifting the tax abroad until we review the terms-of-trade argument for tariffs in Chapter 11.) Nor is the main trouble the higher prices that consumers pay for the quantity of domestically produced import-type goods that they would have bought even under free trade, for this money is simply transferred from consumers to their fellow-citizens and is also not lost to the country.* In fact, this transfer to domestic producers is usually a leading purpose of the tariff, whether the legislators who enact it think about the matter in just this way or not. But transfers of income or wealth within the country are not the whole story. In addition, there is a dead loss from the national point of view. It centers on the amount of goods that would have been imported under free trade but are kept out by the tariff.

Consider the amount of discontinued imports of some one product, widgets. This amount is worth more to consumers than it would cost. Under free trade, consumers buy imported widgets at whatever amount per time period makes the value to them of the "last" one bought (a loose but convenient term) just equal to its cost or price. (At any smaller rate of importing, consumers would still value additional widgets at more than their cost and so would buy more of them; at any larger rate of importing,

---

*In addition to the higher prices on whatever output was produced domestically even under free trade, the transfer will include some payment in excess of cost on the *expansion* of domestic output due to the tariff.

consumers would cut back their purchases to save more in cost than they lost in value.) On the "last" widget imported per time period under free trade, then, the excess of value over cost is zero. But with a tariff in effect, consumers adjust their buying so that the "last" widget still imported has a value of the "last" widget imported exceeds its cost from the national point of view by the amount of duty per widget. For the amount of widget imports that the tariff prevents (in comparison with imports under free trade), the per-unit excess of value over cost to the country is somewhere between zero and the amount of import duty. We may roughly estimate this excess value for the "average" widget in the range of discontinued imports by splitting the difference between zero and the full duty per unit. The total loss per time period of value in excess of cost therefore equals approximately the amount of import shrinkage times half the duty per widget. Whether or not this approximation is close, a valuable opportunity definitely goes to waste because the tariff falsifies the price signals that guide consumer purchases. This dead loss is something distinct from and in addition to the already mentioned transfers from consumers to their government and to domestic widget producers.

The dead loss has two components, sometimes called the *consumption cost* and the *production cost* of the tariff. They are associated with two components of the import shrinkage, namely, the cutback in total consumption of imports and import-type domestic goods combined, and the replacement of some imports by increased domestic production of similar goods. The consumption cost occurs because the cutback in total widget consumption means that consumer purchases shift away from widgets onto other products that would yield as much satisfaction only at higher cost. Although the "last" widget consumed under free trade has a value to consumers just equal to the cost to the country as a whole, the "last" unit consumed under protection has a value exceeding its cost by the full amount of the duty; and the "average" widget in the range of discontinued total consumption has a value to consumers exceeding cost to the country by roughly half the duty.

The production cost of the tariff consists of how much more the increase in domestic widget production costs the country than the imports it displaces. Domestic production expands, though costing more than imports, because the tariff enables producers to collect an increased price; the need for a price increase to call forth this additional domestic production suggests that expanding production does raise costs per widget. Because the tariff-increased price is necessary to let domestic producers cover their costs on expanded output, the higher prices consumers pay on the additional output (beyond the output produced and bought domestically even under free trade) do not represent merely a transfer into domestic earnings; in part, they are a dead loss. We can estimate this loss in a way paralleling the estimation of consumption cost. Under competitive conditions, output per time period tends to be such that one more widget would involve an extra cost just equal to its selling price. At any smaller output, expansion would add less to cost than to sales revenue; at any larger output, a cutback would cut costs more than sales revenue. The "last" widget per time period produced domestically under free trade, therefore, has a cost (a so-called "marginal cost") equal to the free-trade price. Similarly, the "last" one produced under protection has a cost equal to the protected price, which exceeds the free-trade price of imported widgets by the amount of the duty. Over the range of expansion in domestic output, then, the "average" widget has an excess cost of roughly half the amount of duty. This average excess multiplied by the expansion of domestic output approximates the total excess cost of producing these widgets directly rather than obtaining them indirectly through production of export goods.

The production and consumption costs of a tariff bear a close analogy to each other. The tariff displaces a lower-cost foreign source of supply by a higher-cost domestic source; a given quantity of widgets requires a larger sacrifice of other things under protection than under free trade. The tariff also diverts some consumption from widgets to other things. Just as people can "produce" widgets either directly or else by producing exports with which to buy widgets abroad, so people can "produce" satisfactions for themselves by consuming either widgets or other things. Imported bananas and domestic apples, or imported wine and domestic beer, are alternative methods or "ingredients" for "producing" consumer satisfactions. Accurate price signals let consumers choose to obtain satisfactions in the cheapest available way. But a tariff falsifies these signals and makes consumers choose a higher-cost product source of satisfaction.

Since the tariff imposes a dead loss equal to roughly half the duty per unit on the "average" widget in the ranges of both total consumption cutback and domestic production expansion, and since these two changes add up to the import shrinkage, the sum of consumption and production costs roughly equals this shrinkage multiplied by half the duty on each unit. We already reached this same result when considering the import shrinkage as a whole, before splitting up the damage done by the tariff into its two parts.

MEASURING THE ALLOCATIVE LOSSES

This method of estimating the allocative harm done by tariffs admittedly ignores a number of complications. Some are examined in the following section. Even allowing for these complications, however, we are led to a general conclusion about trade barriers that may seem both surprising and disturbing. The allocative harm done is probably quite small in comparison to anything as large, say, as national income. Before condemning the method of estimate for this reason or jumping to any other conclusion, the reader should wait for the interpretations offered in Chapter Five. The losses that seem so small are simply those connected with the misallocation of resources—the diversion of demand onto higher-cost sources of products and satisfactions. Whether there are other benefits of trade and other costs of protection, not subject to numerical estimate but nonetheless genuine and important, is something else to consider.

A few sample figures will suggest how to estimate the allocative damage of tariff protection. Suppose that a country levies a 25 percent duty on the prices paid foreigners for its imports.* As a result, we assume, trade shrinks by 33 1/3 percent of its free-trade volume (the percentage is the same whether trade is measured in physical units or in money value at pre-tariff prices). Remembering to use one-half of the duty on each unit as a measure of average dead loss, we see that the total dead loss equals 1/2 x 1/4 x 1/3 = 1/24 of the value of imports under free trade. If the same rate of duty caused imports to shrink by 50 percent of their free-trade volume, the total dead loss would be 1/2 x 1/4 x 1/2 = 1/16 of free-trade import value. If the 25 percent duty was just barely high enough to shrink trade to nothing, or by 100 percent, the dead loss would be 1/2 x 1/4 x 1 = 1/8 of free-trade import value. (The government would then collect no tariff revenue, and the increased prices collected by domestic producers of import-type goods might largely represent a necessary inducement to expand their output at increasing cost, and not just extra earnings on what they were already producing.)

As this example suggests, the more price-sensitive the demand for imports is, the more deeply a tariff eats into the gains from trade. Another thought might suggest the opposite: a high price-sensitivity of demand could mean that the imports are not "urgently" needed, so that shrinking them would cut welfare correspondingly little. This second consideration does apply to an import quota: the more readily consumers would have done without a good in response to a price increase, the less they suffer from an import cutback of a predetermined size. In other words, the more

---

*This percentage is either a uniform rate of all goods or some sort of "effective" average of different rates. On the difficulties involved in using such an average, see below, "Some Complications." Furthermore, the divergence of the individual rates from the average makes the damage done greater than it would be if all the individual duty rates were equal. See pp. 65-66 below.

price-sensitive imports are, the lower the rate of duty is that would be equivalent to a definite quota. But for a definite rate of import duty, how sensitively trade shrinks is the dominant consideration. One more extreme case makes this intuitively clear. If import demand were so insensitive to price that a tariff caused *no* fall in imports either by expanding domestic production at their expense or by cutting back total consumption, there would be no dead loss, but just a transfer from consumers to the government as tariff revenue and to domestic producers as higher prices on their unchanged output. This contrast between the extremes of high and zero price-sensitivity reminds us, incidentally, of the familiar case for raising necessary revenue, other considerations being the same, by taxing things whose quantities respond to price only slightly.

Now consider imports and dead loss expressed as a percentage of national income. As before, suppose that an average duty of 25 percent shrinks imports by 33.3 percent of their free-trade volume. If imports had in turn amounted to 20 percent of national income (a high figure for most countries in the real world), the dead loss would be only $1/2 \times 1/4 \times 1/3 \times 1/5 = 1/20$, or .83 percent of national income. If imports shrank more sensitively, or by 50 percent of their free-trade level, the dead loss would still amount to only 1.25 percent of national income. Of course, this figure refers only to the harm a country does to itself with its own tariffs; it does not count the harm the country inflicts on others or the harm it suffers from the tariffs of others.

A few economists have made estimates of this sort for actual countries. Arnold Harberger has done it for Chile. In an impressionistic way he judged that Chilean tariffs and other trade restrictions amounted to the rough equivalent of a 50 percent average import duty and that imports actually amounting to about 10 percent of national income would double to about 20 percent under free trade. The excluded imports are therefore worth about 10 percent of national income; and this, multiplied by half the rate of duty, gives 1/40 of national income, or 2 1/2 percent, as a rough estimate of dead loss.[6]

Harberger's estimate is in line with estimates that have been made of the gains expected through better resource allocation in an economically unified Europe. Tibor Scitovsky's estimate was "less than one-twentieth of one percent of the gross social product of the countries involved." Harry Johnson "estimated the gain to Britain from the formation of a Free Trade Area as at most 1 percent of national income."[7] Both these estimates, like Harberger's, are admittedly rough and open to objections and refer only to the gains from improved resource allocation, not counting the even harder-to-assess benefits hoped for from economies of scale, greater exposure to ideas about improved production methods and competitive pressures to adopt them, and so forth.

Finally, let us estimate what the United States might gain by moving to free trade. Instead of trying to come as close as possible to the true figure, though, we shall shade our guess in the direction of overstating the significance of the tariff. In 1970, industrial imports subject to most-favored-nation rates of duty amounted to just over 2.60 percent of national income, while dutiable MFN imports of agricultural goods amounted to 0.45 percent.* (Total industrial and total agricultural imports together accounted for about 96 percent of the value of all imports.) If these imports would have *quadrupled* under free trade—which assumes far more price-sensitivity of demand than any expert on U.S. trade has ever, to our knowledge, suggested as realistic—the industrial and agricultural imports excluded by the tariff amounted to 7.8 and 1.35 percent of national income, respectively. Taking 12.1 and 12.4 percent as the estimated average rates of duty on the two product categories, we obtain a dead loss of .5 x .121 x .078, or .004719, and .5 x .124 x .0135, or .000837. Adding the two dead losses, we get .005556, or slightly more than one-half of 1 percent of national income lost on account of tariffs. As we said, this result is more likely to overstate than to understate the correct figure.[8] On the basis of different and more detailed assumptions about the price-sensitivity of U.S. import demand, Stephen Magee estimated the annual rate of damage inflicted by U.S. tariffs, based on 1971 data, as between $178 million and $493 million.[9] These estimates imply a dead loss of between .02 and .057 percent of national income for that year.

SOME COMPLICATIONS

Several questions arise over the validity of these calculations, one of which concerns the assumptions that underlie our comparisons of the gains and losses of different people. Admittedly, we count these gains and losses equally per dollar's worth. Another question about our method of estimating the misallocation-harm of a tariff concerns whether it covers not only the import shrinkage but also the export shrinkage that sooner or later matches it. The answer is yes. Or, rather, there is no *separate* damage on the export side. Exports benefit a country not in themselves but only as a means of

---

*Most-favored-nation rates are the rates of duty estimated by the International Trade Commission in its study cited below, note 8. For the meaning of the expression "most-favored-nation," see below, p. 270. The great bulk of trade falls into the MFN category.

paying for imports. Import prices in money represent import prices paid in export goods or in other goods forgone to produce the exports, and our method does take into account how a tariff distorts these prices.* If imports were affected not only by import duties but also by separate duties on exports, then this distortion as well would have to be taken into account in assessing the damage. But, in simple numerical examples, it is convenient to use the term "tariff" or "import duty" to stand for the total divergence between the national and private views of how expensive imports are in terms of exports, a divergence due not only to import duties in the strict sense but also to whatever export duties there may be.

A few more qualifications remain to be considered. First, one-half of the duty per unit overstates the wasted average excess of consumer value over free-trade cost if the duty is more than high enough to cut off imports completely. A duty of $200 a pair on shoes surely would not impose an average dead loss of as much as $100 a pair. Even with imports completely shut out, consumers would not value a "last" pair of shoes at as much as $200 above the world price, since domestic production at much lower cost would almost surely keep shoes from being *that* scarce and valuable. At the margin where the last bit of import trade is just barely cut off, the relevant excess of value to consumers (equaling home production cost) over world supply price is equal to the duty that would just barely cut off imports; and the average dead loss per unit over the range of excluded imports is roughly equal to one-half of this just-barely-prohibitive duty.

Our method of estimating the loss from a tariff has a different bias when none at all of the commodity would be produced at home without protection. The bias concerns the production cost of the tariff. Earlier we supposed not only that the "last" unit produced at home under protection had a cost exceeding the foreign supply price by the full amount of duty but also that the "last" unit produced at home under free trade had a cost exceeding the foreign supply price by zero. Now, however, when no domestic

---

*While the method commits no gross error of improperly just forgetting the export side, some doubt about accuracy does creep in here. The changed volume of export-type production associated with shrunken trade may well affect the costs per unit of export-type goods and in turn affect the real quantities of goods in general that correspond to the estimated money costs of the tariff. On usual assumptions about how costs vary with output in export-type production as in other production, this is one reason why the estimate of loss may be an overstatement. (See W. M. Corden, "The Calculation of the Cost of Protection," *Economic Record,* April 1957, pp. 41, 45-46.)

production would take place under free trade because even its cheapest unit would cost more than the foreign supply price, we can no longer estimate the average excess unit cost of domestic production in the import-replacing range simply by splitting the difference between zero and the duty per unit; instead, we must find the average of some positive figure and the duty per unit.

The last two biases, in summary, run in opposite directions. Half the duty per unit times the import shrinkage overstates the total loss from a higher-than-prohibitive duty and understates the loss from a duty essential to any domestic production at all of the import-replacing commodity. It would be arguing *too* loosely to suppose that the first bias for some goods and the second bias for other goods (and, conceivably, both biases together for still other goods) pretty much offset each other when we try to estimate the damage done by a country's entire schedule of import duties. But at least the two biases do not reinforce each other.

Suppose that, instead of a tariff, the government imposed an import quota or persuaded foreigners to impose "voluntary" restraint on their exports of some good to us. Although the losses due to a quota would seem at least as great as those due to an equally restrictive tariff, Congressman Phil Landrum of Georgia was apparently serious when he asked:

> Would it not be more nearly complete free trade under an arrangement that would allow a stabilized amount of a given product to be imported than it would be to try to erect a tariff barrier in the first place to keep it out?... If we legislate quotas, are we not getting a little closer to free trade in these modern times than we have ever been before?[10]

Contrary to whatever the Congressman may have been thinking, a quota causes as much consumption and production loss as a tariff set just high enough to cause an equal shrinkage in imports. In addition, however, a quota allows what would otherwise be tariff revenue for the government to go instead to importers or foreign exporters in the form of a "quota profit." When this profit is captured by foreign exporters, it clearly causes the home country's total dead loss to exceed its loss from an equally restrictive duty. Where importers capture the profits the total dead loss for their country as a whole is no greater, but the transfer of real income from consumers to privileged importers rather than to the government would itself seem to be an added disadvantage.

Related to this added disadvantage are the problems of allocating import privileges under a quota system, the creation of inflexibilities and not-particularly-deserving vested interests, the lessening of competitive pressures for efficiency if the privileges are rigidly allocated according to some historical formula, and so forth. In short, limiting imports by quantity imposes various genuine but hard-to-measure costs in addition to the costs from an equally restrictive ordinary import duty.

A practical difficulty connected with the harm done by quotas is that of calculating the equivalent rate of duty. Because no one knows just how price-sensitive the demand for imports is, there is no sure way to determine how high a duty would be required to shrink imports to the level permitted under quotas. In his 1971-based examination of U.S. quantitative restrictions, Stephen Magee estimated a total loss to the United States (inclusive of quota profits captured by foreigners as well as consumption and production costs) of $3.555 billion or about 0.44 percent of national income.[11] Since 1971, voluntary restraints on steel and import quotas on oil have been eliminated, but textile quotas have been extended to encompass wool and man-made goods. The full scope of quantitative restrictions, particularly those of the "voluntary" kind, is not always known.

Still another bias now comes to mind. A method may be valid for assessing the effect of a duty on one single good under otherwise complete free trade, but is it still valid for assessing many duties on many goods at once? An import duty on pork may increase or help maintain imports of beef; and if a duty on beef has been holding its value to consumers above its foreign supply price, any imports maintained represent a gain partly offsetting the direct damage from the beef duty. At the same time, the beef duty, though harmful in itself, helps lessen the harm done by the pork duty. On the other hand, a duty on golf clubs would worsen the harm from a duty on golf balls; and similarly, duties on tires and gasoline would reinforce each other's harm. A different type of interrelation is illustrated by a protected industry using dutiable imported raw materials. Removing all tariffs would harm this industry in one respect but benefit it in another. The net gain thereby achieved would depend on the whole complex of such relations among dutiable imports, some being substitutes for each other, others being used together, and still others being ingredients for domestic production.

An extensive literature on the concept of "effective protection" formalizes the relations between tariffs on final products and tariffs on imported ingredients of their domestically produced substitutes.[12] This literature recognizes that what really receives tariff protection is not a commodity itself but the domestic activity of producing it. Protection works by making value added domestically exceed what it would be at free-trade prices (if the domestic industry could somehow exist under free trade). "Value added" is the value or cost of output in excess of what is attributable to what we might call "processed inputs" or "purchased inputs," that is, raw materials, fuels, parts, and other ingredients bought either from other sectors of the home economy or from abroad. The value of output beyond the cost of these processed or purchased inputs is the value added by the home industry's own activity, which is attributable in turn to the labor, land-use, money capital, entrepreneurship, and similar ultimate or primary factors of production employed directly in that industry (as distinguished from factors employed *indirectly* through their embodiment in purchased inputs).

Suppose that a widget salable for $1 under free trade has 75 cents of this value attributable to purchased inputs and 25 cents attributable to labor, profit-earners, and other factors employed directly in the domestic industry. Now suppose an import duty raises the selling price of a widget to $1.40. With processed inputs remaining duty-free and their cost remaining at 75 cents, the value of output available for the directly employed factors rises from the original 25 cents to 65 cents ($1.40 minus 75 cents). The 40 percent duty on imported widgets amounts to a 160 percent subsidy to domestic widget production (the percentage by which 65 cents exceeds 25 cents). ("Subsidy" is a convenient but imprecise word, since the government does not literally subsidize domestic widget production. Rather, its restraint on foreign competition makes possible an increase in price and in domestic value added.) The industry's scale of operations and employment of ultimate factors expands by more than one would guess from considering merely the rate of import duty on widgets.

In general, however, the magnification of apparent into effective protection is not as dramatic or simple as in this example; and the effect may just as well run in the reverse direction. Complexity, in fact, is one of the key lessons of the whole analysis. The example supposed no duties on purchased inputs. If, however, tariffs raise the costs of purchased inputs sufficiently relative to the price of widgets, then the domestic industry enjoys no effective protection at all, or even negative protection.* Its encouragement by the duty on widgets is just outweighed, or more than outweighed, by discouragement through higher prices of its inputs. Still assuming that purchased inputs and directly employed factors account for 75 and 25 cents, respectively, of widget value at free trade prices, still assuming a 40 percent import duty on widgets, but now assuming a 60 percent duty on purchased inputs, we find that domestic widget production bears effective protection at a rate of *minus* 20 percent. The duties increase the selling value of a widget to $1.40 and the cost of purchased inputs to $1.20, leaving only 20 cents as domestic value added, or 5 cents (20 percent) less than before.

---

*This point does not depend on how much of the purchased inputs is literally imported from abroad. A protective duty tends to raise the prices of domestic import-competing goods along with the prices of actual imports, and the widget industry buying them suffers to the same extent.

As our numerical examples suggest, value added in domestic widget production receives effective protection at a rate higher than, the same as, or lower than the nominal duty rate on widgets according as the duty rate on purchased inputs falls short of, equals, or exceeds the widget rate. (If various purchased inputs bear different rates of duty, the rate to use in this comparison is a weighted average of the rates on the individual inputs, the weights being the shares of the respective inputs in total cost of a widget at free-trade prices.) The applicable formula is as follows: effective protection rate on domestic value added equals nominal duty rate on widgets *minus* average duty rate on purchased inputs times their share in total cost at free-trade prices, all divided by the share of domestic value added in total cost at free-trade prices. This formula assumes that the various duty rates are no higher than those that would completely exclude imports—that they have no "water" in them—that the foreign supply prices of our imports are constant (the formula abstracts from terms-of-trade effects such as are considered in Chapter 11), and that the physical mix of the various ultimate factors and purchased inputs remains unchanged, despite the duties, from what it would be at free-trade prices. Even if this last assumption held true in the real world, assessment of the effective protection accorded to various lines of production would be extremely complicated. Realistically recognizing the variability of the input and factor mix would make this assessment all the more complicated. Complexity is, in fact, one of the points of the whole analysis. Recognizing the concept of effective protection increases our skepticism that economic and econometric experts—let alone politicians—could devise a tariff structure anywhere close to one that would be ideally compensatory in the sense discussed in Chapter 12 below.

One consequence of the effective protection analysis is to complicate still further the measurement of the net social harm due to protection. Ronald McKinnon has argued that dead loss measurements which treat all imports as consumption goods are unrealistic "since all imported goods are generally subject to some domestic value added before they are consumed" and are therefore "in some sense intermediate inputs even when not formally classified as such." According to McKinnon, the gains from trade are much larger when intermediate goods are used in nearly fixed proportions with the cooperating ultimate factor of production and when intermediate goods are much cheaper to import than to produce at home.[13]

In fact our original formula for dead loss may either overestimate or underestimate the harm done by the imposition of a tariff on a final good which itself uses other dutiable imports in production. The consumption cost of a less-than-prohibitive tariff on a final good is unaffected by any duties that may be imposed on intermediate factors of production. As long as the tariff-inclusive price of the final good remains sufficiently low, import duties levied on intermediate factors of production will merely cause domestic consumers to substitute imports for domestic production of the final good until domestic producers have fully absorbed the duties imposed on their purchased inputs or have shut their production down.* The consumption cost may therefore be calculated, as before, by taking one-half the amount of duty on the final good *only* times the shrinkage in total consumption.

Calculating the production-cost component, however, is more complicated when purchased inputs bear a duty. That component may be either more or less than is suggested by dead-loss calculations not distinguishing between duties on inputs and duties on final products. If we try to allow for this distinction in calculations based on plausible assumptions or assumptions likely to err on the side of exaggerating the loss, we still reach the same conclusion as before: the sum of consumption and production components of dead loss due to U.S. tariffs amounts to only a small fraction of 1 percent of national income.

The concept of "average tariff" requires modification not only on the ground exposed by the theory of effective protection but on another ground also. A simple arithmetical average of duty rates gives equal weight to every item in the tariff schedules, so that if there were three items in those schedules dutiable at 25 percent, 50 percent, and 75 percent, the average rate would be 50 percent.

Suppose that the physical volume of imports shrinks by one percent for every one percentage point increase in duty and that the value of imports in each of these categories accounts for one-twentieth of national income.† Then import shrinkages due to each duty would be 25 percent, 50 percent, and 75 percent respectively, and the dead loss as a fraction of national income could be calculated for each as follows: (1) $.5 \times .25 \times .25 \times .05 = .0015625$, (2) $.5 \times .5 \times .5 \times .05 = .00625$, (3) $.5 \times .75 \times .75 \times .05 = .0140625$. Adding up

---

*The duties will be absorbed in the form of reduced wages, rents, interest payments, profits, and other returns to the ultimate factors employed directly in producing the final good at home. If the tariff on the final good were prohibitive, that is, high enough to bar all imports of it, then consumers could not substitute imports for domestic production, and they would have to bear part of the duties imposed on intermediate factors of production. The resulting consumption cost would be one-half that part of the input duties borne by consumers times the shrinkage in total consumption. However, that consumption cost would be different from and additional to the consumption cost directly attributable to the barely prohibitive tariff on the final goods.

†Our assumption of a one percent shrinkage in imports for each one percent point of duty merely simplifies the arithmetic. Imports could

these figures gives .021875, or 2.1875 percent, as the fraction of income lost. Yet if we try to measure dead loss by using the arithmetic average of all three tariffs and the total observed shrinkage in imports, we get .5 x .5 x (.25 + .5 + .75) x .05 = .01875, or only 1.875 percent. By using the "average" tariff we underestimate the actual dead loss.

This "aggregation bias" results from the fact that the dead loss caused by a particular duty is proportional not to the duty rate itself but to its *square*. Increasing a duty increases the dead loss in two dimensions that get multiplied together—the loss per unit of trade shrinkage and the amount of trade shrinkage. To emphasize this proportionality to the square of the rate, we may rewrite the calculations for the three separate categories of the preceding paragraph as (1) .5 x $(.25)^2$ x .05 = .0015625, (2) .5 x $(.5)^2$ x .05 = .00625, and (3) .5 x $(.75)^2$ x .05 = .0140625.

The great diversity of rates in actual tariff schedules makes it tempting to work with the assumption of a single average rate. Yet doing so yields, as we have seen, an *underestimate* of dead loss. The calculation would be accurate only in the trivial case in which all individual duty rates are equal to each other and so to their average.*

A final difficulty concerns the overall balancing of trade. The total import shrinkage from a whole range of import duties is not as great as the sum of the separate amounts by which each single duty would shrink imports of the

------

respond more or less sensitively without affecting the proportionality of the dead loss to the square of the duty rate. Readers familiar with the concept of elasticity will see that the formula for dead loss expressed as a proportion of free trade import value is one-half times the square of the duty rate multiplied by import demand elasticity. Here, the duty rate is expressed as a proportion of the free trade import price, and the elasticity is calculated with price and quantity changes related to the free-trade price and quantity. If we know the free-trade total value of each import expressed as a fraction of national income, we can readily reexpress the dead loss from each duty as such a fraction also. The square-of-the-duty-rate principle obviously does not depend on assuming any particular volume of imports.

*Another possibility would be to construct a special weighted average duty rate, with high rates and rates on imports in highly elastic demand carrying bigger weights in the construction of the average than low rates and rates on low-demand-elasticity imports. Constructing and using such a weighted average rate would be just as complicated a job, however, as calculating and adding up the individual dead losses caused by the individual duties.

dutiable product if it were the only duty. The reason is that the tendency of all the duties together to make imports fall short of exports would be resisted by inflation of the country's price and money-income level or a rise in the foreign-exchange value of its currency. (Again we must anticipate what Chapter Six explains.) These developments would tend to keep trade in balance not only by restraining exports but also by resisting the fall in imports. Some domestic industries would therefore expand less under general protectionism than one would suppose from estimates that did not take these repercussions into account. The converse holds true for a general move away from protectionism: some industries which seemed dependent on protection would in fact survive under free trade. Imponderable repercussions like these further increase the difficulty of judging which industries really are protected and how much protection they receive.[14]

NOTES

1. Frank H. Knight, *The Ethics of Competition* (New York: Kelley, 1951), p. 234.

2. Jagdish Bhagwati, *Trade, Tariffs and Growth* (Cambridge, Mass.: MIT Press, 1969), pp. 150-52.

3. See, for example, Jacob Winer, *Studies in the Theory of International Trade* (New York: Harper, 1937), pp. 533-34; Charles P. Kindleberger in *Foreign Trade Policy* (1958), (see Chapter 1 note 5), p. 82; and William Penfield Travis, *The Theory of Trade and Protection* (Cambridge, Mass.: Harvard University Press, 1964), p. 142.

4. O. R. Strackbein, *The Tariff Issue Reviewed and Restated* (Washington: National Labor-Management Council on Foreign Trade Policy, 1951), p. 2.

5. 1973 HW&M VI 1781. (See Chapter One, note 8.)

6. Arnold Harberger, "Using the Resources at Hand More Effectively," *American Economic Review,* May 1959, pp. 134-46. Harberger also tried to estimate the loss due to domestic monopolistic distortions in Chile and concluded that it, too, was small compared with national income. For somewhat similar studies, see J. Wemelsfelder, "The Short-Term Effect of the Lowering of Import Duties in Germany," *Economic Journal,* March 1960, pp. 94-101, and J. H. Young, *Canadian Commercial Policy* (Ottawa: Royal Commission on Canada's Economic Prospects, 1957).

7. Harry G. Johnson, "The Cost of Protection and the Scientific Tariff," *Journal of Political Economy,* August 1960, pp. 338-339n, citing Scitovsky's *Economic Theory and Western European Integration* (Stanford: Stanford University Press, 1958), p. 67, and his own "The Gain from Freer Trade with Europe: An Estimate," *Manchester School of Economic and Social Studies,* September 1958, pp. 247-55. Johnson also finds that the percentage loss of national income under self-sufficiency is rather small unless the economy is both naturally heavily dependent on international trade and inflexible in economic structure. See his "The Costs of Protection and Self-Sufficiency," *Quarterly Journal of Economics,* August 1965, pp. 356-72.

8. Data used to make these and certain other calculations below were taken from U.S. Tariff Commission, *Trade Barriers,* Chapter IV, pp. 27, 34, 89, and the *Economic Report of the President* (Washington: U.S. Government Printing Office, 1974), p. 266.

9. Stephen P. Magee, "The Welfare Effects of Restrictions on U.S. Trade," *Brookings Papers on Economic Activity,* 1972, p. 681. These are Magee's estimates before he adjusts for

the "aggregation bias," which we describe above and below, pp. 65-66. After adjusting for such bias, Magee obtains allocative losses of between $510 million and $1,415 million, or of between .06 and .16 percent of national income.

10. 1970 HW&M XI 3091. See Chapter 1, note 1. Congressman Landrum's witness replied that he thought this was the first time he had "heard it suggested that quotas would be a step toward free trade" and that he "would like to ponder that a bit."

11. Magee, op. cit., 673. Of the total welfare loss, the quota profit captured by foreigners was estimated to be $1.2 billion.

12. See, for example, Harry G. Johnson, "The Theory of Effective Protection and Preferences," Economica, May 1969, pp. 119-38; W. M. Corden, "The Structure of a Tariff System and the Effective Protection Rate," Journal of Political Economy, June 1966, pp. 221-37; and articles by W. M. Corden, Ronald W. Jones, Ronald Findlay, and L. Clark Leith in the February, May, and August 1971 issues of Journal of International Economics.

13. "Intermediate Products and Differential Tariffs: A Generalization of Lerner's Symmetry Theorem," Quarterly Journal of Economics, November 1966, pp. 606, 609.

14. W. M. Corden, Economic Record, April 1957, p. 40.

The relatively small allocative effects of protectionism, as estimated in the preceding chapter, should be kept in perspective. The *total* gain from trade is admittedly both immense and incalculable. The whole character of the modern world, including the size, geographic distribution, and culture of its population, depends on past and present trade. Trade transmits not merely goods and capital but also ideas—ideas not merely about technology but also about standards of living and whole ways of life, including political and social arrangements. It transmits the results of diversified experimentation. Without it, the world's people would be much fewer and poorer than they are now.

True as this is, it does not bear directly on current policy, which concerns changes in trade barriers, rather than trade as a total. Not even the most rabid protectionists propose to wholly scuttle international trade. No one lobbies for protective tariffs on coffee or bananas or other products in which the United States has an unquestionable disadvantage. However, the United States has participated in an International Coffee Agreement for the protection of the coffee-exporting countries. For this reason, among others, it is pointless to stress figures purporting to show how much the United States depends on imports of certain vital materials, on how individual states and cities benefit from foreign trade, on how many jobs directly and indirectly depend on export and import trade, and so forth. In plain truth, neither a movement to complete free trade nor a return to a degree of protectionism that has any important political support would make any great difference to the United States—so far as the most narrowly defined allocative gain is concerned. Exaggerating this gain or loss invites easy rebuttal.

TRADE AND TECHNOLOGY

The relatively small allocational gain likely under complete free trade may be due in part to a scientific and technological "revolution" that, according to some writers, has been narrowing gaps in comparative advantage and undercutting the benefits of international specialization.[1] According to this view, technology and capital equipment have been gaining ground relative to natural conditions and resource endowments in determining what things can be economically produced. Technological progress and international trade are alike in widening the range of alternatives in production methods and in consumption. Synthetic materials diminish dependence on countries producing their natural counterparts. In the consumption patterns of economically advanced countries, farm products have grown less important relative to manufactures, whose production is not so closely tied to geographical conditions, and also relative to services, which move in international trade less readily than commodities. Convertibility of industrial plant among different types of production also reduces an advanced country's dependence on particular import supplies and export markets. Improved storability of seasonal goods may also lessen the importance of trade.

These points are related to the now-fashionable argument that the market economy has largely given way to planning by a "technostructure" of managerial and technical elites (see above, p. 29). Technological innovation brings with it the "need" for innovating firms to have organizational control over their economic environment—that is, their suppliers, their customers, and so forth. This need in turn implies a need to grow—to assimilate within the firm transactions that would otherwise take place within the market economy and disrupt well-laid plans to implement technical progress.

It is particularly crucial, according to this argument, for the firm to insulate itself from the vagaries of international trade. Unexpected foreign competition and excessive dependence on import supplies, which might capriciously evaporate and thereby sabotage some intricate capital project, "must" be avoided.* One author observes how U.S. automobile producers

---

*According to this rhetoric, the large firm "must" get what it "needs." Apparently, the idea is to prove the existence of control by the firm over its environment by using language that presumes the existence of such control in the first place. ("Things that need to go right must be made to go right;" Galbraith, *Economics and the Public Purpose,* [Boston: Houghton Mifflin, 1973], p. 39).

have established foreign plants from which they obtain components for final assembly here. By thus acquiring their own low-cost sources of supply, these producers have been able to curb foreign car sales in the United States.[2] The versatile technology of automobile production has permitted them to substitute an internal transaction for trade between foreign producers and domestic consumers and thereby to gain a greater degree of control over their environment, in which further technical progress (and, we may presume, further substitutions for trade) are made possible.

This reasoning is supposed to provide a rationalization for a rather old-fashioned protectionist doctrine. Since large firms have been able to insulate themselves from foreign competition—so the rationalization goes—other firms should have the same privilege. Tariffs or, better still, quotas should be used to provide stable markets and prices for all those industries (such as, perhaps, textile manufacturing) in which many small firms share the market. Commodity agreements and quotas "only do for producers in such industries what transnational corporations accomplish far more efficiently for the planning systems."[3]

We will consider in greater detail (below, pp. 173-80) the general issue of foreign investment and the multinational firm. For now it suffices to observe that the existence or nonexistence of a "technical revolution" or "technostructure" that may operate in some instances to reduce the scope for trade has no bearing on the question of whether trade should or should not be further regulated. Just as we should not exaggerate the allocative damage that any politically feasible protectionist measure is likely to inflict, neither should we deny such damage outright. The allocative gains available from trade liberalization are not simply repealed at the mention of technological progress.

For one thing, we must beware of the "fallacy of composition." (This fallacy deserves attention because it will be mentioned again in later chapters. The fallacy is the supposition that anything true of the part or individual must also be true of the whole or group. One person in a crowd can see a parade better by standing on a box, but not everybody could see better if everybody stood on a box.) While technological progress might increase the share of *some* things, it will not necessarily increase the share of *all* things that a firm or country can economically produce for itself. Despite modern technology, alternatives remain alternatives: producing more of some things still means producing less of others. Even if any of a wide range of industries could flourish in a country without some having pronounced economic advantages over others, the case against specialization and for extreme diversification still would not be decisive. (Ten men marooned on a desert island might have identical abilities for all the different tasks; yet specialization would still pay.) Especially so far as economies of scale of plant or industry or market apply, international specialization remains advantageous.

Some technological developments probably *increase* dependence on particular geographical sources of necessary materials. Uranium for atomic energy may be one example, although atomic energy may also reduce a country's dependence on hydroelectric sites and coal and oil fields. Fast transportation and improved preservation of perishables tend to increase trade. Finally, insofar as technological progress raises real incomes and makes people more aware of the world about them, consumers' wants become more diversified, and so do the materials and intermediate goods used in satisfying them. On this account, as people become more nearly satiated with the essentials of life and begin to demand such things as exotic foods, household decorations, and sporting equipment, international trade gains importance.*

Trade and technology are alike in expanding the range of opportunities and making any particular opportunity less important than before. It does not follow, though, that trade opportunities are *especially* unimportant. Suppose we agreed that as far as the narrow matter of resource allocation is concerned, it would make no great difference to the welfare of the United States if tariffs were abolished or, say, tripled. Now that we have synthetic rubber, no great harm would come from restricting imports of natural rubber; now that we have dacron, orlon, and kodel, as well as sheep, tightening the import barriers on woolen goods will do no great harm. Since the Pinto and Gremlin show that the United States can produce Volkswagen-sized cars, there is no strong reason not to put a quota on foreign-car imports. For that matter, now that we have dacron and Pintos, restrictions on orlon and Gremlins would do no great harm; now that electric stoves are available, gas stoves are dispensable; now that we have television, we could get along without radio.

In short, the more new opportunities we have, the less we would suffer from losing some old ones. Yet whatever valid arguments for protectionism there may be, the smallness of the marginal gain from trade expansion is not in itself an argument for throwing the gain away. The smallness of the gain is connected, anyway, with the small (though growing) volume of trade in the United States relative to national income. Relative to national income, the gain from having the Memorial Bridge across the Potomac River is also very small, but this is no reason for blowing it up. In absolute terms, the harm done by tariffs and quotas may not be so small, after all. One percent of national income in 1974 was over $11 billion. As Professor Ronald Coase

---

*On the one hand, it is sometimes argued that mass marketing promotes standardization and conformity. Also, the satisfaction of nonessential demands is regarded by some as a defect of trade. See, for example, Galbraith, *Economics and the Public Purpose,* pp. 151-52.

once said in conversation, it is not very reassuring to learn how small a percentage of national income is wasted by protective tariffs or any other particular type of unwise policy; so many types of waste are possible. "After all, we have only 100 percent to lose."

The relatively small amount of damage done by tariffs has a corollary that should be welcome to persons who regret any need to interfere with a basically free market economy. This is the apparent fact, noted above (p. 28), that monopoly distortions do not destroy a very large fraction of national income, either. The essence of monopoly is restriction of the alternatives open to buyers. Well, if the additional alternatives provided by international trade are relatively unimportant because so many alternatives are already provided by domestic trade and modern technology, then domestic monopoly would seem correspondingly unimportant also. Most of the points that the "modern-technology" case uses to argue the diminished importance of international trade—substitute materials, the potential competition implied by the wide range of goods that a country could produce economically, the rise in the relative importance of services— also argue a diminished scope for the exercise of monopoly power. Apparently the free-enterprise system is a hardy plant, with a way of growing around obstacles or making the best of them or providing incentives for the development and use of substitutes for whatever goods trade policy or monopoly may have interfered with. We need not be alarmed just because economic systems in the real world do not meet textbook standards of perfection.

"NONALLOCATIVE" GAINS FROM TRADE

The estimates mentioned so far have referred to a pecularly narrow kind of gain or loss associated with whether or not people are free to allocate given resources among alternative lines of production, according to known methods of production and existing opportunities for specialization. For all its merits, especially in exposing protectionist fallacies, this traditional analysis is incomplete. In addition to the allocative (or "static") gains traditionally analyzed, trade provides several kinds of "nonallocative" (or "dynamic") gain that may be more important. Trade barriers inflict harm akin to the nonallocative harm from monopoly examined in Chapter 3 under the label "X-inefficiency."

Trade links together markets in different places. It serves as a kind of safety valve or shock absorber, allowing random economic disturbances in different places to partially offset each other. A local crop failure or a local temporary glut of a particular product is less serious in a world united by trade than in an isolated local market. In this way, trade resembles insurance. Just as a loss spread over many policyholders through insurance premiums is less damaging than the loss each person would otherwise risk having to bear alone in full, so spreading around the risk of local disturbances is advantageous. Furthermore, the interconnection of markets is self-reinforcing: opportunities for trade promote the development of specialized trading firms, warehousing, commodity specialists and communications and market-reporting services, standardization of commodity grades, organized commodity markets with the futures trading and hedging facilities that they provide, arbitrage and speculation, banking facilities geared to the needs of international trade, credit reporting, international parallelism in commercial law, and commercial arbitration facilities. It also keeps businessmen alert to new markets for their goods and services, and alert to new ideas they may discover abroad and adopt at home.

Second, a market broadened by trade may make production cheaper and more efficient in several ways besides reallocation of resources in accordance with static comparative advantage. In some industries, a bigger market may offer scope for economies of mass production. Plants that had manufactured a large variety of goods may cut costs by specializing in fewer. Plants or companies that had themselves carried out several different stages in producing finished goods may cut costs by specializing in particular stages and more extensively buying and selling materials, semifinished goods, and component parts. This process of "vertical disintegration" illustrates the truth for companies as well as for workers of Adam Smith's dictum that "the division of labor is limited by the extent of the market." An expanded market may also offer scope for specialization and cost-cutting by promoting standardization of some consumer goods. This does not mean imposing "conformity" on unwilling consumers or depriving them of variety; on the contrary, trade broadens their range of choice. It broadens the scope not only for cost-cutting within firms but also for so-called "external economies" connected with the fuller development of transportation, communications, banking, research services, trade publications and other information services, trade associations, and technical schools and other facilities for training workers. Even the fuller development among managers and workers of attitudes and traditions and readiness for specialized knowledge, including an informally absorbed familiarity with their own industries and with industry in general, counts among the noteworthy external economies. Loosely speaking, the development of each firm or segment of the economy radiates influences that make development easier for other firms or segments; and a broadened market offers broader scope for these interactions.

Greater room for competition and its benefits in an expanded market counts as a third category of gains. Even if a country had only one or a few companies in a particular industry, their fewness would not matter much under free trade; competition from imports would restrain monopolistic pricing. Protectionism, by contrast, holds an umbrella over at least tacit monopolistic price agreements. Arrangements even with potential foreign competitors become more practical when tariffs shelter monopoly at home. Anticompetitive government policies, of which tariffs are a conspicuous type, also confer some respectability on cooperation among erstwhile competitors, and in the field of political pressures as well as in the market. There is some truth in the maxim, variously attributed to President Cleveland and to the sugar magnate Henry Osborne Havemeyer: "The tariff is the mother of trusts." Professor Gottfried Haberler finds "free international trade...the best anti-monopoly policy and the best guarantee for the maintenance of a healthy degree of free competition." Free trade *inside* the United States has probably outweighed the antitrust laws in making its economy "highly competitive compared with most other countries... Instead of pursuing a policy of harassing business leaders in law courts and before Congressional committees for alleged 'profiteering' and monopolistic practices," Haberler recommends subjecting them "to still stronger competition from abroad by reducing barriers to imports."[4]

A case history of the monopolizing effects of international trade barriers has been provided by Professor Joel Dirlam of the University of Rhode Island. Dirlam describes how the acceleration of steel imports during the early 1960s challenged the price leadership policies of U.S. Steel, causing a rapid *deceleration* in U.S. domestic steel prices (which had previously risen at twice the rate of average wholesale prices), and even some instances of "punitive price cutting." However, when "voluntary" quotas on foreign steel shipments to the United States were imposed in 1969, price leadership was reasserted (this time by Bethlehem Steel), and steel prices began once again to accelerate. Not only were the monopolistic practices of the U.S. steel industry reinforced (or salvaged), but also foreign steel producers were forced into collusive arrangements for carving up the shrunken U.S. market.[5]

In a famous speech of February 1953 advocating free trade, Henry Ford II quoted a statement that his grandfather had made in 1930, which is still relevant today:

Business thrives on competition. Nobody does his best if he knows no one is competing with him. Comfortably tucked away behind a tariff wall which shuts out all competition and gives industry an undue profit which it has not earned, the business of our country would grow soft and neglectful.... We need competition the world over to keep us on our toes and sharpen our wits. The keener the competition, the better it will be for us.[6]

Ford's point about tariffs is similar to the point Harvey Leibenstein has been making about tariffs, monopoly, and anticompetitive practices in general. We may recall (above, p. 30) that, according to Leibenstein, such practices create an "X-inefficiency" that is different from and greater than their allocative effects. The traditional static theory of comparative advantage describes how foreign competition promotes a more economic allocation of resources among definite lines of production employing *known and unchanging methods*. The firm is assumed to obtain the "maximum output obtainable from various factor inputs given the state of knowledge."[7] The X-inefficiency argument emphasizes, instead, how competition prods producers into finding ways to get a *greater* volume of output from given inputs—into putting monetary ahead of nonmonetary goals and profits ahead of leisure and corporate comfort. When forced by competition to make profits or go broke, the firm tries to find out about *new* or *previously neglected* methods and to discover and invent and develop new and improved products and to make technological and organizational improvements in production and marketing.

Here again, the American steel industry provides an illustrative case study. In testimony before Congress, Professor Walter Adams of Michigan State University observed how "for many years, especially during the 1950's, the American steel industry was technologically backward, not only in terms of invention but also in terms of innovation." Noting that the Austrians developed the basic oxygen process for steel making in 1950, Adams asked rhetorically:

Do you know that United States Steel, mighty United States Steel, did not install a basic oxygen furnace until 13 years later, namely 1963?...
I submit to you very respectfully that the American steel industry began to wake up to the need for technological adaptation under the stress and spur of the import competition that began to develop in the early 1960s.[8]*

When applied to international trade, the X-efficiency argument means not only strengthened competitive incentives, through the removal of trade barriers, but also an increase in the means and opportunities of responding to them (a characteristic that should be of special value to underdeveloped

---

*Contrast this with the argument reviewed earlier in this chapter that technological and organizational advances increase concentration by forcing the firm to exercise greater control over its environment.

countries). It means the conveyance not only of material means such as machinery but also of intangibles such as technological ideas and skills and business and managerial abilities.[9] In a survey of the benefits of dynamic competitive pressures to be expected from European economic integration, Professor Tibor Scitovsky emphasized an upward leveling of national differences in work habits, commercial and industrial practices, and awareness of technological and market opportunities. He envisaged a pervasive spirit of competition, in which corporate relations become more impersonal and therefore conducive to one firm's poaching on another's markets and in which the "quiet life" of high mark-ups, low turnover, and contentment with the "old ways" of doing things give way to keener competition and an increased flow and utilization of knowledge.[10]

The same qualifications attached to the X-inefficiency argument in Chapter Three apply here. Narrowly defined as the sacrifice of profits for leisure and other non-monetary benefits, certain alleged X-inefficiencies may be consistent, after all, with an expanded definition of efficiency that takes into account the legitimacy of some corporate amenities and of the convention that treats leisure as a consumer good. Those genuine X-inefficiencies which do result from tariffs as well as monopoly will yield in part to the competition for control of the firm which takes place in the capital markets.

A more serious criticism holds against any assumption that barriers to international trade give rise to X-inefficiency. According to this argument, the imposition of such barriers exerts conflicting effects on efficiency, from which no net effect, positive or negative, can be presumed on purely theoretical grounds. Tariffs and nontariff trade barriers cause real income and the rate of return to effort (as measured by profits, wages, and other factor rewards) to rise in import-competing firms but to fall in exporting firms.* "Effort," which Corden equates with "efficiency," tends to fall because of the higher real incomes enjoyed by import-competing firms (whose management can now afford to "consume" more leisure and exert less effort than before) and because of the lower rate of return to effort in the exporting firms. But, on the same account, effort tends to rise because of the lower real incomes enjoyed by exporting firms (whose managements can now afford to consume less leisure and more effort than before) and because of the higher rate of return to effort in the import-competing firms. "The efficiency effects of protection can go either way. Quite specific

---

*Measures that restrict imports tend, indirectly, to hamper export sales as well. Changes in exchange rates or price levels produce this result. A fuller explanation must await Chapter 6.

assumptions must be made to lead to the result that tariffs reduce efficiency."[11]

Corden himself recognizes a number of conditions that may bring this result after all. In particular, he mentions "made-to-measure" tariffs that are "adjusted as finely as possible to the 'needs' of the protected industries."[12] A policy of setting trade barriers just high enough to keep a protected industry in existence but not so high as to confer excess profits encourages members of that industry to tolerate X-inefficiencies in order to conceal any excess profits that might otherwise result from unintentionally excessive protection. (This is similar to the point attributed to Alchian and Kessel, above, p. 31, whereby the threat or reality of governmental regulation encourages firms having a degree of monopoly power to tolerate inefficiency and otherwise enjoy nonpecuniary amenities rather than pursue maximum money profit.)

A number of additional considerations favor, on balance, the presumption that trade liberalization increases efficiency. These considerations call into question certain assumptions made by Corden, to the effect that efficiency depends strictly on managerial effort and that firms are purely competitive price-takers. In such a world, competition *within* the import-competing or exporting industry is so intense that existing levels of effort are already "efficient" in any meaningful sense of that word. The excess profits created by higher trade barriers may temporarily cause an "inefficient" substitution of leisure for effort by import-competing firms, but the entry of new firms and expansion of old ones to take advantage of the generally higher price now received for import goods will eventually cause excess profits and the scope for X-inefficiency to disappear. (Remember that any *allocative* harm done by the trade barrier is separate and permanent.) Similarly, the pressures put on exporting firms to intensify effort (inefficiently?) due to temporary losses will disappear as established export producing firms shut down or contract their operations.

The enduring nonallocative consequences of import barriers are those which affect the degree of monopoly in different industries, and, in turn, the firm's inclination to cut prices and costs, to introduce new and better products, and to discover and make technological improvements.* Import barriers cut off some foreign competition with import-competing domestic

---

*Corden does consider the possibility that protection will increase the degree of monopoly and therefore the level of inefficiency. He does so, however, within the relatively narrow confines of his own effort-leisure calculus. ("The Efficiency Effects of Trade and Protection," in *Studies in International Economics,* p. 6.)

producers and also (by repercussions working through exchange rates or price levels) effectively shrink the home country's export markets. The representative domestic producers of import-competing goods thus gain increased shares of the markets they sell in, which suggests that each faces a less price-sensitive demand for his own output than before. He gains more scope for quasi-monopolistic pricing and for enjoying the proceeds in money profit or X-inefficiency, as he prefers.*

A trade barrier imposed at home exerts parallel effects abroad, shrinking the volume of foreign-country as well as home-country imports. As a result, the representative individual foreign producer discovers that he accounts for a larger share of total sales in his market than he did before and that the price sensitivity of demand for his output has fallen. He has more scope for quasi-monopolistic pricing and for wallowing in X-inefficiency.

One thought might seem to discredit what we have said so far. Tariff protection increases the demand for domestic import-competing goods and so may attract new firms into the industries producing them, thus *reducing* business concentration. Again, though, we must beware of the fallacy of composition. Just because the number of firms increases in some industries, it does not follow that the same can happen in all. On the contrary, some industries shrink, for tariff protection reallocates resources instead of creating them. To the extent (perhaps slight) that protectionism reduces real income at home and abroad by impairing allocative efficiency, it tends to increase concentration, on the whole. It reduces the number of firms that the home and world markets can accommodate if those firms are to take full advantage of any economies of large-scale production. Even in import-competing industries that do expand, less concentration does not mean more competition; after all, competition from foreign rivals has been banished or weakened. Trade barriers go part way toward carving up each industry's world market into separate national markets, within which a representative producer, even if facing more competition from his

---

*A qualification is necessary concerning producers of export-type goods. Although the trade barrier reduces the export share and increases the domestic share of their total sales, we cannot be sure that the export demand is more price-sensitive than the domestic demand and that, accordingly, the overall price sensitivity of demand declines. Supporting the presumption just implied, however, is the likelihood that the shrunken market can accommodate only fewer export producers. If so, fewer firms are experimenting with new methods and new products, and there are fewer potential sources of ideas that might be worth imitating, as well as fewer sources of competitive pressure impinging on laggards.

fellow-countrymen, faces less competition overall than under free trade. Suppose each state in the United States were to protect domestic producers against out-of-state competition. An individual producer would face less actual and potential competition overall, even if more in-state competitors were to appear (and, as we have said, the latter could happen only in some but not all industries). Think of what a car would cost if each state had its own protected automobile industry. Think of how local monopolies might prey on consumers. Think of how alertness to new products and methods would lose importance relative to lobbying at the state capital.

Connected with promoting competition is what free trade might do to help restrain inflation, particularly in its wage-push and administered-pricing aspects (considered in Chapter 3), which supposedly force the monetary authorities to choose between unemployment and monetary expansion. Unions are not profit-seeking institutions and need not worry, in the same way that business firms must worry, about whether a price increase on what they sell may go too far and shrink total profit. Unions, according to a widely accepted diagnosis, keep pushing for "more," even when the demand for their members' labor has not increased. A leader keeps pressing for wage increases to look successful in comparison with leaders of other unions and with potential rivals in his own. These upward pressures squeeze businessmen and make them anxious to pass on higher costs to consumers. The chances of doing so are better when one's competitors are facing similar cost increases. Free trade, however, exposes domestic producers to competition from foreign producers unlikely to be facing similar wage demands at the same time. Even in competitive industries, "the spur of foreign competition...stiffens the employer's resistance to inflationary wage demands...."[13] Unrestricted foreign competition joins domestic competition in promoting the kind of market in which a producer cannot be confident of success in passing on cost increases and in which wages and prices cannot be set at levels out of line with supply and demand. (We do not deny, though, that inflation is *basically* a phenomenon of money rather than market structure. As noted further in Chapter 6, inflation results basically from the growth of government activities and from the way that the resulting budget deficits are [indirectly] financed.)

TRADE POLICY AS A KEY SYMBOL

Free trade symbolizes a broad range of issues—competition versus protectionism of all kinds, the free-enterprise system versus detailed governmental intervention. If existing barriers to international trade constituted the only departures from free trade in the broadest sense, their harm would be tempered by the opportunities left open in other sectors. But, as we saw in Chapter One, protectionist restrictions abound even in the domestic economy.

Trade policy is a key symbol of governmental economic policies in general, because international trade is the sector where protectionist pressures have traditionally been the most intense and successful, where false patriotism, emotion, and sophistry have flourished in the guise of argument. That sector is the very citadel of protectionism, from which it sallies forth to conquer new territories whenever the opportunity arises; it is the place where protectionism must be beaten if it ever is to be beaten decisively.

Mr. Warren S. Richardson, General Counsel of the Liberty Lobby, put his organization on record as favoring "a return to the dynamic principles of the free-market system on which free enterprise is based." But then he betrayed a misunderstanding of what free enterprise is all about:

> Liberty Lobby is four square behind the tariff system limiting the import of goods and services produced by foreign countries with lower wage scales and poorer standards of quality....
>
> We recommend that the tariff policy of the United States of America be high enough to equalize in a general and not a specific sense the price paid here for foreign imports.
>
> We believe that not only should this be our Government's policy, but we also believe that the tariffs should be high enough to give American industry a slight advantage in our own markets.[14]

Such an idea, literally applied and carried to its logical conclusion, would eliminate all trade between each "free enterprise" country and the rest of the world, leaving only the socialist countries to trade with each other. As Secretary of State Dean Rusk once said:

> Either we believe in capitalism, in the freedom of individual enterprise, or we do not. And we do not if we hold with massive government intervention to distort and freeze the operation of the market. If we look to government to rig the game we may as well look to it to play the hands. If we mean to discourage the forces of free enterprise all around the world, I can think of no better way of doing it—without even stirring from our chairs—than to shrink from competition behind unrealistic tariff walls.[15]

Free trade is an important symbol in another but related way. As an issue, it tests whether reason can prevail in public affairs. Regardless of how much or how little material harm results from heeding fallacious arguments, it is disheartening to see them accepted. This, we suspect, is the main reason why economists have traditionally paid so much attention to trade policy. This is not to say that all protectionist arguments are nonsense, but the refined academic subtleties and theoretical curiosities considered in later chapters are hardly the arguments that carry most weight in practical politics.

Henry George is one of the older economists who emphasized free trade for just these reasons. Nowhere in his book *Protection or Free Trade,* for example, does he actually assert that free international trade, by itself, would contribute a great deal to the American standard of living. Instead, he stresses "a question of direction—a question which of two divergent roads shall be taken," namely, "whether labor is to be benefited by governmental restrictions or by the abolition of such restrictions."[16] "The Ohio of the tariff question flows into the Mississippi of the great social question."[17] "Free trade cannot logically stop with the abolition of custom-houses. It applies as well to domestic as to foreign trade."[18]

To Henry George, free trade and protectionism epitomized not merely rival approaches to economic policy but also differences in political philosophy. Protectionism

> conflicts with those ideas of natural right and personal freedom which received national expression in the establishment of the American Republic, and which we have been accustomed to regard as distinctively American. What is more incongruous than the administering of custom-house oaths and the searching of trunks and handbags under the shadow of "Liberty Enlightening the World?"[19]

If Jones and Smith voluntarily exchange goods, both must expect to gain; and only some rather special reason can justify outside interference. If Brown now asks the government to interfere so that Jones will have to trade with him instead of with Smith, the presumption is against its complying. How does it matter if transactions become more complicated—if money is used and if many people take part, some of them foreigners? Why doesn't an American have as much right to buy English pottery as, say, to trade his apples for another American's cow? Maybe the principle *is* different; but if so, the protectionist should explain what justifies one interference and not the other.

The Joint Economic Committee of Congress once recognized this issue:

> It is hard to see why consumers should not have the right to choose such goods as are desired, without regard to their origin or their foreign cost. Until we presume to replace freedom with a controlled system where people are no longer their own masters, this must be so. No group of producers should be allowed to have a

vested interest in the right to dictate what our people shall consume.

... There is no reason why we should not spend our money if we choose for foreign sports cars, lightweight bicycles, handmade laces, particular wines and cheeses, jeweled movement watches, or hand-cut glassware.

Our ability to command exotic products is one measure of our progress and freedom from previous limitations in the pursuit of happiness.... For a Government official to make a moral judgment on how we ought to spend our money is an invasion of liberty and privacy which is acceptable only where obvious public harm follows....[20]

Importing is not wrong in itself. Even some respectable returning American tourists wonder why it is wrong, as well as illegal and risky, to smuggle purchases past the customs officers. Should a government unnecessarily prohibit or limit or penalize something not otherwise morally wrong, especially when doing so is in effect heeding Brown's plea that it hamper trade between Jones and Smith? As Henry George wrote,

To make that a crime by statute which is no crime in morals, is inevitably to destroy respect for law; to resort to oaths to prevent men from doing what they feel injures no one, is to weaken the sanctity of oaths. Corruption, evasion and false swearing are inseparable from tariffs. Can that be good of which these are the fruits?[21]

One rebuttal to skepticism about government activity stresses the idea that government exists to meet demands that cannot be met by private firms. The marketplace does an adequate job of providing some goods such as coffee and shoes, which consumers must pay for to get them. But the benefits of some other goods, such as national defense and law enforcement, cannot be restricted to paying customers. All Americans benefit from the deterrence to foreign attack that the armed forces provide. An effective police force protects everyone against crime, not just the robbery victim whose stolen property is recovered or the old lady whom the timely appearance of a cruising patrol car saves from a beating. Well-defined property rights and a stable legal framework permit a developed economic system that benefits everybody, not just the minority who ever have occasion to file a lawsuit.

Government, on this interpretation, is a mechanism of cooperation in buying services that private enterprise cannot conveniently provide. It is not at all scandalous, therefore, that individuals should use the political process to get some of their wants served. Indeed, it is not scandalous for some citizens to seek benefits that actually harm others, for these others may be receiving benefits from the first group. In effect, the two groups may be making an exchange that gives each of them more benefit than harm. Exchanges agreed to through the political process may be no more harmful than those agreed to through the marketplace.[22]

This interpretation of government serves as a useful caution to free-trade propagandists. If they rant about the perversion of government to serve individual interests, they invite the rebuttal: "Well, then, whose interests should government serve? Some mysterious collective interest? The interests of some superhuman 'society' distinct from and superior to actual people?"

Phrased carefully, though, the traditional strictures against protectionism on grounds of political philosophy still have force. The voluntary-exchange theory does indeed illuminate one important aspect of democratic government, especially as an ideal; but it is an incomplete theory. Government is not *merely* a mechanism for cooperating to buy certain services and for trading acceptance of special-interest measures in such a way as to serve the interests of practically all citizens. Not even democratic government fits the absurd slogan, "After all, we ourselves are the government." On the contrary, the government is a distinct group of people who, like other people, specialize in their own particular line of work. Ideally, to win votes, the politician must serve the citizen well; just as the businessman, to win profits, must serve the consumer well. Ideally, a "citizens' sovereignty" operates in parallel with "consumers' sovereignty."

Interfering with the operation of this citizens' sovereignty are the realities of the political process. Citizens are more sensitive to their interests as producers than as consumers and have stronger incentives to press their wishes by lobbying and otherwise. Politicians heed the special-interest pressures actually exerted on them more than the unexpressed wishes and even unrealized interests of the majority. Voters send their

> representatives...to the capital to get things for them....The politicians, compelled to buy their re-election with public money tend to become under the law of survival of the fittest the kind of men who like to do that and have no other idea of the public service.[23]

Instead of trying to get rid of special privilege, politicians are tempted to appease each clamoring interest by helping it to boost the prices of what it sells and then compensate others by doing the same for them. The game of privilege and counterprivilege sets up a constant tendency for governments to expand their activities and powers. Policy combinations get adopted that would not have commanded a majority if considered as a whole. While the result may sometimes accord with the voluntary-exchange ideal, examples such as American tax, farm, and trade policy make us doubtful of getting good results generally.

Neither democracy not any other form of government assures wise policies. The chief point in its favor is that democracy provides for peaceful change and in so doing makes rational discussion and attempts at persuasion relevant. Citizens dissatisfied with the existing administration have a recourse other than revolution. Parties out of power have incentives to monitor what the current rulers are doing, which puts some check on abuses of power. It is an impossible and questionable ideal that government policy should respond quickly and accurately to the prevailing array of individual tastes and views, however that array might be defined or measured. The important thing, instead, is that the sustained and strongly held views of a substantial majority can prevail (as they will, sooner or later, if discussion does not change them) without any need for violence.

The case for democracy need not invoke any mystical belief in the rightness of majority views. According to a philosophy that puts a high value on individual freedom, even majority rule is unacceptable when it is not essential and when members of the majority and the minority could go their own separate ways. A philosophy of individual freedom therefore favors devising social and economic institutions that as far as possible avoid clashes among the separate pursuits and goals of individuals; it prefers the market over the political process whenever the market can work.

The case for democracy is simply a case for making political decisions in a particular way; it is not a case for unnecessarily politicizing more and more aspects of life. The more numerous and complicated the functions of government, the greater the chance of their drifting into the hands of "experts" and the smaller the chance of the effective control by the citizens. If we separate the *methods* of democracy (that is, majority rule, representative government, and so forth) from the *content* of government policy, we see that the former is no guarantee of individual freedom. Paradoxically, government action may be more ruthless under democracy than under other forms of government precisely because it is thought to represent some sort of "general will." It is absurd to suppose that controls cannot restrict freedom so long as they are enforced by a government in whose election each adult citizen may take part. This idea is totalitarian also—totalitarian in considering a man's most important freedom to be his freedom to act as a member of the state.

Here we are back to our general point about the *political gains from trade:* Government should attempt to serve a conception of the public interest that weighs positively the individual's taste for freedom as well as for national defense and other services which government may be best equipped to provide. The public interest is better served the further we go toward reversing the attitude, traditional in discussions of foreign economic policy, that the government can and should do everything.

A manifestation of this attitude is provided by an exchange between Congressman Charles Vanik and Secretary of the Treasury George Shultz:

> Mr. Vanik. Now getting back to the question of agricultural products, I am very much concerned about our trading off essential agricultural products needed in our own country.
>
> Secretary [of Agriculture] Butz says he wants to export everything he can. I am afraid he might be exporting beyond our capacity to export we might find our own cupboards bare at home [sic].
>
> What provision do we have in this bill that the export of agricultural products will be at such a rate that we will not upset the domestic market and our own needs?
>
> What assurance do we have, for example, that we are going to have enough wheat, enough bread, enough meat, and the other things that are developed on the farm?
>
> Secretary Shultz. We have the assurance that we have a sensible Congress which will produce reasonable farm policy. These things are all connected with each other. Not everything in the world is accomplished by the trade bill.[24]

The congressman's answer to his conception of the problem of farm exports, already subject to governmental controls, is to lay on additional controls. Secretary Schultz says that Congress can always take care of farm exports once the trade bill is passed. Neither recognizes the possibility that the marketplace is better able than Congress to decide what volume of agricultural goods is "essential" for home consumption or what our "capacity" to export really is. It is a forgone conclusion that Congress is the best judge of such matters. The only question is whether it should provide for them now or later.

Special-interest policies and promises tend to sap political morality *cumulatively*. A voter may regret the self-defeating scramble for special advantage through government but feel that he must join in to have any hope of recouping a part of what other special interests take away from him. He has no accurate indication of how much special advantage he is ethically entitled to seek in self-defense. The more he and others in similar positions seek and obtain, the more still other groups will feel entitled to have in *their* self-defense. The feeling grows that ordinary ethical standards lose their force when individuals act through the political process.

Such thinking often surfaces in Congressional testimony. According to Congressman Dave Martin of Nebraska, "American cattlemen are the last free and completely independent segment of our American economy. They do not want Government controls, nor do they want price supports." Yet the controls already available under the Meat Import Act of 1964 and the "voluntary" restraints that several offshore meat-producing countries had imposed on their exports to the United States were not enough. According to the Congressman, these countries were circumventing the controls by shipping to the United States via Canada, which had not voluntarily restrained its meat exports. The only recourse, therefore, was to create still more controls, to impose quotas on hitherto unrestricted meat products and on products exported from countries not imposing "voluntary" restraints. Otherwise, the government would have "to regulate the production of meat in the United States" and set up "another costly price support and subsidy program."[25] Simply leaving the free-spirited cattlemen to their own fates at the hands of a free market was apparently an unthinkable response to their predicament.

Other examples abound. Mr. Leonard Appleman, former Indiana farm boy, smalltown Ohio businessman, and President of the Green Olive Trade Association, came to the House Ways and Means Committee to complain that the Spanish had taken to shipping olives to the United States in small jars, rather than in bulk. This, it seems, amounted to a grievous circumvention of the U.S. tariff laws, whose authors, not anticipating Spanish cunning, had imposed a duty on olives by the bulk, but not on the "glass, the cap, the labor, anything else."[26]

Political struggle for special economic advantage makes for something worse than petty bribery and grafts. Yet buying votes by dispensing special privilege is so familiar and is done on such a large scale that people are not accustomed to think of it as scandalous. As Professor Henry Simons once remarked, the kind of corruption that "stinks" has much to recommend it, relatively. The large-scale kind debases the whole character of business and political life. Diversion of energy from production to politics is self-accelerating because as the struggle for political privilege becomes a more and more rewarding activity, the men who are especially good at that sort of thing will increasingly come to the fore. Men who are competent both in the political struggle and in production will respond to the increasing rewards attaching to the former and the increasing relative penalties attaching to the latter.[27]

Adopting free trade would be one step toward this process. It would help undo the overburdening of democratic government and the unnecessary politicalization of so many aspects of life.

NOTES

1. For example, see Samuel Lubell, *The Revolution in World Trade* (New York: Harper, 1955); the book has an enthusiastic foreword by Bernard Baruch. For a prewar statement of a partly similar thesis, see Dennis H. Robertson, "The Future of International Trade," *Economic Journal,* March 1938, reprinted in American Economic Association, *Readings in the Theory of International Trade* (Philadelphia: Blakiston, 1949), pp. 497-513.

2. Galbraith, *Economics and the Public Purpose* (Boston: Houghton, Mifflin, 1973), p. 168.

3. Ibid., p. 259.

4. Gottfried Haberler, *International Trade and Economic Development* (Cairo: National Bank of Egypt, 1959), p. 11; *Inflation, Its Causes and Cures* (Washington: American Enterprise Association, 1960), pp. 33, 82.

5. 1970 HW&M VI 1850-56. (See Chapter 1, note 1).

6. *Vital Speeches,* March 15, 1953, p. 328.

7. W. M. Corden, "The Efficiency Effects of Trade and Protection," in *Studies in International Economics,* I. A. McDougall and R. H. Snape eds., (Amsterdam: North-Holland Publishing Company, 1970, p. 2.

8. 1973 HW&M IV 1180. (See Chapter 1, note 8).

9. Cf. Gottfried Haberler, *International Trade and Economic Development,* op. cit., pp. 10-11.

10. Tibor Scitovsky, *Economic Theory and Western European Integration,* especially, pp. 22-32 and Chapter III. Cf. Scitovsky's contribution to E.A.G. Robinson, ed., *Economic Consequences of the Size of Nations* (New York: St. Martin's Press, 1960), pp. 285-87, and Bela Balassa, *The Theory of Economic Integration* (Homewood: Richard D. Irwin, Inc., 1961), Chapters 5-8, especially p. 166. Balassa reviews several mutually contradictory efforts to estimate how important the effects of a broadened market are.

11. Corden, op. cit., p. 10.

12. Ibid., p. 6.

13. Haberler, *Inflation: Its Causes and Cures,* p. 34.

14. 1970 HW&M VI 1631. One wonders why Mr. Richardson didn't want to go ahead and provide American industry with a *big* advantage.

15. "Foreign Policy and Trade," address before the Chamber of Commerce of Charlotte, North Carolina, February 21, 1962, in *Vital Speeches of the Day,* April 1, 1962, p. 360.

16. Henry George, *Protection or Free Trade* (New York: Doubleday, Page, 1905), p. 3.

17. Ibid., p. 243.

18. Ibid., p. 306.

19. Ibid., p. 18.

20. Report of January 5, 1956, quoted in *Foreign Trade Policy* (1958), pp. 996-97. (See Chapter One, note 5.)

21. George, op. cit., p. 37.

22. James M. Buchanan and Gordon Tullock, *The Calculus of Consent* (Ann Arbor: University of Michigan Press, 1962), give an excellent presentation of the voluntary-exchange ideal and of alternative constitutional provisions, including voting rules, that might make government conform more to the ideal than it does in reality.

23. Walter Lippmann, *The Method of Freedom* (New York: Macmillan, 1934), p. 84.

24. 1973 HW&M I 315.

25. 1970 HW&M XIII 3679.

26. 1970 HW&M XV 4347-48.

27. Cf. Murray Rothbard, *Man, Economy, and State* (Princeton, N.J.: Van Nostrand, 1962) II, 818.

6

In applying the logic of the price system to international trade, we have so far assumed that imports and exports pay for each other, so that their money prices indicate the real terms of exchange. Now we must question this assumption and either justify or modify it.

PROTECTIONISM AND INTERNATIONAL IMBALANCE

Questions do arise out of the problems of unbalanced trade and capital movements that have plagued the world since the beginning of the Great Depression in 1929 and even more conspicuously since World War II. During the 1960s the United States imposed capital controls (subsequently removed), and in August 1971, President Nixon imposed a temporary 10 percent surcharge on U.S. imports to prod foreign countries into revaluing their currencies and thereby alleviate swelling U.S. deficits. The major monetary events of the early 1970s—the breakdown of the Bretton Woods system of fixed exchange rates, the quadrupling of oil prices, and the phenomenon of worldwide inflation—have given rise to widespread alarm. Out of this alarm demands are sometimes made for the imposition of tariffs and other barriers to international trade. Section 122 of the Trade Act of 1974 gives the President authority to impose temporary surcharges and quotas "to deal with large and serious United States balance-of-payments deficits" and "to prevent an imminent and significant depreciation of the dollar."

Measures like these cause the same sorts of economic and political harm as we have already attributed to protective tariffs and other trade barriers. May they not be necessary, however, to avoid still greater harm? Any such question about balance and imbalance in international payments ties in with the issue of free trade versus protection. If the reader will be patient with a bit more abstract analysis, he will soon see how crucial it is.

THE BALANCE OF PAYMENTS

A balance of payments is a two-sided summary of a country's recorded or estimated international transactions during a given time period, usually a year. The "plus" column lists exports and other transactions of kinds ordinarily requiring payments from foreigners to residents of the home country; the "minus" column lists imports and other transactions ordinarily involving payments from residents to foreigners. Each transaction appears in one list or the other according to which way payment for it would *ordinarily* go. Exporting a commodity ordinarily brings an inpayment from foreigners and so counts on the "plus" side. An export transaction still counts as a "plus" even if the goods go as a gift or are sold on credit and will not be paid for until next year—or never will be paid for because the foreign buyer defaults. Loans and gifts to foreigners count on the opposite side, the "minus" or import side, since, if made in cash, they would ordinarily involve an outpayment. Extinguishing an old debt owed to foreigners also counts as a "minus." (Just because the interpretation is so strained, it aids the memory to think of loans and gifts and repayments to foreigners as imports of foreign IOUs and thank-you letters and our own cancelled IOUs; these imaginary imports of pieces of paper belong on the same side as imports of ordinary merchandise.) Loans and so forth still count this same way even if not made in cash, even if a loan takes the form of credit granted in the sale of merchandise or if a gift is given in merchandise.

As these examples suggest, every transaction has two aspects, after all. They are equal in amount but appear on opposite sides. A commodity export must be matched on the opposite side somehow—by credit extended to its foreign buyers, by a gift of its value to foreigners, by taking commodity imports in exchange, by actually taking payment in home or foreign money (which means foreign disinvestment in previously acquired home-country bank balances or new home-country investment in foreign bank balances), or in some other way. The value of a gift to foreigners appears on the side for aspects of transactions that usually involve outpayments (the commodity-import or "minus" side); but the form in which the gift is transmitted, such as commodities, appears on the export or "plus" side. If the foreigners instead take and hold money of the giving country, they are investing in claim on that country, so that even this way of their accepting the gift counts as a "plus." In effect the giving country is borrowing back the value of its gift to foreigners; the money transferred to foreign ownership represents IOUs "exported" to them.

Definitions of a balance of payments and of how its parts interlock with each other admittedly seem paradoxical and contradictory at first. Yet the perplexed reader could eventually become accustomed to balance-of-payments usage and find everything consistent.

The main point to grasp, so far, is that the two sides of a balance of payments add up to the same total amount. They would, anyway, if all figures were complete and correct; statisticians use a fudging item called "errors and omissions" to make the two sides equal, as in principle they must be. They must be equal for the same general reason that both sides of a company's balance sheet or income statement must: it is a matter of interlocking definitions.

What, then, could a balance-of-payments *deficit* mean? The answer hinges on distinguishing between "ordinary" transactions and "settlement" (or "stopgap") transactions. These are sometimes called "above-the-line" items and "below-the-line" items, respectively, with reference to a way the figures are sometimes arranged. Ordinary or "above-the-line" items include trade in goods and services, travel, borrowing, lending, investing, repaying, and other transactions decided on a business basis, and, in general, all transactions other than those motivated by concern with the country's payments and currency position. Even most government transactions count as ordinary; defense spending abroad and foreign aid are examples, since their motives are military, political, or humanitarian. When the total of all these ordinary transactions on the "minus" side of the balance of payments exceeds the total of all similar transactions on the "plus" side, the difference is called a *deficit*. In other words, a country has a deficit in its balance of payments when the total of its imports and all other above-the-line minus items exceeds the total of its exports and all other above-the-line plus items. Being out of balance in the opposite direction is called a surplus; but, to be more definite, let us continue talking only about the deficit. This deficit must be matched—or, as it is often said, must be "settled" or "financed"—by an excess of plus over minus items below the line. What are these below-the-line settlement items? Most characteristically, they are transactions carried out by government agencies or the central bank out of concern for the country's balance of payments and, more specifically, in order to shore up the value of its currency in terms of foreign currencies. The central bank may be selling gold or foreign currencies from previously accumulated reserves and taking payment in its own money, thus bolstering the latter's value on the foreign-exchange market. Like exports of ordinary commodities, these official sales of gold or foreign currencies count on the "plus" side of the balance of payments; but, unlike ordinary exports, they count *below* the line. Some arrangements of the figures also count certain private transactions below the line. These private transactions are ones supposedly most subject to desired influence by government interest-rate policies or other policies adopted in view of the country's payments and currency position.

No hard and fast or "natural" line separates the settlement items from the ordinary transactions. The classification depends pretty much on presumed differences in the motives underlying the transactions. Just where the statisticians draw the line must be a matter of judgment and conventional practice. The same follows for the size of a country's deficit (or surplus). The figure reported cannot be a hard-and-fast, objective historical fast; it unavoidably depends on rather arbitrary classifications of doubtful items. In the reports of most countries, the below-the-line financing that matches and settles a deficit on account of ordinary transactions includes drawing down official reserves of gold and foreign money and official stopgap borrowing abroad. Also included in some arrangements of the U.S. figures is a buildup of debt in the form of foreign holdings of quickly cashable claims on Americans. Reclassifications of transactions are often proposed and occasionally made. There is no one indisputably "right" way of arranging the numbers and of measuring a country's balance-of-payments deficit (or surplus) in a particular year. Still, the general idea of a deficit (or surplus), depending as it does on the distinction between ordinary and settlement transactions, is meaningful in principle. This is true when exchange rates are fixed, anyway; under a pure system of freely floating rates, settlement transactions are absent, so that the concept of deficit or surplus lacks meaning.

A deficit is equal to and measurable by the amount of its below-the-line financing because of sheer definitions and arithmetic. It may be helpful, though, to consider the development of a deficit by a country that had previously been in balance. Now, for some reason, its people and businesses begin to spend more than they receive from the rest of the world in *ordinary* transactions. This excess of "minuses" above the line must be matched by an exactly equal excess of "pluses" below the line. In other words, the deficit in ordinary transactions must be getting financed somehow; otherwise it could not even exist. Should the country run out of gold and foreign-exchange reserves and exhaust all its other means of financing its deficit, it would unavoidably revert to spending no more than it was receiving in ordinary transactions. A sudden adjustment of this kind might be very unpleasant, just as it might be for a family that had been spending beyond its income and whose checks had begun to bounce. Ideally, the government could smooth out the balancing process by drawing on its official reserves of gold and foreign exchange and by engaging in official stopgap borrowing from foreign governments and international monetary institutions. Funds so obtained would cover and thus permit the deficit. By the same token, they would permit the government to avoid the use of protectionist devices and perhaps postpone adjustments in the incomes of residents and in the internal price level or in the exchange rate. How long it could do so would depend on the size of its international reserves and on the willingness of foreigners to furnish loans.

BALANCING PROCESSES

How can a deficit ever plague a country as a whole?* The country's balance-of-payments position with the rest of the world is simply the total of the individual positions of all the individuals, families, companies, and other government and private organizations that make up the national economy. Each such unit can be regarded as having a balance of payments with everyone else, fellow-citizens and foreigners lumped together. Any deficit for the country as a whole must mean that deficits outweigh surpluses in these individual positions. One might expect people's ordinary motives to keep them from developing alarming deficits, that is, from running their assets down on their debts up to an alarming extent. Even reckless persons would find their deficits limited by the sizes of their bank accounts and the limited willingness of others to go on making risky loans to them. How, then, can the country as a whole be in balance-of-payments trouble when its people are experiencing no particular trouble? The answer is that official below-the-line transactions interlock with ordinary transactions. More than mere arithmetic explains this interlocking. How much overseas military spending—an "ordinary" transaction—a government undertakes may partly depend, for example, on how big a gold or foreign-exchange reserve it can draw on. Less obvious but more interesting is how official below-the-line transactions influence private ordinary transactions. Official transactions in gold and foreign exchange affect the money-holdings, price levels, foreign-exchange rates, and interest rates that guide private decisions about buying and selling

---

*The opposite imbalance, a surplus, can also be troublesome in its own way, especially if large and persistent; but for simplicity, we shall stick to the example of a deficit.

and borrowing and lending abroad, as well as at home. When the government is running down its gold and foreign-exchange reserves, it is unintentionally skewing private decisions towards what, from the national point of view, is excess importing.

Drawing a sharp contrast will help explain this. Suppose *no* below-the-line transactions are taking place. Total "pluses" and "minuses" in ordinary transactions must then be equal. What reconciles this arithmetically necessary balance with the freedom of individuals, companies, and so forth to undertake whatever transactions they see fit in the light of their own circumstances? To simplify the explanation without affecting the key principles involved, let us assume that commodity imports and exports are the only kinds of ordinary transactions that take place. Balance or imbalance in "trade" thus coincides with balance or imbalance on account of all above-the-line transactions.*

One method whereby trade comes automatically into balance may be explained by considering a single state and its trade with the rest of the United States. To see why an imbalance in its trade could not last long or amount to much, it is convenient to suppose that one does develop temporarily. (To avoid contradicting arithmetic, we must allow some *nonofficial* below-the-line financing, after all: to some extent, people can spend more than they currently earn by drawing down their bank accounts or going into debt.) Suppose, then, either that the out-of-state demand for Virginia's livestock products and chemicals collapses or that something happens to divert some Virginian demand from home onto out-of-state goods. Either way, some Virginians find their incomes reduced, cut their own spending, and so cut the incomes of still other Virginians. Furthermore, the temporary trade deficit is being financed by net transfers of money to outsiders (or by borrowing from outsiders). With their incomes fallen and cash balances shrunken (or debt swollen), Virginians cut down their buying not only from each other but also from outsiders. Reduced business at home also spurs efforts to make sales outside the state. Virginia's imports and exports thus come back into balance at a new level. If the original disturbance were large and the correctives feebler and slower than they are in reality, still another aspect of adjustment

---

*Alternatively, we could broaden the terms "imports" and "exports" to include not only purchases and sales of goods and services (even counting travel and the capital "services" for which interest and dividends are paid) but also lending and repaying, borrowing and receiving repayment, and all the other ordinary items on the two sides of the balance of payments.

would be noticeable. Shrinkage of Virginia's money supply through net outpayments would deflate prices and costs. The change in price relations would lead some people both in and out of Virginia to switch some of their buying away from out-of-state goods and onto the relatively cheapened Virginia goods. This effect, too, would help restore balance.*

The fall in income because of a deficit does not *necessarily* mean a fall in employment and production. If prices and wages fall flexibly enough to bear the entire brunt of a disturbance and make resources shift among occupations, total production and employment can remain at their old levels. A fall in money income would correspond to a fall in the prices that translate real income produced into money income. In the real world, however, prices and wages are not so completely flexible. They move down only stickily. In reality, then, a fall in money income corresponds partly to a fall in employment and production as well as in prices.

For a very few decades before 1914, most major countries were on an international gold standard. Their currencies were not so closely tied together then as the dollars used in Virginia and the other 49 states are now, but the link was fairly close. The link would be complete under the imaginary system in which gold coins were the only kind of money used in all countries. Their movement out of countries with balance-of-payments deficits and into countries with surpluses would play the same role in adjustment as the movement of dollars between Virginia and the other states. A gold standard of the historical type works less surely and automatically than this, since each country's money supply consists not of gold alone but of paper money and bank deposits pyramided onto a fractional reserve of gold. No longer are money and gold actually the same thing; rather, the redeemability of money in gold links the two together. When a country is running a balance-of-payments deficit, the foreigners probably will not take payment entirely in the paper or bank-deposit money of the deficit country. They will want gold. The money-redeeming authorities of the deficit country must supply it. And since their gold reserve is only a fraction of the country's total money supply, the gold may run out before the balance-of-payments deficit corrects itself. This danger spells balance-of-payments trouble for the country as a whole, even though its people, as individuals, may be in no particular trouble.

---

*If the original disturbance were in the opposite direction, making a temporary surplus in Virginia's balance of payments, the adjustments just described would work in reverse. The rise in local incomes and cash balances and perhaps even in prices would work to increase imports and reduce exports.

One thing about the country's trouble needs emphasis: it is connected with official below-the-line transactions of the kind we have so far assumed away in demonstrating the automatic balancing process. Drawing on official reserves to keep the currency's value tied to gold makes up these settlements or "stopgaps."

Even under a fractional-reserve gold standard with these stopgaps occurring, the adjustment processes of the Virginia example *may,* after all, work powerfully and swiftly enough to cure a deficit before the country's gold is all gone. Imports and exports may balance themselves more or less automatically and adequately—most of the time—even though the linkage between the money supplies of different countries is far from rigid. But the looser the linkage, the greater the danger of balance-of-payments trouble. To play perfectly safe, the money authorities must allow or cause the country's total money supply to fall not merely by the same amount but rather in the same proportion as the fractional reserve of gold. Gold losses must have a magnified impact. To safeguard a 20 percent gold reserve, the authorities must allow or cause a $1 billion gold loss to shrink the money supply by $5 billion.

Many people who yearn for the days before World War I have an exaggerated idea of how long the international gold standard was in effect, of how smoothly it worked, and of how free from interference trade was in those days. Imports and exports kept in balance as well as they did because governments made this balance, together with preserving the gold redeemability of their currencies, the overriding goal of financial policy. They had little scope to manage money supplies to suit themselves, even if domestic full employment and price-level stability had been their objectives. Money supplies, prices, employment, production, and incomes had to respond to the requirements of keeping foreign trade balanced. Each country had to let deflation and inflation at home keep generally in step with world-wide monetary conditions. The unquestioned dominance of a single financial center, London, had much to do with the fact that the system worked as tolerably well as it did.

A quite different system of international monetary relations is not only simpler to explain but simpler to operate. This other system stands at the opposite extreme from monetary linkage as tight as under the imaginary 100 percent international gold standard or as the linkage between Virginia and the other states. Yet it also avoids official settlement transactions in gold or foreign exchange.

Under freely floating exchange rates, governments and central banks refrain from fixing or influencing exchange rates through purchases and sales of gold or foreign currencies. Each country has its own independent money, regulates its quantity to suit itself, and leaves its value free from a fixed tie to gold or to any foreign currency. Unmanipulated supply and demand continuously determine exchange rates. Different currencies exchange on the market in rough proportion to their purchasing powers over goods and services. With no "below-the-line" settlement transactions taking place, a balance of payments cannot be in deficit or surplus.

To see how this system works, let us call the home currency the dollar and the currency of all other countries, lumped together, the crown. At the start, imports and exports are in balance at an exchange rate of 4 crowns per dollar. Now something—inflation at home, depression abroad, a shift in preferences from home to foreign goods—something makes our import expenditures tend to exceed our export earnings at the old exchange rate. Dollars are in excess supply and crowns in excess demand. Under this pressure, the dollar depreciates to 3 crowns, say; the crown appreciates to 33-1/3 cents. Translated into dollars at the new exchange rate, the prices of our imports and exports rise. Import purchases become less attractive and export sales more attractive to us. From the viewpoint of foreigners, lower prices of imports and exports in crowns motivate increased purchases from us and reduced sales to us. (The same things happen in reverse if the initial disturbance is one that tends to put foreigners' trade in deficit and ours in surplus. The exchange rate moves to, say, 5 crowns per dollar. Translated into dollars at the new rate, lower prices make imports more and exports less attractive for us. Translated into crowns at the new rate, higher import and export prices motivate foreigners to cut their buying and push their selling in trade with us.)

This condensed description oversimplifies automatic adjustment through freely floating exchange rates, but it captures the essentials. The relations between prices of home and foreign goods adjust through the exchange rate that makes them comparable, not through rises and falls in whole national price levels. Price changes in each local currency occur more selectively where they are needed, in the foreign-trade sector, and not through overall inflation or deflation. General expansions and contractions of employment, production, and incomes are also unnecessary for balance-of-payments adjustment. Each government can, if it wishes, insulate its country's money supply from external domination and stabilize its size or its growth rate as suits domestic conditions.

The exchange-rate mechanism of balancing imports and exports makes it all the clearer why even countries with low average productivity can compete successfully in selling some goods abroad and why even countries with high average productivity can be undersold at home by foreigners on some goods. It also helps puncture the worry about cheap foreign labor and explain why no country need be generally uncompetitive, regardless of how high its wages and prices are. With the exchange-rate mechanism allowed to operate, imports and exports, broadly defined, do pay for each other. Their money prices do correctly reflect real costs (assuming no serious domestic price distortions). The standard demonstration of the gains from trade applies, and businessmen do have the price and profit incentives for the trade that reaps these gains. These same conclusions hold true when the trade-balancing mechanism of close monetary linkage is operating instead, except that this other mechanism operates less swiftly and surely.

INDECISIVE POLICIES

It is hardly an oversimplification to blame the balance-of-payments troubles of the last few decades on the failure of governments to make up their minds about which set of automatic adjustment processes they will allow to operate. By and large, governments have rejected any monetary linkage as close as among the states of the United States now or even as close as among countries before 1914. They dislike the threat of deflation of money supplies, prices, production, and employment transmitted through foreign trade. They prefer to pursue their own full-employment policies. On the other hand, they have not been willing, except as a last resort, to untie their own currencies and avoid all official dealings in gold or foreign exchange. The quasi-fluctuating (or "dirty-float") system now in effect came about by default in March 1973 as the major industrial countries finally abandoned their efforts to defend the crumbling fixed-exchange-rate system. These efforts had persisted for an unduly long time, with inflationary consequences (see pp. 100-03, below); and now the operation of flexible rates is impaired by a "joint float" that keeps some European currencies nearly fixed in relation to each other, by continued pegging of many currencies to the dollar, and by central-bank intervention even in the markets for floating currencies. With this intervention at work, we cannot deny the possibility of balance-of-payments deficits and surpluses as confidently as we could if rates were floating freely. Even so, the definition and meaning of a deficit or surplus is much less nearly clear-cut than under a regime of firmly fixed exchange rates.

When governments do fix their exchange rates, they finance this fixing by drawing down (or in times of balance-of-payments surplus, building up) their accumulated reserves of gold, foreign exchange, and Special Drawing Rights issued by the International Monetary Fund. Official borrowing ekes out skimpy reserves. In cases of stubborn imbalance, governments sometimes modify their domestic money supply, interest rate, and tax-and-spending policies as the old-fashioned gold standard would have required. Sometimes they make official exchange-rate adjustments, though one major difficulty with fixed-but-adjustable rates is that the system gives speculators practically a "heads-I-win-tails-I-break-even" opportunity to profit at the government's expense. When an adjustment in a fixed exchange rate appears necessary, there is little doubt about its direction if it is made at all.

When countries let their currencies float, they are often tempted to iron out fluctuations by intervening in the exchange markets. The idea is that central bankers can prevent excessive or destabilizing movements in the exchange rate by buying or selling foreign currencies in appropriate amounts. The difficulty is that temporary intervention, once begun, can easily recur and that no clear line separates the effects of or the motives behind central-bank intervention from those of private speculation. In this connection, John Pippenger has observed that

> the relatively small surplus in the second quarter of 1973 . . . suggests that, on balance, central banks sold dollars and tended to accentuate the depreciation of the dollar. If speculators had followed the same policy, their actions probably would have been described as destabilizing.[1]

One of the advantages of a fluctuating exchange rate is that it gives speculators a chance to iron out exchange-rate movements instead of giving them assurance about what direction an official adjustment would take. If a central bank resorts to exchange-market intervention, the question arises why central bankers are more able than private speculators to anticipate future movements, and, if they are, why they do not use their superior insights to make private fortunes of their own. If the intervention is infrequent, one wonders why it is necessary at all; and if it is frequent, it begins to influence speculators' behavior much as a policy of fixed-but-adjustable exchange rates does. Intervention under fluctuating exchange rates manifests the fundamental ambivalence of governments between the rules of the old-fashioned gold standard on the one hand and those of freely fluctuating exchange rates on the other.

The same ambivalence also appears in tariffs, import and export quotas, capital controls, and comprehensive requisitioning of foreign exchange earned and rationing of foreign exchange to be spent. A compromise system, lacking the automatic adjustment mechanism of either extreme system, is prone to suffer chronic balance-of-payments deficits or surpluses. The only apparent cure may take the form of controls over those real trade and capital flows which symptomize the underlying chronic imbalance.

Theory and experience have time and again shown that three things are not permanently compatible: (1) fixed exchange rates, (2) independent national monetary policies, and (3) continuous freedom of trade from controls to force imports and exports into balance. Before World War I, countries generally sacrificed the second of these. Nowadays, in the spirit of indecisive compromise, countries are generally sacrificing each to some extent. People who understand the value of free trade should especially insist on a clear cut choice between fixed exchange rates and monetary independence.

PROTECTIONISM AND WORLDWIDE INFLATION

For several years after World War II most countries other than the United States were beset with troubles collectively known as "dollar shortage." They seemed continually in danger of overimporting and of using up their scanty reserves of gold and dollars. Many a government was fixing the value of its own currency against the dollar at a higher level than would have prevailed in free market. In countries where this was the policy, people found goods imported from the United States and a few other "hard-currency" countries a great bargain in local currency, while their own exports seemed expensive in hard-currency markets. Hence the tendency to overimport and the need for controls. Even today these troubles plague quite a few countries, particularly in Asia and Latin America.

The 1950s, however, saw great improvements, particularly in Europe. Postwar economic recoveries, slowdowns in inflation, a degree of informal coordination in domestic monetary policies, a few further exchange-rate adjustments following the widespread ones of 1949, continued heavy overseas spending by the U.S. government, and some lucky coincidences— all permitted progressive relaxation of currency and trade restrictions. Balance-of-payments crises caused setbacks only occasionally.

Significantly, American balance-of-payments troubles came to the fore as European troubles abated. The small U.S. deficits of 1951-1956 had caused no alarm, for they gave foreign countries an intended opportunity to rebuild their gold and dollar reserves. In 1958, however, the deficit grew to $3½ billion and was mostly covered by a gold loss, amounting to about one-tenth of the stock on hand at the beginning of the year. The deficits thereafter fluctuated in size (alternating with occasional surpluses on one definition or another) but reached staggering levels in the early 1970s, exceeding annual rates of $40 billion in the third quarter of 1971 and the first quarter of 1973. Gold sales to foreign central banks were formally suspended in August 1971, and the dollar was devalued in

December 1971 and February 1973. Throughout this period, the major foreign central banks attempted to support the dollar at officially set rates. They finally gave up after the inflationary consequences of doing so, as well as pressures in the foreign-exchange markets, became unbearable. By March 1973, these central banks set the dollar afloat.

The following months brought a number of unfortunate, though not necessarily related, developments—the oil crisis, the spread of balance-of-payments deficits to other industrial countries, and the phenomenon of double-digit worldwide inflation. These developments, combined with the fact that the United States had begun in 1971 to run occasional deficits even in its balance of merchandise trade, have greatly expanded the protectionists' repertoire of arguments.

In testimony before a Congressional committee Representative John H. Dent offered his own definition of the balance of payments:

> A country's balance of payments can be simply computed by any eighth grade economist by deducting the value of imports from the value of exports.
>
> But it is not that simple. For instance, a very simple equation would be the matter of cotton that is sold to Japan. If you sell $800 million worth of cotton and you only buy back $500 million worth of textiles, do we have a balance of trade? We do if we are measuring it in money.
>
> But in an economic complex such as we live in, it must be measured in the amount of labor displayed [sic]. You cannot measure trade any longer by dollar volumes.[2]

After trying several other challenges to a witness's testimony opposing tariff quotas on zinc, Congressman John Duncan asked,

> Are you interested at all in the zinc imports strain on the United States balance of payments, or do you have no interest in that?
>
> Mr. Fox. I think we should import raw materials when we need to import them, and export manufactured products as concessions.
>
> Mr. Duncan. What would you propose to do about the balance of payments?
>
> Mr. Fox. About the balance of payments?
>
> Mr. Duncan. Yes, sir.
>
> Mr. Fox. That is rather a broad question, sir.
>
> Mr. Duncan. Of course, zinc imports have a great bearing upon our deficit in the balance of payments.[3]

Congressman James Burke fears large oil deficits and the consequent disruption of industries

> that will cause a wholesale loss of jobs in other areas where we are importing goods that we do not need and putting ourselves in a position of having an imbalance of payments and large deficits in trade, that we might have to look down the road of quotas in order to bring about an orderly marketing policy here in the country.[4]

Contrary to such arguments, the balance-of-*payments* deficit or surplus is measured by the difference between the total of all the above-the-line transactions on the two sides of the balance of payments. The difference between exports and imports measures the balance of *trade*. If imports exceed exports, the balance of payments itself can be in surplus if the deficit in the balance of trade is more than offset by net surpluses elsewhere in the balance of payments, as in the capital account. Certainly, it is misleading to attribute the deficit in the balance of payments to any one item in the trade account. The deficit does not exist because we import too much zinc or even too much oil; it takes time for corrective processes to respond to extraordinary disturbances and bring above-the-line transactions into balance.

Even the quadrupling of oil prices that took place in 1973 and 1974 does not explain the general trend toward higher world-wide rates of inflation, which became recognizable well in advance of the October 1973 embargo. Of ten major industrial countries—Belgium, Canada, France, Germany, Italy, Japan, the Netherlands, Switzerland, the United Kingdom, and the United States—the percentage rise in the consumer price index was greater in 1972 than in 1971 for all but three (Japan, the United Kingdom, and the United States) and greater in 1973 than in 1972 for all ten. This trend illustrates the inflationary bias of exchange-rate pegging. During several years of last-ditch defense of that system, unprecedented U.S. balance-of-payments deficits were matched by surpluses abroad, where domestic money was created on a massive scale as central banks and governments bought up U.S. dollars in efforts to keep exchange rates fixed. (During the single year 1971, foreign authorities bought more U.S. dollars than they had bought cumulatively through all history until then, and further spurts of domestic money creation ensued.) With a lag, as usual, price trends responded.[5] In the United States, one element of lagged response to earlier money-creation was the further impetus to price increases resulting from two devaluations and then the downward float of the dollar. In a way, the United States was reimporting the inflation it had exported earlier, but without undoing the damage already inflicted on other countries. Once a country has become hooked on rapid inflation, however innocently, its addiction is hard to cure, for the withdrawal pangs (recession and unemployment) would likely be severe.

Discouragingly often in monetary history, observers blame unsatisfactory economic conditions on the floating exchange rates that remain after rate-pegging has collapsed, even when that pegging had contributed to the unsatisfactory conditions. This misinterpretation is rampant again as many observers blame inflation on floating rates. We do not maintain, on the contrary, that the last-ditch defense of the pegged-rate system has been the sole source of inflation; but we do regret the evident danger that the United States and the world will not salvage anything, not even a correct lesson, from their recent monetary traumas.

A country's balance-of-payments problems have nothing to do with the size of any one traded item (and certainly not with the amount of labor displaced by that item, as Congressman Dent suggested). Instead, those problems signify basic monetary and exchange-rate difficulties. In our case, if we wanted to pin the blame on any one item, it would have to be the large speculative capital flights that took place from the United States during the early 1970s, encouraged no doubt by the "sure bet" that the dollar was subject to further depreciation. That speculation had a basis in "fundamentals," in inflationary policies. American errors were particularly harmful to the outside world because the dollar was a reserve currency, the currency most widely used for official transactions on the foreign-exchange markets.

THE PROBLEM OF PETRODOLLARS

The quadrupling of oil prices in 1973-1974 exerted unusual strains on the international financial system. Total exports of the oil-exporting countries (including roughly $5 billion worth of products other than oil) had amounted to $29 billion in 1972; in 1974 they amounted to $139 billion. The oil-exporting countries' shares of total Free World exports rose from 8 percent or less in the early 1970s to 17.8 percent in 1974, while their import share rose to only 4.6 percent. The trade deficits of the oil-importing countries and surpluses of the exporting countries amounted to as much as $70 billion in 1974.[6] This gap between the oil countries' exports and imports, together with the question of how the oil-importing countries are going to cover it and what the oil-exporting countries are going to do with their surplus revenues, is the problem of "petrodollars."

Whether or not the imbalance in *trade* due to petrodollars leads automatically to a balance-of-*payments* problem depends in part on whether exchange rates are fixed or floating. The idea of such a problem is meaningful if exchange rates are fixed long enough for total above-the-line transactions to become unbalanced. Under freely or even "dirtily" floating rates, however, it is difficult to identify any reliable measure of the deficit or surplus, simply because overall balance constantly tends to be restored through adjustments in exchange rates. According to the "official settlements" measure of the balance of payments the deficit consists in part of increases in liquid liabilities of foreign governments. But with most of the oil exporting being done by governments these days, it is not clear that such increases represent "settlements" rather than business transactions. As a matter of sheer arithmetic, the oil-exporting countries must either lend, invest, give away, or simply accumulate whatever revenues they do not spend. If they are willing to use their revenues in these various ways, then, in a sense, settlement transactions are unnecessary.

Still another presumed problem arises out of the fact that the oil-exporting countries do not invest in each oil-importing country precisely the amount of their trade surpluses with that country. Rather, they invest more of their trade surpluses in a few financially leading countries and in the Eurodollar market and less in others. These others, if they are to finance their trade deficits, must obtain loans, investments, or gifts from the countries that are receiving disproportionate shares of the oil exporters' funds. Whether and how this will be possible enters into the problem of "recycling." One specific worry is that deposits of oil revenues will be concentrated in a few banks, that banks will get into trouble by accepting deposits on short term while lending long, and that the ratios of banks' capital to deposits and to loans are shrinking.

Banks nevertheless have incentives to avoid such difficulties. They can avoid excessive concentration of their deposits and loans and excessive imbalance between their deposits and loan maturities through the interest rates they pay on deposits and charge on loans. The biggest banks, wary of getting themselves into unsafe positions, will leave opportunities for the smaller banks to capture their own share of the oil-revenue deposits. Furthermore, recycling can take place not only through banks but also through purchases by the oil-exporting countries of money-market instruments, longer-term securities, real estate, and other business properties in the oil-importing countries. As it turns out, banks and financial markets have probably done a better job of recycling petrodollars than they were generally expected to do.

Suppose, however, that recycling does become a more serious problem in the future. Well, the most seriously affected countries just cannot—again as a matter of arithmetic—keep on running trade deficits that they are unable to finance. Under the logic of floating exchange rates, the consuming countries least able to attract capital inflows will cover their oil deficits by running trade surpluses with the countries most able to attract capital inflows. Under the logic of market processes, high oil prices, as translated at the exchange rates of the importing countries, will promote economies in oil use and the development of domestic substitutes. The consumers and industrial users most in "need" of oil at the margin will stick in the market bidding for it and for the corresponding foreign exchange, as well as for whatever available loans they consider it prudent to obtain. Intense bidding for foreign exchange to pay for oil would indirectly, through resulting exchange-rate adjustments, restrain other imports and promote exports. A pattern of interest rates and exchange rates would develop at which urgent oil "needs" would get paid for by a combination of surplus exports of other goods and services and by borrowing.

THE FUTURE OF WORLD PAYMENTS

At this writing (August 1975), the future of the world payments system is still undecided. The dollar continues to float, but "dirtily," and more as a result of breakdown in the old system of fixed exchange rates than as a deliberate policy choice. Meanwhile, protectionist claims appear sounder whenever the dollar sags in the exchange markets or whenever the latest deficit in the balance of payments or trade is posted. The major trading countries hold meetings with a view to restoring "order" in world payments, the United States being a notable exception to a widespread official desire for a return to some compromise system of fixed exchange rates.

Of the various arguments bred by current crises, probably the least tenable are those linking payments to commodity imports. Aside from the question of whether overall deficits have any meaning at all when currencies are floating, it is not even clear whether the imposition of trade barriers offers relief. While tariffs and other barriers do initially discourage imports, they also tend to draw resources from exporting and non-import-competing industries. By raising prices in general and through input-output relations among production processes, they might even tend ultimately to worsen balances of trade and payments at a given exchange rate.[7]*

---

*In a less-than-fully-employed economy, the imposition of a trade barrier may tend to reduce imports and move the economy closer to full employment. But see also below, pp. 109-10.

Other arguments are aimed at the world payments system itself. A few champions of the old-fashioned gold standard still support a return to the pre-1914 system of fixed exchange rates.[8] Still others see a need for (or the inevitability of) some kind of international money but favor, instead, an expanded role for the Special Drawing Rights issued by the International Monetary Fund.[9] By institutionalizing a "paper gold" system of international money, the world might enjoy the advantages of a fixed exchange rate without at the same time suffering the disadvantages of an old-fashioned gold standard or any of the various compromise systems that have surfaced in recent years. In particular, according to the argument, the IMF could relieve the world of any dependence on gold supplies or U.S. dollars for international reserves by issuing money of its own. It makes more sense, on this view, to tie exchange rates to a monetary unit managed by world monetary experts than to tie them to some commodity or national currency.

As the world economy and world trade continue to grow, so will the balance-of-payments deficits developing from time to time under fixed exchange rates and the quantities of gold or other reserves needed to finance official exchange-rate fixing. A gold standard provides no assurance that just enough gold will be produced each year to satisfy the growing demand for reserves. A leading trouble with a dollar standard is that growth of the dollar reserves of foreign governments and central banks requires chronic deficits in the balance of payments of the United States. Yet these deficits undermine confidence in the dollar, particularly when outmoded exchange rates swell these deficits and the resulting foreign acquisitions of dollars to sizes considered excessive. A restored dollar standard might break down again, as it did in the period 1971-1973.

In order to end the reserve-nonreserve currency relationship between countries that caused the old fixed-exchange-rate system to operate as an engine of inflation, it was necessary to create a different relationship in which exchange rates were free to fluctuate. As the dollar depreciated under this system, foreign countries were freed from earlier policies of supporting it at the sacrifice of monetary restraint at home, while the United States was forced either to exercise monetary restraint or absorb the full measure of its own expansionist policies. This set the stage, finally, for generally greater monetary restraint and lower rates of inflation than had been possible before. The fact that exchange rates were set free to fluctuate around the same time that inflation reached double-digit levels proves not that the fluctuation of exchange rates was at fault but rather that it had become necessary to discontinue rate-pegging because of its inflationary consequences (recall pp. 102-03, above).

We do not believe that the world is necessarily headed toward greater monetary stability just because exchange rates can float upward or downward. It is one thing for countries to have the opportunity for carrying out sensible monetary policies and another for them to exercise that opportunity. We simply wish to dispel any notion that the old compromise system of fixed exchange rates was itself any more likely to yield greater stability than the compromise dirty float that displaced it.

THE CHOICE FACING US

By now it is no secret that our own preferred solution to the problems surveyed would include allowing exchange rates to float freely. One difficulty with the existing compromise system of dirty floats is that it does not go far enough—it tolerates enough central-bank intervention to prevent a truly automatic balancing of international accounts. Our experience to date with floating rates, thrust on us as they were by default rather than choice, has already dispelled many of the old fears that such rates would disrupt trade and capital flows. Any inconveniences about which bankers and foreign exchange dealers might complain seem small in comparison to the advantages to be gained from a commitment to free rates. The United States could easily make such a commitment on its own, letting other countries fix their currencies to each other or to the dollar, as they saw fit.

In addition to the economic interrelations among policies concerning trade, exchange rates, and employment, considerations of political tactics are worth attention. Fixed exchanges promote protectionist sentiment by hiding how import barriers harm industries other than those directly favored. The balancing of imports and exports under a system of fixed rates is complicated and is understandable only with study. Under free rates, by contrast, people can see how tightening import duties or quotas would tend to make the home currency appreciate against foreign currencies. It is clear that while a higher tariff on one import would benefit the competing home industry, the effect of the tariff on the exchange rate would stimulate *other* imports and discourage exports. Under free exchanges, businessmen damaged by tariff privileges given to others could make definite, understandable, timely complaints.

Two economists have phrased the point pithily: "... free trade and fixed exchange rates are incompatible in the modern world, and all free traders should be in favour of variable exchange rates.... The central argument in favor of flexible exchanges is identical with the traditional case for free trade."[10]

EMPLOYMENT AND MONEY

Although this chapter is mainly concerned with international monetary issues, a few words about domestic policy are in order. Analysis and historical evidence continue to accumulate suggesting that the so-called business cycle of boom and depression is mainly a matter of monetary instability. Besides measures to preserve a competitive price system,* the key to stable prosperity apparently lies in stopping erratic spurts and sags in the country's money supply and adopting, instead, a steady trend in line with the real growth of the economy and compatible with a fairly stable general price level. Even if the best attainable monetary policy were less rigid than this one, it would almost surely have to avoid sharp major deviations from steady, moderate monetary growth. Deliberate monetary management is hardly radical or socialistic; government taxing, spending, and debt management, as well as central-bank operations, cannot help but profoundly influence a country's money supply, total spending flow, business conditions, and price level. The idea of monetary stabilization is not that the government should influence these things more powerfully than it does already but that its power should be tied down by a well-chosen rule rather than be used haphazardly and harmfully. Gold standard supporters sometimes forget that the rule of keeping the dollar tied to gold at a definite price is no less a rule than one for stabilizing the price level or the growth rate of the money supply. Nor is the gold-standard rule self-enforcing and proof against violation. In the long run, the rule that can best enlist informed opinion to make the government keep obeying it is whatever rule makes best sense economically.

A stable money policy is important not only to avoid the wastes, injustices, and frustrations of inflation and recession but also to guard against protectionist sentiment. When labor, factories, and machinery stand idle in a recession, people are not likely to care about the lesser wastes due to trade barriers. They are likely to swallow arguments that tariff protection safeguards home industry against foreign competition, saves jobs, and so on. Free-trade arguments "pointing out that protective tariffs make necessary more work to obtain the same result" forget that most people in developed countries, being hired by others rather than self-employed, "are accustomed to regard work as a thing to be desired in itself, and anything which makes more work as a benefit, not an injury." Against this rock free

---

*This provision refers to the possible conflict between full employment and price-level stability mentioned in Chapter 3.

traders "waste their strength when they demonstrate that the effect of protection is to increase work without increasing wealth . . . . The growth of the protective spirit as social development goes on" is due less "to the influence of the manufacturing interests which begin to arise" than to "habits of thought engendered by the greater difficulties of finding employment."[11]

Such habits of thought can mesh with at least one rather sophisticated line of reasoning. For certain theoretical purposes, imports, like saving, can be thought of as a leakage from the country's stream of spending and money income; exports, like investment spending, can be thought of as an injection into the stream. A surplus of exports over imports achieved by higher tariffs would be a net injection into the country's income stream. The export surplus might even have a "multiplier" effect, raising national income by more than its own amount. Another way of putting the whole theory is to say that an export surplus might bring more money into the country or into existence, or else make the country's existing money supply get spent faster, or both. The extra spending would help bring recovery from recession and so reduce unemployment.

Several reservations apply to this theory. First, the export surplus can last only a while. In the long run, exports and imports pay for each other. We can have an export surplus only until foreigners use up their reserves of dollars or gold or only as long as we keep giving or lending foreigners the money to buy our exports with. Second, tariffs cannot usefully be raised again and again. Once tariffs have cut down imports severely, little room remains to make an export surplus by putting tariffs still higher. Third, import barriers to promote employment are a trick that foreign countries can easily copy if they too do not know any better. If we try to "export our unemployment," other countries can retaliate. All countries can't have all export surpluses at once. As the 1930s showed, the main result is likely to be a wasteful overall shrinkage in trade. Fourth, the tariffs-for-employment theory is applicable, anyway, only when fixed exchange rates are blocking an independent monetary policy.

Wanting import barriers to remedy unemployment shows poor understanding of what causes and cures recessions. Imagine—trying to become prosperous by getting rid of goods worth more than those you get! As J. M. Keynes once suggested, a tariff can do nothing against unemployment that an earthquake could not do better. Recession and the accompanying unemployment are essentially a matter of too little spending. Inflationary recession is largely a consequence of double-barreled monetary mismanagement: excessive spending, due to excessive money-creation, occurred relatively far back in the past and turned, more recently, into too little spending to buy a full-employment output of goods and services at the inflated and still-rising prices. An inflation-addicted economy needs continual fixes to stave off withdrawal pangs. To vary the metaphor, following Nobel laureate

F. A. Hayek, rapid inflation is like holding a tiger by the tail—there is no satisfactory way to let go. Sound monetary management must be restored, but the transition is not easy. Tariff-tinkering is off the track.

One variant of the tariffs-for-employment argument suggests that import controls or special tariffs can help ward off deflationary balance-of-payments deficits when depression abroad shrinks exports. But controls or tariffs are unnecessary when the exchange-rate mechanism is allowed to keep trade balanced. With this insulation from foreign monetary mismanagement, a country can avoid the international contagion of depression as well as inflation. It cannot escape all ill effects when depression abroad shrinks trade opportunities; but it can stabilize its money supply independently so as to avoid general recession at home, no matter what happens elsewhere.

NOTES

1. "Balance-of-Payments Deficits: Measurement and Interpretation," *Federal Reserve Bank of St. Louis Review,* November 1973, p. 13. Pippenger is referring to the U.S. balance of payments.

2. 1970 HW&M XI 3108 (see Chapter 1, note 1).

3. 1973 HW&M IX 2954-55 (see Chapter 1, note 8).

4. 1973 HW&M XII 4019.

5. For evidence and reasoning along this general line, see David I. Meiselman, "Worldwide Inflation: A Monetarist View," in *The Phenomenon of Worldwide Inflation,* David I. Meiselman and Arthur B. Laffer, eds., (Washington: American Enterprise Institute, 1975), pp. 69-112. Meiselman saw some hope for an eventual easing of price inflation in the fact that rates of monetary growth began to decline abroad after rate-pegging was abandoned in 1973.

6. *International Financial Statistics,* August 1975, pp. 38-39, and Federal Reserve Bank of Chicago, *International Letter,* April 18, 1975. Whether or not the value of oil sold on credit is counted as part of current revenues is one explanation of divergence among various estimates of unspent oil revenues.

7. Mordechai E. Kreinin, *International Economics* (New York: Harcourt Brace Jovanovich, Inc., 1971), p. 250; Harry G. Johnson, *Economic Policies Toward Less Developed Countries* (Washington, D.C.: Brookings Institution, 1967), p. 75n.

8. See the papers by Patrick M. Boarman, Miroslav A. Kriz, and Donald L. Kemmerer in *World Monetary Disorder,* ed. by Patrick M. Boarman and David G. Tuerck (New York: Praeger Publishers, 1975).

9. A similar idea was advanced under a different name by Robert Triffin, *Gold and the Dollar Crisis* (New Haven: Yale University Press, 1960).

10. J. E. Meade, "The Case for Variable Exchange Rates," *Three Banks Review,* no. 27, September 1955, p. 6, quoted in Paul Wonnacott, *The Canadian Dollar, 1948-1958* (University of Toronto Press, 1960), p. 24; and Egon Sohmen, *Flexible Exchange Rates, Theory and Controversy* (University of Chicago Press, 1961), p. 116. Also see Milton Friedman, *Capitalism and Freedom,* Chapter IV. The slight differences of meaning

sometimes expressed by the terms "freely fluctuating," "variable," "floating," and "flexible" exchange rates are unimportant here.

11. Henry George, *Protection or Free Trade* (New York: Doubleday, Page, 1905), pp. 200-201, and footnote.

7

Although the case for free trade looks strong, protectionism persists in practical affairs. As the old saying goes, free traders win the arguments while protectionists win the votes. This chapter examines the nature and content of those protectionist arguments that carry the most weight politically.

THE CLAIMS OF "PRACTICAL KNOWLEDGE"

It is politically unfortunate that "The case for free trade is primarily rational and unspectacular. To appreciate it calls for a broader and deeper understanding of economics than most people possess, or care to acquire... The most fallacious of the protectionist arguments are the ones which carry the greatest popular appeal."[1] Protectionist fallacies and half-truths can be stated forcefully and briefly, while the answers to them tax most people's patience. The free trader is at a disadvantage in generally knowing better than to use arguments as simple, appealing, and false as those of the protectionists. The protectionist can exploit what J. E. Cairnes called "the prejudices of mere experience." He can point to "facts": here is an industry that has thrived under tariff protection; here is one that has suffered after a tariff cut. He can coolly ignore the harm done to consumers, exporters, and others by the tariff and the benefits given them by the cut. Precisely because this neglected harm or benefit is by its very nature diffused, the free-trader cannot "prove" it with spectacular "facts." He can show the results of protectionism by valid reasoning able to stand critical inspection, but his reasoning goes to waste on people who will not pay attention.

The protectionist actually takes pride in his narrow viewpoint. He sticks to plain facts—clear examples of damage from foreign competition and benefit from protection. He does not concern himself with remote, intangible, *theoretical* consequences. Thank God, he is no impractical theorist who never met a payroll! If he happens to be a watch lobbyist, he must struggle for patience with congressmen who never had practical experience retailing watches. If he manufactures fishing tackle, he pities the ignorance of trade-agreements negotiators who never had practical experience in that line.[2] He scorns the theorist's concern with how all parts of an economic system interconnect and with the remote as well as obvious repercussions of policy measures. He sticks to the down-to-earth, case-by-case approach. In so doing, he refuses even to consider the economic heart of the tariff controversy. Professors are his special bugbear.

Congressman James Burke, after failing to draw a sympathetic response to several points he was trying to make about trade and unemployment statistics, told Professor Hendrik Houthakker of Harvard:

> I like Harvard. I have a great deal of respect for it. I think sometimes you have a tendency to get behind those ivy covered walls over there, and you look out over the beautiful Charles River flowing down there with the boys rowing up the river and sailing up the river and think everything is hunkey-dorey.

Later he added:

> You see, we are confronted with this. I have to go before my people a year from next November and give them an accounting of my stewardship. I won't have a group of bright-eyed young students sitting before me listening to me in admiration of the great free trade philosophy that has been taught in all of our great universities since the 1940s.
>
> I am faced with realistic facts. That is why I would expect a place like Harvard, the great brilliant men you have over there and I respect you, believe me. I am not being disparaging about Harvard, but I think there is a tendency in these great universities to do all their studying and speculating on statistics, and believe the facts and fiction given out by government.[3]

According to Andrew Biemiller of the AFL-CIO, "Textbook theories of foreign trade—and government policies based on such theories—are increasingly irrelevant in the real world of trade and investment in 1970."[4] Said the vice president of the United Glass and Ceramic Workers: "Unfair import competition...gains its advantage from lower wages paid abroad. Let no economist with fancy degrees tell you otherwise."[5]

Messrs. Burke and Biemiller are not without allies in the academic world. Professor Galbraith, also of Harvard, argues strongly for international commodity agreements and takes the position that tariffs "cannot be excluded on doctrinal grounds." Like Burke, Galbraith sees most economists as captives of irrelevant theories who calmly ignore the suffering of others while basking in personal comfort.[6]

Free traders and academics should not be intimidated. They should ask the protectionists just what it is that makes their practical knowledge so important. Insinuations are not enough. The protectionist should show how his knowledge refutes the economist's case for free trade. Or is it so special that words cannot convey it? Any such claim would be sheer mysticism—literally—like the claim of religious mystics to have acquired transcendentally important but ineffable knowledge in their trances. Knowledge that cannot be written down is the opposite of scientific knowledge, since it lacks the public character that lets different investigators check and build on each other's factual and logical contributions. A practical man who sneers at "theorists" on the basis of his own superior but incommunicable knowledge is undermining rational investigation.

One kind of information that protectionists can and do communicate in overwhelming abundance is statistics—masses of statistics on wage rates and fringe benefits in the United States and foreign countries; on costs of production in individual industries here and abroad; on imports and exports; on sales and employment trends in import-competing industries; on domestic and import shares of the markets for particular products; on operating rates of American industries as percentages of some sort of "capacity"; on productivity; on use of machinery and power in various industries and countries; on the labor content of various commodities; on tariffs and other trade barriers, as well as subsidies, maintained by foreign countries; on tariff reductions accomplished by U.S. trade agreements; and so on. Such masses of material can be impressive when paraded before Congressional committees. They dramatize the supposed contrast between ivory-tower speculation and down-to-earth fact. Free-traders are often lured into this act; and they pile up statistics on such things as the large number of jobs supposedly dependent on exports and the small number supposedly jeopardized by freer trade; on how greatly business in individual Congressional districts depends on trade with Ruritania in particular or with foreign countries in general; on the large percentages of total supplies of vital materials obtained abroad and the large percentages of important kinds of American production, particularly farm production, sold abroad; on the populations, incomes, living standards, and growth rates of various countries inside and outside of common markets; on the sales and employment of individual firms that have made an easy adjustment to import competition; and so on. Many of these statistics and counterstatistics are interesting from some points of view and relevant to some questions, but their total effect can be misleading. Their very abundance suggests that all these facts and figures must somehow contain the real answer to the tariff issue. Otherwise, why would people put so much effort into gathering and computing and pondering them? Motley facts and figures take on a seeming relevance and spurious authority, overwhelming and burying the really crucial points.

The opposition often alleged between theory and fact is a false one. Both are necessary to correct analysis. But just any old theories and any old facts are not good enough, even if correct. They must also be relevant. Let us admit that widget workers' wages are only one-tenth as high in Slobbovia as in the United States, that the poor competitive position of the American gadget industry cannot be blamed on technological backwardness or managerial inefficiency, and that Ruritania discriminates shamefully against imports of American cars and chickens. So what? No case for protectionism emerges of its own accord out of facts and figures alone. Choosing and interpreting them depends on theories about which ones are relevant, and how. Anyone presenting a fact or figure has *some* idea, presumably, of how it fits in, of what difference it makes; and that is his theory. The real contrast is not between people who theorize and people who use only facts but between people who theorize with the advantage of knowing what they are doing and people who theorize without realizing it. Facts chosen and presented on the basis of half-formed, unrecognized theories are likely to be worse than useless. However correct they may be, irrelevant facts clutter up a discussion and sidetrack attention away from what really matters.

The thing to ask about a presentation of statistics is what difference it makes. What difference would it make if the results of an investigation had turned out to be the opposite? Laborious statistical investigations used in controversy between free-traders and protectionists are likely to give the impression that the considerations on the two sides are delicately balanced and that a correct decision depends on certain hard-to-pin-down facts that might quite conceivably have been different from what they actually turned out to be. Asking about relevance guards against such an impression.

None of these remarks are meant to disparage facts. The free-trade case *does* rest on facts, as well as on analysis of their interconnections and on value judgments. Some of these facts are: that resources are scarce in relation to people's practically limitless wants; that people desire goods and services, or the opportunity to have them; that more than one factor of production exists and that the law of diminishing returns holds true; and that prices do influence decisions about production and consumption. These facts, and others, underlie all economic analysis. Free-traders also take account of less universal facts, such as that technological progress gives rise to new products and production methods, with results generally considered "good," or that countries differ in natural resources, population characteristics, and standards of living. In addition, they take account of any other facts whose relevance protectionists actually do try to show with reasoned arguments.

Somebody will doubtless object that these are not what he means by facts; they are just trivial truths known all along. Actually, facts are not trivial just because no one disputes them or just because they hold true in widely different places and historical periods. It so happens that the main body of economic analysis, and the free-trade case in particular, does rest on these basic facts and not on mere historical details of particular times and places. What science looks for are propositions of *generality and depth,* ones that apply widely and are fruitful in yielding insights. Such propositions necessarily must rest on truths of *general* validity. If economics consisted of nothing but descriptions of what was true in specific historical circumstances, it would not be a very interesting subject. As Professor Ludwig von Mises once commented about an elaborate statistical study of the demand for watermelons, no principles of economics would be shaken in the least if no such commodity as watermelons ever existed. We might add that the basic case for free trade would stand unshaken if the spread between American and Japanese wage rates were ten times or one-tenth as big as it is, or if the volume of textile imports or the number of jobs dependent on exports were likewise vastly different from what it is, or even if no such country as the United States of America had ever existed.*

Tariff arguments with any claim to respectability describe circumstances in which tariffs would be beneficial and explain how. But if such circumstances are not even plausibly imaginable, what could it be that elaborate statistical and historical studies are looking for? Of course, such studies may touch off chains of thought that lead ultimately to well-formulated theories of beneficial protectionism; but this would be pretty much a matter of how ideas originate rather than of whether they are valid. One suspects that the protectionist parade of details of recent economic history is a more or less unconscious diversionary tactic designed less to lay down a positive case for protectionism or to meet free-trade arguments squarely

---

*Admittedly, the *basic* case for free trade is not always conclusive by itself. Considerations of defense or of cold-war strategy, for example, may conceivably override it. As a matter of fact, however, most of the confusion over the issue of free trade versus protectionism centers on failure to grasp this basic case. It is what most requires emphasis.

than to contrast sharply with free-trade agruments and subtly to disparge them as merely theoretical. To meet this tactic, the free-trader is entitled to say to the protectionist: "You show me an argument that would be persuasive if certain facts were true. Then I'll take seriously the question of whether those facts are true." One cannot legitimately slip out of theorizing, or out of an examination of arguments, by piling up facts. The question is what kind of facts are needed, and how they would have any bearing on policy if they turned out one way or the other.

Free-traders, like everyone else, are tempted to give their analysis and recommendations a veneer of topicality by decorating them with current facts and figures. This public-relations advantage is bought at a price. A parade of detailed facts about particular activities in particular times and places—facts that are rather difficult to come by and that refer to continually changing conditions—suggests that the free-trade case applies only under rather special circumstances whose presence or absence must continually be checked by detailed investigations. (The protectionist arguments examined in Chapter 12 do come close to implying this.) If the free-trade case really did have such limited relevance, it would hardly be worth bothering about. The general case for the price-and-profit system—of which the free-trade case is just a particular application—would likewise be uninteresting.

Admittedly, some detailed historical facts, like those bearing on how great and painful the adjustments to free trade would be, are relevant. But they are relevant to questions about how to make the transition, or, at most, to whether transitional difficulties would be so great as to outweigh the benefits of finally having free trade. But this is different from the question whether free trade, as such, is desirable and whether protectionist arguments are sound or not. So far as some tariff arguments, like the defense argument, do depend on specific historical circumstances, then detailed facts are relevant. But here, too, a distinction holds: the fact that such circumstances may argue for exceptions to a general free-trade policy is not to say that the positive case for free trade is itself history-bound.

A distinction between empirical science and metaphysical speculation is justified. But we should not overdo the current fashion of carrying the supposed methods of natural science uncritically over into the social sciences. Natural scientists and economists alike are looking for facts of more general validity than those tied to specific historical circumstances. As the chemist and economist Michael Polanyi once said, a measure of the speed at which water is running in a particular gutter, no matter how painstaking and precise, is not science. By and large, natural scientists have to arrive at their broad, generally valid, non-history-bound propositions by inference from painstakingly precise experimental measurements of many kinds. In economics, it so happens, the general universally valid propositions can be derived from more direct observation, including introspection. It is illegitimate to identify hard-won facts with solid empiricism and facts of everyday experience with useless metaphysical speculation. Failure to see the differences as well as the similarities between economics and the natural sciences leads almost to identifying a difficult investigation with an especially worthy one, an obscure and hard-to-dig-out fact with one particularly worth having. Actually, the truth would seem to be nearer the opposite in economics proper (as distinguished, for example, from economic history). Obscure and uncertain facts that quite well may not hold true in times and places other than those in which they were found seem like a shaky basis for propositions of generality and depth. Saying this is not at all to scorn historical and statistical work in economics. Such work may help, for example, in judging the relative strengths of opposing influences described by theory. (One strand of theory teaches that the risks of a fluctuating exchange rate hamper international trade; another strand teaches that a rate which always equilibrates supply and demand is more conducive to transactions than a fixed and hence often disequilibrium rate. It may be useful to know which influence appears to have been the stronger in particular experiences with fluctuating rates.) But in the natural sciences, judging the relative strengths of influences already understood qualitatively is less characteristically the role of measurement; there, measurement is essential to provide clues about even the qualitative state of affairs.

Sometimes protectionists are interested in neither theory nor facts. When presented with statistical evidence tending to support the case for free trade, they lash out at the free trader for being unfeeling or unpatriotic. Thus, after listening sympathetically to protectionist claims of trade-induced unemployment in the steel industry, Congressman Burke launched this attack against the opposting testimony of Professor Joel B. Dirlam:

> Mr. Burke....
> I admire you for sitting there so complacently and taking this great optimistic view of the future, but I don't see where it is going to take place.
> Dr. Dirlam. This was based on my detailed examination of the statistics of the steel industry, which failed to show that imports had caused any unemployment.
> Mr. Burke. I think what you should do is go down to Pennsylvania and go down among the steelworkers and talk to them. Forget about the statistics. Get down and talk to human beings who are being affected.
> You might have a different view on it.
> Dr. Dirlam. I got the statistics on unemployment in every steel center. This failed to show—
> Mr. Burke. Forget about statistics. Go right down into the areas and talk to the steelworkers and find out what their problems

are. Then you might get a little bit of a different point of view on it.

I think you have presented a great deal of statistics here. In fact, they are overwhelming. I should think it would be a very costly venture to get all these statistics together. But as you have told me, this is purely out of your salary as a professor at the University of Rhode Island and you give a strong talk that would indicate, you almost sound to me like—and of course I would never accuse you of this, but you have given a great argument in favor of Japan.[7]

Still other protectionists claim that facts, though relevant, have to be acquired in a particular way. Thus, Representative John Dent, who apparently enjoys junketing around the world, regretted in testimony before the House Ways and Means Committee that he hadn't had a chance to visit Japan *this* year to get the latest figures on steel wages—"and that, my dear Mr. Chairman and members, is the only way you will ever find anything out about wages that go into steel or wages that go into any product. You have to be on the scene."[8]

For Representative Mendel Rivers, it is a matter of having *worked* in a particular industry:

If anybody knows something about the textile industry, it is Mendel Rivers, because I worked in them. I don't know what contribution I made but I worked 11 hours a day. I understand they don't work that long these days.

The workers in these plants are fine people. They have a fine life to live. Their wages are good. Our workers in America have the highest standard of living of any workers on earth, and you know it. Get out on the highway any weekend and see how many of our employees are out with their trailers on the back and motorcycles on the back of the trailer headed for the mountains of South Carolina, often with the trailers carrying boats.

They go out to get recreation starting Friday evening, your American workers. All they want is a chance to survive. I want to save them. God bless them.[9]

These examples show why the devotee of facts and anecdotes is the worst theorist of all—an unconscious one.

The plain man—I do not think this is an overstatement—calls a "theory" anything he does not understand, especially if the conclusions it is used to support are distasteful to him.... It is only because he does not understand "theory" that the plain man is apt to compare it unfavourably with "practice," by which he means what he can understand . . . .

The practical man is apt to sneer at the theorist; but an examination of any of his most firmly-rooted prejudices would show at once that he himself is as much a theorist as the purest and most academic student; theory is a necessary instrument of thought in disentangling the amazingly complex relations of the external world. But while his theories are false because he never tests them properly, the theories of science are continually under constant test and only survive if they are true. It is the practical man and not the student of pure science who is guilty of relying on extravagant speculation, unchecked by comparison with solid fact.[10]

If a man really believes that a conversation with unemployed steel workers, or a visit to Japan, or a trip to the Carolina mountains really has some bearing on U.S. trade policy, then he should explain why. He should be prepared to say what difference it makes to the case for and against free trade if the steelworker says that steel imports have put him out of work, or if the visit to Japan shows that wages there have changed since last year, or if the fraction of mountain-bound trailers carrying motorcycles seems to be falling off lately. The amateur theorist who calls himself a practical man should be held as accountable for his theories (however unconsciously he may be enslaved by them) as any professional. Free trade cannot be dismissed as "a beautiful ideal."[11] A theory that does not square with practice must have a flaw in it, which the objector need only point out. Few things are so practical as a correct theory; few so impractical as an isolated fact or anecdote.

FAIR VERSUS UNFAIR COMPETITION

Perhaps the plea most commonly used in Congressional committee hearings is that such-and-such an industry is suffering from "unfair" foreign competition and must be saved by a higher tariff or an import quota. At the very least, existing protection must be maintained. The typical witness points out how his old customers are shifting to the cheaper imports and how his workers face unemployment. Very likely he will emote a little: his workers have rare skills gained by a lifetime of specialized work in the widget industry; they are good, loyal American citizens, the backbone of the nation, who live along elm-lined streets in peaceful little towns, own their own homes and recreational trailers, support the schools and churches, and have sons guarding the nation on duty in the armed forces overseas. Such stories are effective: the unfortunate widget workers are definite people, while others who bear the diffused harm of protectionism are nameless and forgotten.

A statement by Mr. Victor Bates, President of Bates Nitewear Co., provides a good example of an emotional argument, infused with altruism:

> I came to this country in 1920 from Greece at the age of 16. I came here because I thought this country was a land of opportunity. I still have this basic belief. My first job was as a delivery boy in the sweatshops of the cut-and-sew industry. I have never backed off from a fair fight and I have thrived on fair competition, but it is now apparent to me that this fight is no longer fair because of the standard of living which all of us, including our employees, have come to enjoy.
>
> For the past several years, our company has made it a policy to offer college scholarships to our employee[s'] children....
>
> I am afraid that the influx of imports will hurt our profit structure and I am sure that it will if same continues. We would be forced to discontinue this wonderful educational benefit for our employee[s'] children.[12]

"The bicycle industry is not an inefficient industry clamoring for 'protection' from efficient foreign manufacturers," said Mr. William Hannon of the Bicycle Manufacturers Association. "We only ask for a chance to compete fairly—on an equal basis—with imported products."[13]

The National Association of Scissors and Shears Manufacturers has "never asked that an embargo be placed on the import of scissors and shears. All we have requested, and all we want, is a fair, competitive opportunity in the U.S. market."[14]

Some Congressmen do question the damages asserted by such witnesses,[15] but if evidence is produced, many seem to regard the case for import barriers as airtight. Indeed it is, if based on a frank value judgment that the short-run welfare of the people in the import-competing industry overrides all other considerations. Occasionally something near this is hinted at. According to a wallpaper spokesman, for example, "no significant purpose is served by the withholding of tariff protection required in this industry. Our industry is so infinitesimal a segment of the American economy, that the tariff protection which will save this industry from destruction cannot possibly impair the general reciprocal trade program." Protection "would appear to be mandatory as an extension of the well-founded principle of procedural fair play. It is difficult to understand how anyone can withhold tariff relief in a fact situation in which the economic necessity for such relief has been adequately established."[16] Usually though, instead of avowing any special value judgment, people competing with imports suggest that what is good or bad for them is good or bad for the country also. During a tirade against a Japanese microscope priced about 60 percent below the equivalent American model, Senator Malone conceded that

> We could buy the cheaper one and allow the Japanese and the Germans to manufacture all the precision instruments. It is a fine theory as long as you only have that one industry—it is not a large industry, not a large employer—but if you follow that through, you kill all the industries, and then the United States and all of our businesses are down to that same level.[17]

Such arguments fall into the familiar "fallacy of composition" (see p. 71).

A particular industry may plainly suffer from competitive imports, but it is a fallacy to conclude from this that the American economy as a whole is suffering and would benefit from protecting the afflicted industry. Protecting it makes consumers pay higher prices and so may cut their buying power as customers of other industries. It also hurts industries into whose costs the protected goods directly or indirectly enter, whether as raw or semifinished materials, tools, means of transportation, or items in their workers' cost of living. Most important, import barriers, change the *pattern* rather than raise the *level* of production and employment throughout the economy. The fear that imports could kill off all American industries implies that foreigners give us all the goods we want free, taking nothing in return except perhaps dollars that they are never going to spend, dollars that our government and banks could then advantageously create out of thin air. The idea is pleasant but absurd. Actually, foreigners will not send goods to us unless we send goods to them.

Protectionists forget that industries are not *ends* in themselves, but rather *means* for partly overcoming obstacles that stand in the way of human well-being. The purpose of a food industry is not to provide work—not to call forth effort—but to overcome hunger. The purpose of a clothing industry is not to exercise the brain and muscle of managers and workers but to overcome nakedness and shabbiness. The purpose of a transportation industry is not to employ labor but to overcome distance. Protectionists seem to approve of obstacles because overcoming them gives employment. Otherwise, why would protectionists oppose food and clothing imports unless they approved of anything that kept hunger and nakedness difficult to overcome? To judge from the tariff on soap, Congress positively cherishes the dirt that supports the American soap industry. To judge from the tariff on fire hose, Congress considers arsonists public benefactors. To judge from the tariffs on medicines and surgical and dental instruments, Congress would deplore any improvement in the health of the American people. "Economically, what difference is there between restricting the importation of iron to benefit iron producers and restricting sanitary improvements to benefit undertakers?"[18]

William Graham Sumner pointed out that an industry dependent on protection is hardly an industry in the usual sense of the word. It thrives only because government interference with the freedom of buyers has turned capital and labor out of other channels where they would otherwise have been more productive. A protected widget factory is not so much a means of providing widgets as a means of making widgets more expensive behind a tariff wall than they would be under free trade. Under special circumstances (considered in later chapters) a case of sorts can be made for imposing this extra expense on consumers, but in general Sumner is right: a protected industry is a nuisance. "The bigger it is the sadder it is."[19]

The "unfairness" of permitting low-cost imports to compete with domestic goods is often attributed to low foreign wages. Thus, the Copper and Brass Fabricators Council does not seek protection "against fair competition from foreign fabricators."

> If it were possible for Congress to develop a flexible tariff system which would encourage foreign mills to observe our labor standards and which would do no more than offset the lower foreign production costs which result from low labor rates, our domestic mill industry would welcome the opportunity to complete with foreign mills in our domestic markets. We ask only for the opportunity to compete on a fair basis.[20]

Representative James Corman of California is one member of Congress who has expressed sympathy for this idea. On the theory that quotas "do away with whatever there is that makes a free economy tick," Corman would set tariffs just high enough to "level out the labor cost differences."[21]

Other protectionists consider *any* basis for low foreign prices to be unfair. Thus, wool growers, in a plea for greater protection, once cited a Tariff Commission finding that Australian sheep raisers have the advantage of cheap *land*. The chairman of the House Ways and Means Committee has sympathized with American growers of hothouse tomatoes and cucumbers because their Mexican and Cuban competitors were free from the expense of heavy investments in hothouses. A witness from the bicycle industry has complained that his foreign competitors enjoyed the low costs of mass production to meet a large demand. The coal industry has agitated against imports of heavy fuel oil; since this residual oil is a by-product and so has no well-defined cost of production, its competition with coal is unfair. U.S. mink ranchers have complained about the lower costs of feed ingredients enjoyed by their Scandinavian competitors.

The U.S. tariff law of 1930, still in effect though much amended, pays homage to the theory that low foreign production costs are harmful, regardless of their cause. Its Section 336 (little used and now still applicable only to duties never modified in trade agreements) laid down procedures for adjusting tariff rates within certain limits to offset differences between the production costs of American goods and competing imports. The Tariff Commission had the task of studying production costs both at home and abroad and recommending suitable new tariff rates to the President.

Even aside from the many possible meanings of "cost," the differences among costs even of producers within a single country, and serious practical difficulties, the very idea of cost investigations is absurd. Steady importing of some commodity proves by itself that the foreign cost is lower (unless the foreigners are "dumping" the commodity or subsidizing exports of it, a separate but related matter examined below, or unless the American pricing is monopolistic). Senator Malone apparently understood how necessary cost investigations are when he proposed a flexible tariff that would have just brought the price of an imported commodity up the price of the corresponding American commodity.

In recent years, quotas, rather than tariffs, have become the vogue. Why even bother to calculate price-equalizing tariff rates when Congress can directly control the volume of foreign goods brought into the country? The Mills Bill of 1970 and the Burke-Hartke Bill (Foreign Trade and Investment Act), introduced with considerable support in 1971 and 1973, would have tied imports to some historically determined fraction of domestic production.*

All such proposals seem "fair." Don't set tariff rates (or quotas) too high (or too low)—just high (or low) enough to offset the foreigner's advantage or to restrict him to his "fair share" of the American market. Ac-

---

*The 1971 Burke-Hartke Bill (sponsored by Congressman Burke and Senator Vance Hartke of Indiana) would have limited U.S. imports, both by product categories and by countries, to a fixed percentage of domestic production based on average imports and production over the period 1965-1969. A proposed Foreign Trade and Investment Commission could have tightened any quota on imports found to be "inhibiting the production of any manufactured product" or relaxed quotas on the intermediate factors or production if these restrictions on imports of them were found to be similarly "inhibiting" to U.S. industry.

cording to the National Cotton Council of America, the Mills Bill "is not a repressive, backward-looking measure." Rather, it permits foreigners

to share in the growth of our markets, taking only their reasonable pro rata share of the growth.... It looks forward to expanding trade, in which our foreign friends can have their full share and thus serve the American consumer more in the future than in the past. It would just not destroy the ability of our own economy to be healthy and progressive and to compete for a chance to serve its own consumers.[22]

Others have used more picturesque language. As lobbyist O. R. Strackbein once suggested, "Let the goods come in and compete on a fair competitive basis in this country. Let the best goods win." "We do not match one man with a blackjack and brass knuckles against another with boxing gloves," said Lewis E. Lloyd, complaining about the "unnatural advantage" that low foreign wages give foreign producers. An "equalizing tariff" would take away their "overwhelming advantage" and "put domestic producers on an equal footing."[23]

According to broadcaster Ed Wimmer,

If they [foreigners] come into this market in a willingness to compete on even terms, and are willing to pit their products and salesmanship against our products and merchandising abilities, ... let them come, and let there be no limits put on them for the amount of goods they are able to sell.[24]

The notion that foreigners should be required to charge a "fair price" or that they should be limited to a "fair share" of domestic markets rests on a false premise. Trade is not like a horse race or a friendly golf game; "fair competition" is not an objective in itself. The purpose of trade is to get goods on advantageous terms. To interfere because of foreign cost or price advantages is to attack the very principle of specialization and trade. Consistently applied, the idea that imports must not undersell domestic goods would almost wholly stop all imports of goods also made at home and would in turn stifle exports. Despite the popularity of quotas nowadays, the idea of limiting foreigners to some predetermined fraction of the home market is no better. Either idea comes close to enthroning national self-sufficiency and guaranteeing protection no matter how badly the import-competing industry wastes labor and other resources. The greater the degree of protection, the greater the waste.

The "fair trade" concept has found its way into legislation such as the Antidumping Act of 1921 and the Trade Act of 1974. Under this legislation,

the President is permitted, unless Congress overrides him, to impose or restore import restrictions on the products of any country, which, in his
opinion

> (1) maintains unjustifiable or unreasonable ... import restric-
> tions which impair the value of trade commitments made to the
> United States or which burden restrict, or discriminate against
> United States commerce,
> (2) engages in discriminatory or other acts or policies which
> are unjustifiable or unreasonable and which burden or restrict
> United States commerce,
> (3) provides subsidies (or other incentives having the effect
> of subsidies) on its exports of one or more products to the United
> States or to other foreign markets which have the effect of sub-
> stantially reducing sales of the competitive United States product
> or products in the United States or in those other foreign markets,
> or
> (4) imposes unjustifiable or unreasonable restrictions on
> access to supplies of food, raw materials, or manufactured or semi-
> manufactured products which burden or restrict United States
> commerce.[25]

The Antidumping Act provides for special antidumping duties, over
and above regular duties, on goods which are being sold at less than "fair
value" and which are causing injury to some American industry by reason
of their importation into the United States. When the Secretary of the
Treasury receives complaints to that effect, he is required, under the Trade
Act of 1974, to decide within thirty days whether to initiate a formal, initial
investigation of sales below "foreign market value." The presumed source
of "unfairness" in a dumping investigation is the sale of some good in the
United States at a price less than it commands in some foreign market,
usually the home market of the exporter. He must then determine within
nine months whether there is reason to believe or suspect such sales and,
upon reaching an affirmative determination, suspend appraisals for assessing regular duties on the suspected goods. A final determination must be
reached within three months of the initial determination.

Although a determination of sales below foreign market value is not
sufficient to establish a case of dumping, the mere suspension of appraisals
suspends imports as well, unless importers are willing to risk having to pay
unforeseeably high duties or unless the foreign exporters guarantee to re-
imburse their U.S. customers. When the importer is related to the exporter,
as, for example, a subsidiary, appraisals can be suspended retroactively
to 120 days before notice was given of the initial investigation. In the past

not even this limit applied, and duties were sometimes imposed on goods imported years before the final decision, even though their appraisal might have been held up for reasons unconnected with dumping.

Numerous problems bedevil the Secretary's task of distinguishing "fair" from "unfair" prices. Sales below fair value supposedly occur if the U.S. importer's "purchase price" or the foreign "exporter's sales price" is below "foreign market value." But in order to get at these concepts it is necessary to take into consideration not only the posted price in the United States and in the exporter's home market but also any related shipping and packaging charges, export taxes, commissions, rebated import taxes, and value added in the United States. When a single good is produced by a "multinational firm" in two countries but sold at a higher price in the first than in the second, the foreign market value may, under circumstances specified by the Trade Act of 1974, be calculable on the basis of the price charged in the first even though the alleged dumping takes place from the second. Other provisions require a complicated "constructed value" to be substituted for "foreign market value" when the suspected goods are sold below cost in the home market of the exporting country or when the foreign exporters are "state-controlled."

If the Secretary finds that there has been dumping, the U.S. International Trade Commission must conduct another investigation to determine, within three months, whether the imported goods are causing injury or are likely to cause injury to a domestic industry or are keeping one from being established. An evenly divided vote in the six-member Commission counts as a finding of injury (which is another clue to how sinister Congress considers dumping to be). When sales at less than fair value and injury have both been determined under this procedure, the Treasury then levies a special antidumping duty on the offending imports. This penalty generally amounts to the difference between the importer's purchase price (or exporter's sales price) and foreign market value. Importers may appeal the decisions of the Treasury or the Commission to the Customs Court and to the Court of Customs and Patent Appeals.

Despite complaints from import-competing interests over the slowness and unreliability of the procedures involved, findings of injury are made with surprising readiness. In a January 1975 decision involving tapered roller bearings from Japan, the Commission made an injury determination despite the dissenting opinion of Commissioner Daniel Minchew:

> The domestic tapered roller bearing industry (domestic industry) was operating at near capacity . . . in the U.S. market. . . . The domestic industry experienced increased sales in every year from 1970 to 1973, which encompasses the dumping period. The domestic industry increased its prices consistently throughout the period

1970 to 1973. In addition, the export sales of the domestic industry
as a proportion of total sales increased during 1973. For me, it is
not possible to establish that an industry which has the above-
mentioned characteristics is being or is likely to be injured by reason of imports at LTFV [less than fair value].[26]

Over the years, the Commission has had to grapple with the problem
of defining a U.S. "industry" as well as that of measuring "injury" to that
industry. In the cast-iron soil-pipe case of 1955, it found injury even though
the "injured" domestic industry accounted for only 8 percent of national
production. Similarly, in 1961, it found that Portland cement was being
dumped from Sweden: in view of the heavy transportation cost of cement
in relation to its value, the Commission decided that certain New England
plants constituted an industry in themselves and that those plants were
likely to be injured by less-than-fair-value imports.

During the period spanning fiscal years 1971-1974, the Commission
completed 66 investigations and found injury in 35. Affirmative determinations were reached in the cases of whole dried eggs from Holland (July
1970), ice cream sandwich wafers from Canada (February 1972), instant
potato granules from Canada (September 1972), canned Bartlett pears from
Australia (March 1973), and picker stickers (yes, picker stickers) from Mexico (May 1974). Some negative determinations concerned chicken eggs in
the shell from Mexico (June 1971), Kanekalon wigs from Hong Kong (December 1972), and collapsible baby strollers from Japan (March 1973).

Even when a negative determination is likely, import-competing interests are encouraged by the law to file a complaint and try to have an investigation made, if only to harass importers for a while. Although a minority of complaints end up having an antidumping duty applied, the harshness
of the law remains as evidence of how heinous an offense dumping is
thought to be. (Before 1921, in fact, dumping was actually defined as a
criminal offense, but the law proved unworkable.)

If the examples cited above are not convincing enough to make the
whole idea of an antidumping action look absurd, then we can simply put
them in the perspective of economic analysis. What difference does it make
to an import-competing industry or to the domestic economy as a whole if
a foreign good is sold more cheaply here than in the exporter's home
market? The harm to the import-competing industry and the benefit to the
domestic economy is the same, regardless of the price charged abroad. It
hardly makes sense to establish an elaborate procedure for processing complaints against foreigners who discriminate *in favor of* Americans. The
circumstances that enable them to discriminate against their fellow country-
men may be regrettable from some point of view; but to Americans, bargains are bargains.

Up to now, we may have overlooked one possible answer to the question of how the *reason* why foreign goods are cheap could possibly matter to the United States. The reason does matter if it affects how permanent the bargains are likely to be. The more persistently and dependably foreigners engage in dumping, the more the United States benefits.

One conceivable type of persistent dumping is noteworthy, even though probably without practical importance in current American experience. This is so-called *preclusive dumping,* practiced steadily over the long run to preclude establishment of an industry in the United States. If the dumping is in fact going to continue, there is no particular economic advantage to having the domestic industry. Whatever its motive and whatever its unattractive name, continuous dumping offers us a more efficient way of getting the dumped goods than making them ourselves.

The most nearly persuasive argument for restricting dumped imports hinges on a higher-than-ordinary degree of uncertainty. Unsteady bargain prices, sometimes offered and sometimes not, could conceivably disrupt the American market and cause a bigger nuisance than the bargains were worth when available.

The worst type of ordinary business-motivated dumping is presumably so-called *predatory dumping,* or what Professor Stephen Enke has called "the traditional atrocity case that is often mentioned but so seldom documented."[27] A foreign competitor cuts his price to drive American producers out of business, then raises his price again and reaps an exorbitant profit thereafter at American expense. To succeed, the foreign seller must be a monopolist or cartel. Furthermore, some irreversibility must exist to keep the Americans from going back into production when the foreigner raises his price to a monopolistic level. Otherwise, except perhaps in a short-run sequence, the foreigner can hardly have things both ways, charging low prices to kill off competition and high prices to reap the fruits of monopoly. Keeping American producers out of business indefinitely would require persistent dumping, about which we have already had reassurance. The conditions necessary for successful predatory dumping seem too improbable to justify an elaborate apparatus of antidumping measures. Determining the actual facts in suspected cases, including the facts about foreigners' motivation, would be complicated, and the authority for special antidumping duties would provide a constant temptation to pervert them on behalf of businessmen vexed by ordinary import competition. In any case, calculations of the home-market prices charged by foreigners are a red herring (except insofar as they are a clue to the permanency of the prices charged here). What matters is the impact foreigners are having in this country, not what they are doing in their own.

Sporadic or *intermittent* dumping somewhat resembles predatory dumping, but without the sinister motive. Bargains sometimes appear temporarily on the world market for the same sorts of reason that explain department-store clearance sales and other temporary bargains inside a country. Ordinary fixed-rate tariffs are no guarantee against this sort of thing unless they are high enough to bar imports of the goods completely. Something could be said in theory for adjustable duties or import quotas to compensate for import price fluctuations; but the practical difficulties of information, timing, and administration would be enormous, not to mention the danger of protectionist abuse. Many commodities rise and fall unpredictably in price on the home as well as the world market, and any ambitious government attempt to stabilize the prices of many individual commodities would undermine the working of the price system. Responding to price changes and coping with price uncertainties is one of the main jobs of businessmen. Especially under free trade, the tasks of coping with domestic and world market price uncertainties would intertwine thoroughly.

If intermittently dumped imports were storable, speculators could profit by buying them when dumping made them cheap and reselling them when the dumping had stopped. So doing, the speculators would steady the home market and still take advantage of the bargains sometimes available. If conditions were not clear enough for speculators to see profit opportunities, they would hardly be clear enough for the government to take proper action.

The countervailing duty law of the United States also reflects the "fair trade" mentality. As recently amended, that law imposes special duties on goods whose importation into the United States is subsidized by any "government, person, partnership, association, cartel, or corporation." As originally written into the Tariff Act of 1930, the law applied only to dutiable U.S. imports, but under the Trade Act of 1974 it has been expanded to apply as well to imports that are found by the International Trade Commission to cause or threaten injury to an American industry. Countervailing duties are to be equal to the amount of the subsidy ("bounty or grant") received by the foreign exporter. The new law attempts to satisfy import-competing interests, impatient with past slowness on the part of the Treasury to rule favorable on their complaints, by requiring a final determination of the existence or nonexistence of subsidy to be made within 12 months of the filing of a complaint. The Secretary may withhold a countervailing duty on items subject to trade negotiations unless Congress overrules him.

The countervailing duty law has been applied sparingly in the past. Since the first statute of 1897 there have been, by one count, 70 "basic countervailing duty orders." Over the period 1934-1969, 200 cases were processed, resulting in 34 countervailing duty orders.[28] Effective September 1974, some 26 items were affected, among them butter from Australia, X-radial steel-belted Michelin tires from Canada, ski lifts and refrigerators from Italy, bottled green olives from Spain, and non-rubber footwear from

Spain and Brazil. The accommodations made to import-competing interests by the Trade Act of 1974 give promise of a more generous application in the future.

As for the economic sense of countervailing duties, the point made about dumping applies: it hardly matters that an import is cheap just because it is subsidized by some foreign government. A subsidy, though probably wasteful to the country conferring it, is just one of many considerations that may combine to make an import a bargain from the American point of view. The possible disruptive effects of an impermanent subsidy are no more sinister or avoidable than any other consideration beyond the control of its beneficiaries. Certainly the absence of a subsidy is no guarantee of an intent not to disrupt—a country could engineer an unexpected rise in the price or cutoff in the supply of a commodity under its control regardless of any subsidy that it may or may not have been conferring. The current oil crisis shows just how impotent the trade laws are in the face of a real challenge.

CHEAP FOREIGN LABOR

Cheap labor is the most commonly alleged foreign distortion. Emphasizing it, protectionists enlist exaggeration as well as purported analysis. According to Congressman James Burke,

> You can't compete with a 10-cent-an-hour wage in our country unless you are going to roll back the clock 100 years, unless you are going back to a 7-day week and 10-hour day and go back to the days of malnutrition and tuberculosis and all the other dread ills of the sweatshops.
>   You can't become more competitive unless you bring yourself down to their level.[29]

Often coupled with the cheap-foreign-labor argument is the idea that imports produced by such labor will eliminate American jobs and destroy the market for American goods. John E. Mara, President of the Boot and Shoe Workers' Union, supports import quotas for "two trenchant reasons":

> ...to prevent the shameless exploitation of cheap labor for the benefit of the entrepreneur at the expense of American shoeworker labor; and to prevent the continuing vision, in the minds of such exploiters-of-labor, of America as a bottomless market for any and all products produced by wages lower than those won in years of struggle and achievement by the American workman and his unions.

What kind of economics is it that persuades anyone to believe that a jobless America can support every low-wage country's output?....

Continued unchecked imports of shoes, and of other products ...will certainly impoverish more of our citizens, your constituents among them.[30]

Mr. Abe Fineglass, International Vice President of the Amalgamated Meat Cutters & Butcher Workmen of North America, has gone to the trouble of calculating the number of jobs his union has lost on account of imports. "Shoe imports over the past decade rose from an annual 18.9 million pairs in 1957-59 to 105.3 million in 1969. This is a 457-percent increase in shoe import volume, representing an export of 33,520 jobs."[31]

Protectionists often combine their complaints about low foreign wages with a humanitarian appeal. In the testimony quoted above, Mr. John Mara claimed that

unchecked imports of any commodity made at the competitive advantage of substandard wages will not only maintain low wages economics of other countries, underdeveloped countries most of all, but will continue the abhorrent practice of child labor and the undermining of human dignity where children work with men for the same low wages. What hope can there be for the development of nations which must depend on the equality of children and adults in cheap labor pools? With both getting child's pay.[32]

Claiming that the average hourly wage for Koreans was 13 cents per hour, Mr. George Baldanzi of the Textile Workers Union told the House Ways and Means Committee that

we are not the benevolent benefactors of the peoples of the developing countries. We are engaged in a cruel and greedy economic game which, far from delivering them from their lives of depredation, we are forcing them on a sophisticated form of medieval exploitation.

...If American workers are expected to compete with this form of economic slavery on any basis, we can do so only if we reduce our own worker to this same outrageous economic state.[33]

Sometimes protectionists imply that the relatively high U.S. wages are themselves the product of American altruism. According to Mr. Lazare Teper of the Ladies' Garment Workers' Union:

Years ago, our industry was notorious for its low-labor standards. As a result of public indignation, legislative intervention, as well as union activity, labor standards have been gradually lifted....

Sweatshop wages, child labor, unlimited hours of work—everything that we have managed to eliminate from the American scene as a matter of public policy, has to be faced by the American worker when apparel comes in from abroad.

It is ironic if after eliminating these conditions at home, we would now consciously permit our labor standards to be eroded by foreign sweatshops.[34]

Such arguments rest on the remarkable notion that real wages or standards of living depend mainly on what somebody decides they should be, not on technological progress, capital accumulation, and business innovation. Apparently productivity doesn't count much, or else it, too, is simply decided upon. Having provided for our current standard of living, our union leaders would be only too pleased to provide every family with two cars, a camper, and a $100,000 house if only we'd let them.

This argument is often taken a step further and applied to foreigners. Since foreign employers and legislators are too mean to decide on decent wages and living standards for their own people, perhaps the U.S. Congress can take the decision out of their hands and compel them to decide in a more humane way. Thus James Burke envisions some kind of legislation "whereby the wage and hour conditions in some of these countries will have to be raised or an import duty will have to be levied in order to encourage these people to raise their working conditions."[35]

Wilbur Mills told one of the witnesses just quoted:

Mr. Baldanzi, if you could speak Japanese and I could speak Japanese, and we could be admitted as citizens of Japan, it wouldn't take us long to correct this situation. I would run for office, hoping to get elected, and you would organize the workers. We would straighten this thing out.[36]

Such whimsical notions aside, support is widespread for something equivalent to a Fair Labor Standards Act in international trade. Leonard Woodcock, President of the United Auto Workers, has been a particularly strong advocate of such a measure. He would include in every trade agreement "a fair labor standards provision substantially similar to the pertinent provisions of the Havana Charter." This document, which was signed by 50 nations in 1948 but never ratified, would have required each member of an anticipated International Trade Organization to "take whatever action may be appropriate and feasible to eliminate...[unfair labor] conditions within its territory."[37] Other supporters of the fair labor standards idea would use the bargaining machinery provided by the General Agreement on Tariffs and Trade and the International Labor Organization to coax low-wage exporting countries into improving "wage levels and working conditions."[38]

The following exchange between Congressman Burke and two representatives of the imported footwear industry provides a good example of protectionist altruism, supported by irrelevant statistics, and the perceptive testimony of one free-trader:

Mr. Burke. What do they get in Taiwan for making the [imported] shoe?

Mr. Beispel. I believe it is in the neighborhood of 10 or 20 cents an hour.

Mr. Burke. Does that permit them enough money to buy a bowl of rice over there in Taiwan?

How many hours does a youngster of the age of 10 of Taiwan work?

Mr. Beispel. I have never been in Taiwan, but I know they work long hours.

Mr. Hemmendinger. You can't raise the level of development of the economy of a foreign country by deciding to enact American-style minimum wages and hours, Mr. Burke. The greatest single engine for economic development probably that exists is the ability of these nations to produce for the developed markets of the world.

...In the long run they will all have much higher levels than they do today. But we have to keep our own doors open, or we will just be erecting a fortress, and we will have to defend it.

Mr. Burke. In other words, what we will have to do is contribute to these inhumane conditions of child labor—

Mr. Hemmendinger. The export industries tend to be the better industries in terms of labor in most of these countries.

Mr. Burke. It kind of bothers my conscience a bit. It seems to me very cruel and harsh that we should be making money on the exploitation of little children who are working 10 hours a day for about 6 cents an hour. That would seem to bother me a little bit.

They talk about these grape pickers out in California, and they talk about their conditions. And here we are in this big wealthy country of ours making money, experiencing a great deal of greed on the part of people. And it does not seem to bother their conscience.

Maybe we have a whole new system around here. We establish a minimum-wage scale in the United States. We raise the working standards, and we eliminated the fire traps and the sweat shops. And now we find that we have a group here in this country who are encouraging this overseas.

What I can't understand is what is the difference between exploiting child labor in the United States and over in, say, Taiwan, Korea, or Hong Kong, where is the difference in human values?

Mr. Hemmendinger. This is essentially a matter for the authorities in those countries. We did not fix a minimum wage of $2 to begin with. We had minimum wages which were far lower. These countries have the right and duty to choose what type of social legislation will help improve their standards. But they have to start with something that is realistic in terms of their existing conditions.

The simple answer to your question, Mr. Burke, is that they would be poorer without this trade, and so would the people of the United States.

Mr. Burke. How much poorer can they get if they are getting 6 cents an hour?

Mr. Hemmendinger. They can get nothing an hour.

Mr. Burke. It seems to me it ought to bother someone's conscience. Maybe I am old-fashioned or something. I am hoping and praying there might be some desire on the part of human beings to lift up the living conditions in these countries....

Don't you think there is something this Government can do to encourage them to raise their standards over there where we are purchasing so much from them?

Mr. Hemmendinger. If they were to adopt the kinds of legislation which is suggested, they would simply go broke in no time through inflation.

Mr. Burke. How would enactment of the textile-shoe bill force them to go broke? They would still have the same business they have.

Mr. Hemmendinger. It would impede the issue toward lower cost sources. This is the interest of all of the nations of the world, as well as the American consumer.

Mr. Burke. We would increase our domestic market, and we would be buying more next year from them than we bought this year....

Mr. Hemmendinger. Indonesia would not get much of a quota.

Mr. Burke. What does Indonesia import into [export to?] the United States?

Mr. Hemmendinger. They sell very little, but some day they will.

Mr. Burke. Are their labor standards lower than Hong Kong's and Taiwan's?

Mr. Hemmendinger. Very much lower.

Mr. Burke. After Indonesia, where do they go?

Mr. Hemmendinger. Maybe Africa.

Mr. Burke. In other words, this is going to be a continuing trend on the part of those who invest in this type of business for possibly the next 50 years, and during those next 50 years they will be establishing the fattest graveyards in the world, where youngsters wouldn't reach the age of 30, where they will die from malnutrition, tuberculosis, and all of the other dreaded diseases because of this type of standard of living.

Mr. Hemmendinger. On the contrary, it is helping to raise it.

Mr. Burke. And we will be accelerating difficulties in these countries.

Mr. Hemmendinger. It is raising standards.[39]

Apparently from the questions that followed, Congressman Burke never got the point that Mr. Hemmendinger tried so valiantly to make: All we can accomplish by restricting the products of cheap foreign labor is to make it harder for the oppressed foreigners to sell their products to us and, in that way, make them even worse off. In particular, historical quotas of the kind that Mr. Burke has championed would bar some countries such as Indonesia from ever penetrating the U.S. market and thereby raise their standards of living. Perhaps, however, the congressman really believes that the real reason for so much misery throughout the world is that there are so few good-hearted men like him around.

Still another twist to the cheap-foreign-labor argument emphasizes the idea of efficiency. It is fine, according to this version of the argument, to import goods produced more efficiently abroad than at home. However, if the foreigner's competitive advantage rests on cheap labor or some other basis, it is spurious; and unregulated international trade positively distorts the use of the world's resources away from the theoretically ideal pattern.

Mr. H. A. Harvey claims that his

paramount problem in competing with foreign produced glassware is their labor-cost advantage.

Of course to meet this challenge it may be argued that we should increase our efficiency through modernization of factories and equipment so that we may increase our output per man-hour. In my company's case we have taken this course of action and built the most modern hand blowing facility in this country.

In addition, we have installed extensive budgetary controls and have maximum utilization of accepted management techniques. I have been told by other industry members that our management is inventive. Our glassworkers are fully skilled and produce at a pace not exceeded overseas.

My point in mentioning these facts is that we have taken steps from an investment stand-point and internally to meet this foreign invasion of our markets. *We are not guilty of inefficiency.* On the contrary, my company has been capable in all instances of competing with domestic sources. Still, without tariff or quota help, we can not, and have not, overcome the foreign labor cost advantage.[40]

Mr. Donald McCullough of the Textile Manufacturers Institute would have little reason to complain "if the items entering this country in such volumes were better designed or more attractive, more durable or more efficiently produced. . . . But the vast majority of imports sell here primarily because they are cheaper; and they are cheaper for one reason only—they are made at wages and under working conditions that would be illegal and intolerable in this country."[41]

COMPARATIVE ADVANTAGE AGAIN

Knowing the principle of comparative advantage, the reader should be able to spot the error in all such theorizing. For trade to benefit the countries engaging in it, a commodity need *not* be supplied only by those that make it most "efficiently" in some real-cost sense. Efficiency comparisons are beside the point. If we Americans can import widgets at relatively low cost, we gain, regardless of what makes the foreign widgets so cheap. But even if for the sake of argument we assume a meaningful comparison of physical efficiencies and real costs, protectionist conclusions do not follow. Producing widgets in the United States cannot be justified by comparative advantage if our efficiency in this industry is only equal to or moderately superior to the efficiency of foreign producers, provided that our superiority is still greater (in some average sense) across the general range of industries.

In output per worker in general or on the average—but *not* in each specific industry and apparently not in the ones represented by Messrs. Harvey and McCullough—Americans have a clear lead over foreigners. Down a long list of commodities, protectionists say that we must protect the American industry because American efficiency is not enough greater to outweigh the wage differential.

. . . wherever we find an industry which is incapable of maintaining that 2-for-1 or 3-for-1 productivity ratio, this is precisely the industry in which America's productive resources should be committed; this is the industry in which we should insure that American jobs and American capital are "protected."[42]

That, as Professor Raymond Vernon shrewdly noted, is what protectionists in effect are saying. Their position amounts to just giving up on maintaining our relatively high average productivity and high living standards. "From now on, we propose to be textile producers or lead producers, producers of all the things which we have demonstrably indicated to the world we cannot really produce with that measure of efficiency that is necessary to retain our prior lead." The protectionist view of high wages as a handicap for America is "faulty on its face." American exports tend to come from industries with comparatively high wages. Import products "tend to compete with American industries in which wages are comparatively low."[43]

With some justification, Vernon paraphrased pretty much as follows the argument that a protectionist had just presented in the same hearing: let's face it; we can't keep ahead in productivity. Let's reconcile ourselves to concentrating on the parts of our economy where productivity growth is slow and where we have the jobs. Who needs more products? We can't eat much more sugar or wear any more shoes.[44]

No free-trader doubts that in many foreign countries the levels of wages and other incomes, translated through the exchange rates into dollars, are wretchedly low by American standards. The free-trader merely sees through the unspoken protectionist *theory* about what facts are relevant. Actually, wage statistics no more make a case for tariffs than would statistics on egg prices in Iceland or rainfall in Patagonia. Low wages in a foreign country typically reflect lower-than-American productivity, not in each industry separately but on the average throughout the economy. Low productivity of labor in turn typically results from a great abundance of labor in relation to comparatively scarce factors of production such as capital, business ability, and perhaps natural resources. Educational levels and the general climate of politics and traditions and attitudes also often have a big influence. The low wages enable the unfortunate foreigners, despite their generally low productivity, to charge prices low enough so that the goods they make with relatively slight disadvantage can sell in the American market. Wages reflecting their low productivity enable the foreigners to export some goods and so earn the dollars with which to buy imports. If they could not do this, their poverty would be even worse.

It is far from a calamity for the United States if cheap-labor imports undersell some American products. A rich country no more loses by trading with a poor one than a tycoon loses by dealing with a poor newsboy. On the contrary, we Americans positively gain by buying cheap foreign goods. We can well use the labor and resources saved. Even from our own selfish viewpoint, it is fine that foreigners will work cheaply for us, trading us many of their goods for few of our own. From the chapter on the balance of payments it should be clear why cheap labor could never let foreigners undersell us on all goods, flooding us with theirs in abundance and taking few if any of ours in return, nice as that would be if it somehow could happen.

No one doubts that some American industries do have a hard time competing with imports while paying their workers at high American wage levels. But what do these high wage levels mean? Other American industries are setting the pace in wages by their competition in employing labor. By and large, these other industries can afford to set the pace only because they are highly productive in transforming labor and other resources into goods and services that consumers value. The very fact that the high cost of labor burdens an import-competing industry suggests that its workers have alternative job opportunities. The high average levels of American productivity and wages give foreigners a competitive advantage in the industries least adaptable to mechanization and mass production. As technology continues to advance, the growing competitive strength of the industries progressing most rapidly means a weakening competitive strength of the relative laggards. As resources are drawn into industries where they can contribute most to the value of output, other industries must feel the burden. Tariffs to preserve industries that need them preserve a less efficient allocation of labor and resources than the one that consumer bidding would determine in a free market. (As already explained, this is not to say that American industries needing tariff protection to survive must be "inefficient" in any blameworthy sense. Comparisons of efficiency properly refer not to industries but to overall patterns of production and resource use with and without tariffs.)

Sometimes the cheap-labor argument directs special suspicion to imports of goods made by foreign workers receiving wages that are substandard even in relation to the general wage levels of their own countries. This twist appears in the 1954 report of the President's "Randall Commission" and, surprisingly enough, has even found some acceptance among academic economists. Professor N. Arnold Tolles of Cornell University, for example, at first correctly explained why generally low wages are to be expected in countries with lower output per man hour than the United States. ". . . the mere fact that the wages in some foreign country are below those paid in the United States," he continued, "does not prove that the foreign competition is unfair."[45] But things are different when the foreigners pay wages that are substandard even in their own country. The charge of "wage dumping" might then be legitimate. What might justify protecting American producers against this unfair competition "is not the mere fact of mere economic injury, but the possibility that the injury is based on substandard wages," wages (and associated labor costs) that "are abnormally low, in comparison with other wages in the country of origin. . . ."[46]

Professor Tolles argues that his distinction is consistent with accepted international-trade theory. If "all wages are in harmony with the productivity of labor in each country," beneficial specialization will occur.

> The case is quite different when cheap goods are offered in international trade on the basis of wages which are substandard in the country of origin. The latter type of competition is unfair because the low wages of the exporter are out of line with true comparative advantage. The workers who are being paid less than their economic value are, in effect, subsidizing the exports and at the same time causing injury to the enterprises and workers of the country which receives the low-cost goods.[47]

One may wonder why the wages are so *especially* low in a particular foreign industry. If the answer is that its workers have especially low ability and skill and are in oversupply relative to their job opportunities, then their low wages accord with supply and demand. Their situation is unfortunate, but their low wages simply reflect this unfortunate reality and constitute no distortion. There would be a genuine distortion only if the especially low wages were due to something else than supply and demand factors (including productivity). It is hard to imagine what this "something else" might be. One conceivable possibility would be an effective conspiracy among employers in the particular foreign industry to hold down wages and keep the workers ignorant of better opportunities in other jobs.* Foreign wages, total costs, and product prices would then be

---

*The foreign employers presumably must exploit their workers in some way other than by merely avoiding competition in hiring them, for that would make employment and production in the particular foreign industry too *low* in comparison with the competitive ideal and make its products, therefore, the reverse of too cheap. The difficulty of devising a plausible example of how exploitation of labor could cause a distortion remediable by an American tariff just emphasizes how unreal the problem is, but we shall waive this objection for the sake of argument. (Price and wage ceilings and floors and external benefits and costs in various foreign industries would provide more plausible examples of foreign price distortions, though still not a persuasive case for American tariffs as a remedy.)

false signals, misrepresenting how much of some products had to be forgone to permit production of others. Removal of the wage distortions and correction of the price signals would benefit the exploited foreign workers and their country as a whole.

A simple two-commodity example will sharpen the issue. Suppose no distortion at home: one unit of clothing costs one unit of wheat both in money and in real alternatives sacrificed. In the foreign country, one clothing costs *more* than one wheat in real alternatives sacrificed but *less* in money, since clothing workers are somehow exploited. Distorted money costs and prices motivate a "wrong" pattern of specialization—we in wheat and the foreigners in clothing. The foreigners only seem to have a comparative advantage in clothing; really, they do not. If the foreigners do nothing themselves to correct their wage and price distortions and their misspecialization, it might seem that they could benefit from a tariff of ours which aimed at the same result, though whether this really could help the exploited foreign workers is a question still to be considered.

Perhaps more interesting is the question of whether a tariff to offset the uneconomic cheapness of the foreign clothing is in *our own* interest. In reply, we need only raise another question, familiar by now: how does it matter to us just *why* foreign goods are as cheap as they are? By using the proceeds of our exports to buy foreign goods for less money than the cost of producing them ourselves, we are in effect "producing" those goods indirectly at a smaller real sacrifice of other things than if we produced them ourselves directly. For us, the prices prevailing on world markets are like the climate and the principles of chemistry and other facts of nature, facts we can take advantage of without any metaphysical inquiry into their basis. (The possibility of improving the terms of trade, and a few other very special exceptions, are considered elsewhere in this book where they best fit in.)

Professor Tolles wants American tariff makers to be able "to separate the justified from the unjustified complaints that low foreign wages constitute unfair competition with American enterprises."[48] Accordingly, he proposes detailed studies of the levels and patterns of wages and fringe benefits *within* foreign countries and exhorts the statisticians to try to overcome the many admitted technical difficulties. In so doing, he unintentionally explodes his own case. If it actually matters to the United States whether the prices of imports are true or false indicators of real production alternatives abroad, it should be possible to make this inference about foreign prices merely by observing what effects imports at these prices have on conditions *within the United States*. To see that we cannot do this and so to urge detailed investigations *within the foreign countries* amounts to admitting, without realizing it, that the basis for the foreign prices does not, after all, matter to us. Cheap foreign widgets present the same opportunities to American consumers and the same problem to employers and employees in the American widget industry regardless of what foreign conditions account for their cheapness.

It is this fact which explodes not only the case for trade barriers based on substandard wages but also the whole gamut of protectionist theorizing examined in this chapter. While other protectionist arguments, examined below, enjoy more plausibility, those based on "fair competition" and "cheap foreign labor" are the ones that are most often heard in the committee rooms of Congress. These latter arguments, as we have seen, have nothing to do with the genuine costs and benefits of those liberalization. Rather, they are, more than anything else, an outlet for some people's misguided horror of bargain imports. Frederic Bastiat, writing early in the nineteenth century, keenly satirized this horror in his "Petition of the Manufacturers of Candles, Wax-Lights, Lamps, Candlesticks, Street Lamps, Snuffers, Extinguishers, and of the Producers of Oil Tallow, Resin, Alcohol, and Generally, of Everything Connected With Lighting." Here, taken from *Economic Sophisms* and condensed to save space, is this imaginary petition to the French Chamber of Deputies. Notice how the candlemakers use the "purchasing power" argument, that the prosperity that protection will ensure them will presently radiate onto all other industries.

> Gentlemen, you are right: you reject abstract theories. As practical men, you are anxious only to free the producer from foreign competition and secure the *national market* to *national labor*.
>
> We now offer you an admirable opportunity to apply your practice. We are subjected to the intolerable competition of a foreign rival whose superior facilities for producing light enable him to flood the French market at so low a price as to take away all our customers the moment he appears, suddenly reducing an important branch of French industry to stagnation. This rival is the sun.
>
> We request a law to shut up all windows, dormers, skylights, openings, holes, chinks, and fissures through which sunlight penetrates. Our industry provides such valuable manufactures that our country cannot, without ingratitude, leave us now to struggle unprotected through so unequal a contest.
>
> Do not repulse our petition as a satire without hearing our reasons. Your protection of artificial lighting will benefit every industry in France. If you give us the monopoly of furnishing light, we will buy large supplies of tallow, coal, oil, resin, wax, alcohol, silver, iron, bronze, and crystal. Greater tallow consump-

tion will stimulate cattle and sheep raising. Meat, wool, leather, and above all manure, that basis of agricultural riches, will become more abundant. Greater oil consumption will stimulate cultivation of the luxuriant olive tree. Resinous trees will cover our heaths. Swarms of bees will gather upon our mountains the perfumed treasures now cast useless upon the winds. In short, granting our petition will greatly develop every branch of agriculture. Navigation will equally profit. Thousands of vessels will soon be employed in whaling, and thence will arise a navy capable of upholding the honor of France. [Note the defense argument.] Paris will become magnificent with the glittering splendor of gildings, bronzes, crystal chandeliers, lamps, reflectors, and candelabras. When we and our many suppliers have become rich, our great consumption will contribute to the prosperity of workers in every industry. No one, not even the poor resin manufacturer amidst his pine forest nor the miserable miner in his dark dwelling, will fail to enjoy an increase of salary and of comforts. There is perhaps not one Frenchman, from the rich stockholder to the poorest match-seller, who is not interested in the success of our petition.

We foresee your objections, gentlemen; but there is not one which you will not have to take from the free-traders and which is not opposed to your own practice. Do you object that the consumer must pay the price of protecting us? You have yourselves already answered the objection. When told that the consumer is interested in free importation of iron, coal, corn, wheat, cloth, etc., you have answered that the producer is interested in their exclusion. You have always acted to *encourage labor,* to *increase the demand for labor*.

Will you say that sunlight is a free gift, and that to repulse free gifts is to repulse riches under pretense of encouraging the means of obtaining them? Take care—you deal a deathblow to your own policy. Remember: hitherto you have always repulsed foreign produce because it was an approach to a free gift; and the closer this approach, the more you have repulsed the goods. You have, in obeying the wishes of other monopolists, acted only from a *half-motive;* to grant our petition there is a much *fuller inducement*. To turn us down just because our case is much stronger than any previous one would be to accumulate absurdity upon absurdity.

When we buy a Portuguese orange at half the price of a French orange, we in effect get it half as a gift. If you protect national labor against the competition of a *half-gift,* what principle justifies allowing the importation of something just because it is *entirely a gift?* You are no logicians if, refusing the half-gift as hurtful to human labor, you do not with double zeal reject the full gift.

The difference in price between an imported article and the corresponding French article is a *free gift* to us. The bigger the difference, the bigger the gift. It is as complete as possible when the producer gives us his goods entirely free, as the sun does with light. The question is whether you wish for France the benefit of free consumption or the supposed advantages of laborious production. Choose, but be consistent. And is it not the height of inconsistency to check as you do the importation of foreign goods merely because and even in proportion as their price approaches zero, while at the same time you freely admit the light of the sun, whose price during the whole day is at *zero?*[49]

In March 1958 Mr. John G. Lerch, an attorney specializing in customs law, appeared before the House Ways and Means Committee to bewail "unfair foreign competition" and oppose renewal of the trade agreements act. Never, he said, had he found in economists' writings "any explanation of why we should permit the introduction of foreign merchandise into our markets at a price which is less than it costs the American manufacturer to produce it." Among the 12 clients he was representing, Mr. Lerch listed The Candle Manufacturers Association. And he was not joking.[50]

NOTES

1. Lawrence W. Towle, *International Trade and Commercial Policy* (New York: Harper, 1948), p. 328.

2. See Hearings before the House Ways and Means Committee, January 1951, pp. 225-28, 601-2.

3. 1973 HW&M IV 1162-63 (see Chapter 1, note 8). Another example from Burke: "They live a rather cloistered life. They really don't get out with reality. Brookings and the rest of these people, and Princeton, the boys from Princeton and the rest of them, it would be nice if they could get down into the teeming tenement districts of America and talk to the fellow who lost his job." (1973 HW&M V 1507).

4. 1970 HW&M IV 1007-8 (see Chapter 1, note 1).

5. 1962 HW&M IV 2315.

6. Ibid., pp. 27, 259, 323-24.

7. 1970 HW&M VI 1898.

8. 1970 HW&M XI 3109.

9. 1970 HW&M XIII 3643-44.

10. Norman R. Campbell, *What is Science?* (New York: Dover Publications, Inc., 1952), pp. 181, 174.

11. Harold Scales, 1970 HW&M XI 3181.

12. 1970 HW&M V 1551.

13. 1973 HW&M VI 1894.

14. J. F. Farrington, 1973 HW&M XII 4120.

15. See, for example, the efforts of Congressman Sam Gibbons, 1970 HW&M VII 2028-36, to pin down some representatives of the American footwear industry.

16. Hearings of 1955 before the House Ways and Means Committee, II 1933.

17. HW&M Committee Hearings on 1951 Extension of the Reciprocal Trade Agreements Act, p. 372.

18. Henry George, *Protection or Free Trade* (New York: Doubleday, Page, 1905), p. 114.

19. William Graham Sumner, *Protectionism* (New York: Holt, 1888), p. 47.

20. 1973 HW&M IX 2958.

21. 1973 HW&M XII 3766.

22. 1970 HW&M V 1496-97.

23. Lewis E. Lloyd, *Tariffs: The Case for Protection* (New York: Devin-Adair, 1955), pp. 86-87.

24. 1970 HW&M VI 1736.

25. Trade Act of 1974, sec. 301 (a).

26. U.S. International Trade Commission, "Tapered Roller Bearings and Certain Components Thereof from Japan," (Washington: ITC Publication 714, January 1975), p. 20.

27. Stephen Enke, in *Foreign Trade Policy* (1958), p. 101 (see Chapter 1, note 5). Besides Enke's survey of types of dumping, see Charles P. Kindleberger's paper in the same volume, p. 78.

28. U.S. House of Representatives, Committee on Ways and Means, *Selected Provisions of the Tariff and Trade Laws of the United States* (Washington: U.S. Government Printing Office, 1970), p. 148.

29. 1973 HW&M IV 1145.

30. 1970 HW&M VII 2068, 2070.

31. 1970 HW&M VII 2132.

32. 1970 HW&M VII 2070.

33. 1970 HW&M V 1293.

34. 1970 HW&M V 1270.

35. 1970 HW&M IV 1035. Although Burke is a leading proponent of import quotas, his idea resembles an argument that Senator Malone used to make in favor of his cost-equalizing tariff: put foreigners in the position where they will have to pay higher wages at home or higher tariffs to the United States, and maybe they'll pay the higher wages instead (Hearings before the Senate Finance Committee on the Trade Agreements Extension Act of 1951, Part I, p. 804).

36. 1970 HW&M V 1297.

37. 1973 HW&M III 873-874.

38. Abraham Weiss, 1970 HW&M VII 2155.

39. 1970 HW&M VII 2126-28.

40. 1970 HW&M XIV 4072.

41. 1970 HW&M V 1220-21.

42. Hearing before a subcommittee of the Joint Economic Committee, in *Foreign Economic Policy* (Washington, D.C.: Government Printing Office, 1962), p. 282.

43. Ibid.

44. Ibid., p. 328. An amusing interchange ensued among Vernon, Mr. Oscar Strack-bein, the protectionist, and others; see pp. 328-38.

45. N. Arnold Tolles, in *Foreign Trade Policy* (1958), p. 819.

46. Ibid., pp. 819-20.

47. Ibid. In *Labor Costs and International Trade,* written with the assistance of Betti C. Goldwasser (Washington: Committee for a National Trade Policy, 1961), Professor Tolles spends most of his space attacking the usual cheap-labor argument on the grounds that the statistical difficulties of implementing a remedial cost-equalization tariff would be insuperable in practice. The most remarkable thing about this pamphlet is that it is intended as propaganda for freer trade rather than for protectionism.

48. Ibid.

49. Condensed from the "Petition," reprinted in Frederic Bastiat, *Economic Sophisms,* trans. Patrick James Stirling (New York: G. P. Putnam's Sons, 1922), pp. 60-65.

50. 1958 Hearings, II, 2115ff.

After examining the case for protectionism in its most naive and popular versions, we may appropriately turn to consider some protectionist arguments that enjoy a degree of legitimacy. One such argument asserts that some import-competing industries are desired not only for what they produce now but also for what they would be available to produce in the event of a future reduction in imports, due, for example, to war or an embargo on some vital raw material. "They also serve who only stand and wait." Yet businessmen cannot charge a price for this valuable service of availability in addition to the prices of the output currently sold. Because private consumers fail to count the full benefits to the country as a whole of buying this output, the industry remains too small from a national point of view. Tariff and quota protection as an artificial stimulus to the industry could correct for this divergence between private and social viewpoints. The attendant current sacrifice of real income may be an insurance premium well worth paying. Adam Smith recognized in 1776 that "defense . . . is of much more importance than opulence. . . ."[1]

STRATEGIC INDUSTRIES

So presented, the defense argument is neither economic nonsense nor a denial of the gains from trade. The typical lobbyist, however, is content with less sophistication: He points out how useful his industry would be in wartime and considers his case established. Since almost all products have *some* national security value, all sorts of industries can make some sort of superficially plausible plea for protection on defense grounds. One protectionist showed no embarrassment in claiming that "nearly every industry has a part to play in defense." Industries are so interdependent that almost none are expendable. "Lower tariffs that dry up any one of these industries, be it labelled 'defense' or otherwise, will cripple our ability to defend ourselves, and other nations."[2] Gloves, pens, pottery, peanuts, umbrella frames, paper, candles, and thumbtacks are just a few among many industries that have stressed their own strategic importance. The ordinary wood-cased pencil, its manufacturers insist, is essential in conducting practically all peacetime and wartime activities. It meets all standards of strategic essentiality except that of direct use in combat. "In a large measure, it is almost like a machine tool: neither is used directly in combat, but both are essential to the manufacture of defense weapons. Huge quantities of lead pencils are currently employed for scientific drawings and in layouts for missiles and space-age vehicles."[3]

Lacemakers once sought increased protection on the grounds that they could convert their machinery to make mosquito netting in case of war in the tropics. A linen thread manufacturer once stressed that the fish netting his industry makes is important to the nation's wartime food supply and that the netting is also used for camouflage. Tuna fishermen have called their boats auxiliary vessels for the Navy. Producers of "schiffli" embroidery have told how they bolster morale by making shoulder patches for soldiers' uniforms. Speaking of morale, sympathetic questioning by Senator Malone once led a witness to mention how important wooden clothespins were to women courageously caring for their families alone while their menfolk were away at war. The defense argument often routinely goes along for good measure with other pleas for protection. Almost everyone pretends to think that his industry is exceptional, and Congressmen hesitate to slap down arguments wrapped in the flag.

A government can hardly know in advance just which specific weapons and materials and industries will be most vital in some future war. Constant technological change characterizes both modern industry and modern warfare. Furthermore, industry has proved agile in converting back and forth between peacetime and wartime production. Among industries that have proved most readily convertible or of greatest defense value are those in which the United States has a comparative advantage, such as computers, industrial machinery, and airplanes. These strategic industries typically do not need tariff protection, and free trade would enlarge their peacetime markets, especially abroad.

By contrast industries that typically clamor for continued or tightened protection—handbags, pottery, flatware, fish, nuts, cheese, olives, hats, furs, pianos, toys, and so forth—can turn less readily to war production. A protected, semifrozen pattern of production and resource use might well prove out of date if war came. General economic strength and flexibility seem more important, even on narrow defense grounds than hothouse cultivation of numerous individual industries for which the country is not especially suited.

Efforts to maintain a diversified "mobilization base" undermine readiness and flexibility to some slight extent. Economic damage caused by such efforts erodes the tax base for supporting actual military forces. Because its allies generally exhibit higher ratios of trade to national income, this damage is likely to be greater for them than for the United States; sparing them this loss would tend to strengthen the overall economic and political position of Free World governments. Our military, defense-support, and other aid programs testify to our concern for the economic as well as narrowly military strength of the alliance as a whole; so should our trade policy.

Some protectionists get so carried away with their constituents' problems that they make tactless remarks, which, if taken seriously by our allies, would have unfortunate diplomatic consequences. "What is the difference," asked Congressman John Dent, "whether the Japanese come in and bomb that plant out of existence in Arnold, Pa., or send their glass over here and bomb those men out of existence? It is that simple."[4] In fact our relations with Japan have been strained in recent years by pressures from the United States to have the Japanese impose voluntary restrictions of their exports. Protectionist measures have been routinely taken against Japan and other countries for the narrowest economic interests at home and at the risk of serious harm to U.S. political and military interests abroad.

Insofar as the long-term struggle with Communism involves rivalry in economic performance, keeping the Free World economy strong, flexible, and free of unnecessary burdens itself contributes to defense. So is maintaining the distinctive character of our economic system, with its chief reliance on markets and prices rather than state control. Free trade provides an important indicator of which path we are following.

Protectionism, on the other hand, injects government decisions into trade, mixes business and diplomacy, widens the range of possible international frictions (even among allies), and raises private frictions into intergovernmental frictions. Lionel Robbins has aptly noted the vulgar spectacle of diplomats flying wildly about in airplanes from conference to conference, conferring a penumbra of high politics on consignments of canned meat and sardines.[5]

Another doubt about the wisdom of protecting "strategic industries" from foreign competition arises over the question of what kind of war we might be protecting them for. In an all-out war between Russia and the United States, a submarine campaign and other actions to deprive the United States of overseas supplies would hardly stand out as a crucial feature. In a nuclear war, each country's capacity for long-sustained military production would count for less than its striking and retaliatory capacity at the very start. Against a background of atomic destruction, any benefit from years of peacetime tariff protection would appear pathetically irrelevant.

In a Korea- or Vietnam-type conflict, with the war limited in territory, participants, and weapons, there is little danger of a submarine campaign by the Soviet Union. The United States would continue drawing supplies from throughout the Free World (except from the specific area of attack, which might not have been a source of supply in the first place). The chief economic danger in a limited war is one discussed in the following section: a cutoff in vital materials supplied by enemy-sympathizing foreign powers on which we had become dependent. The diversion of ships and planes to the actual scene of battle probably would not be a crucial problem. Ships of allied and friendly countries as well as our own would be available for strategic trade; and the larger our ordinary peacetime trade had been, thanks to a liberal trade policy, the more ships would be available.[6]

Even if military planners did consider a long nonnuclear war more than barely possible, did know what products would most be needed in wartime, did worry about interruption of foreign supplies, and did doubt that unprotected domestic industries could convert fast enough into making the needed things, the case for restricting international trade would still not be conclusive. As for actual military goods, the Defense Department is presumably ensuring their production by placing orders all along. As for strategic goods supplied by industries partially dependent on the civilian market, one answer might be stockpiling enough of them from domestic or foreign sources to last through a war. Not having to make them then, domestic industry could concentrate on lines of production in which it was more efficient.

Subsidies are traditionally suggested as an alternative to restricting international trade. Subsidy funds might appropriately go into the defense budget and be allocated by military planners.

The need for fresh appropriations to subsidize defense industries would continually remind Congress of the program's objectives and would keep raising the question whether its expected benefits were worth the costs. This persistent question would help guard against perversion of the defense argument for narrow private ends rather than national ends. Tariffs, by contrast, remain in effect without having to be repeatedly enacted; and the costs they impose are diffused and easy to overlook. To many people, admittedly, "subsidy" is a bad word, suggesting government meddling, special-interest pressures, entrenchment of vested interests, and other abuses. The fact that people *do* realize these costs and possible abuses, however, is precisely one *relative* advantage that subsidies have over tariffs.

A second advantage of the subsidy approach is that it distributes the burden of supporting strategic industries more fairly. If this support really helps defend everyone, why should consumers of particular products, who are doing the country a favor anyway by buying them in peacetime, have to bear the whole burden in tariff-raised prices?

Third, instead of interfering with the comparatively low price set by import competition, a subsidy enables the home industry to compete at this price by making up for its higher production costs. A given expansion of domestic production is less wastefully achieved this way than by a tariff. In the terminology of Chapter four, a subsidy inflicts only the production-cost component of dead loss, whereas a tariff inflicts the consumption-cost component as well.[7]

A further reason why subsidies are relatively economic is that they can be employed more selectively and precisely than tariffs. They need not simply encourage the production of particular products. They can encourage production by particular methods and with the use of particular materials or machines or skilled labor—whatever considerations of convertibility to war production seem to recommend. They can promote research, the training of labor, and the location of strategic industries in relatively safe places. They can be withheld from companies whose location or other characteristics make them undependable for wartime purposes and can be financed by taxing nonstrategic activities that compete with the strategic ones for scarce resources.

STRATEGIC RAW MATERIALS

The Arab oil embargo of 1973-1974, the emergence of the Organization of Petroleum Exporting Countries (OPEC) as an effective cartel, and the threatened cartelization of bauxite, copper, iron ore, and other raw materials underline a broader national security argument for tariffs. This argument recognizes that security depends not just on preparedness for war but also on the ease with which the United States could adjust to a cutoff in supplies of some vital import. The occasion might be a war directly involving the United States, a war in which the direct participants on one side view the United States as a logical target for economic pressure (as in 1973), or just an unexpected but damaging exercise in monopoly power by some foreign cartel. National security may require protection from imports as such, if in fact such protection offers the only escape from excessive dependence on foreign supplies.

Such thinking was the basis for U.S. oil policy for years before the recent embargo and price rises. Import quotas were imposed "voluntarily" in 1957 and mandatorily in 1959, and remained in effect until early 1973, when they were replaced by a small import fee. Ostensibly imposed in order to promote national security by encouraging domestic discovery and production of oil, the quotas had the additional effect of causing the United States to drain its own relatively most accessible oil even though foreign supplies were still cheaply available.

What are the narrow allocative effects on the United States of the 1973-1974 quadrupling of oil prices? Although no exact calculation is possible, we can estimate the damage in a way somewhat analogous to our earlier discussion of the damage done by an import duty. The revenue from an import duty goes to the government of the importing country and does not count as part of the country's dead loss. The oil price increase, however, is like an export duty levied by the exporting countries, which collect the revenue. It imposes a dead loss on the importing countries. This loss, expressed relative to the value of oil imports at the original price, may be estimated at $(d+2)/([e+1]+2/d)$. Here, d is the price increase expressed as a multiple of the original price of oil (so that if the price quadruples, the "export duty" d=3), and e stands for arc elasticity of import demand, a measure of the responsiveness of oil imports to price.

Suppose we take e for the United States at the unrealistically low value of 0.1, meaning that a 1 percent rise in the price of foreign oil shrinks imports by only 1/10 of 1 percent. Then the harm caused by the quadrupling of oil prices is 2.83 times the original money value of imports. Given that oil imports in 1972 were worth 0.37 percent of gross national product, the higher price inflicts an annual harm equal to 2.83 x 0.37 = 1.05 percent of gross national product.

While this allocative loss may be surprisingly small for the United States, (though apparently greater than that caused by all U.S. import duties), it is larger for those countries which depend more heavily on imported oil. For Japan, whose 1973 oil imports amounted to 1.84 percent of GNP, the damage would be 5.21 percent. For Italy (1973 oil imports were 2.61 percent of GNP) it would be 7.39 percent. It should be recalled that we are assuming an unrealistically low import demand elasticity of 0.1 and that with higher elasticities the loss would be smaller.

Our formula for estimating the harm caused by higher oil prices underscores a dilemma which confronts any oil-consuming country that attempts to reduce that harm through a rational exercise of trade policy. On the one hand, it is in the interest of such a country to increase the price sensitivity of its import demand, to which end it should adopt oil tariffs that vary *directly* with the OPEC price. On the other hand, it is also in its interest to provide a degree of stability for its domestic energy producers and its domestic producers of energy-conserving goods. To that end it should adopt a variable tariff that varies *inversely* with the OPEC price. Perhaps some compromise between an all-out policy of restraining OPEC and an all-out policy of self-sufficiency would be the most sensible approach to the problem.

It is even more difficult to prescribe any joint policy that the oil-consuming countries might undertake vis-a-vis the oil-producing countries. Efforts by the United States to work out such a policy have been discouraged by a preference on the part of some oil consumers, particularly the Japanese, for bilateral arrangements.

The idea of multilateral cooperation between oil consumers and producers has much to recommend it, at least on the surface. If the OPEC countries agreed to reduce the price of oil from $11 to something like $7 per barrel, they would have the assurance of a price still far greater than they would get if the cartel broke down, while the oil consumers would get a considerable reduction from what they had been paying since the price quadrupled. As long as OPEC persists on an independent course, the rest of the world might make enormous investments in substitute forms of energy and in ways of economizing on energy use. In the end the consuming countries would have spent tens or hundreds of billions of dollars to achieve self-sufficiency, and the oil in the ground in the Middle East would wind up worth much less than it might otherwise have been. All countries might wind up worse off than they would have if more reasonably priced oil had rendered all those investments in alternative energy sources unattractive in the first place. This, according to Herbert Stein, is the economic basis for discussion between the producing and importing countries.[8]

On the other hand, a multilateral deal with the oil producers would eliminate any possibility of gain through the future collapse of OPEC and would tend to dignify and confer legitimacy on the cartel. Furthermore, there is the danger that such an agreement would end up actually binding only the oil-importing signatories. The wealth of the oil producers may be a target for revolutionaries; and even if the present governments remain in power, there is no assurance that they will live up to their agreements. "The exporting countries have signed dozens of agreements over the last decade, on which their record is absolutely clean—they have violated every one. There is no way to hold a sovereign monopolist to anything."[9]

It would not be totally far-fetched to apply the free-trade arguments made elsewhere in this book even to imports of oil. The key fact about oil, however, is radical uncertainty about its future price. According to the logic of a price system, businessmen have incentives to cope with this uncertainty by building flexibility into their operations, by maintaining convertibility among alternative sources of energy, and by stockpiling fuel. The very unlikelihood of any long-lasting policy of laissez-faire toward oil by the United States or any other major oil-consuming country prevents those incentives from operating successfully.

Even if the government (more specifically, the current Congress and Administration) were to announce such a policy, no businessman familiar with the ways of government would put complete faith in what he was told. Businessmen considering accumulation of oil for sale in an emergency would rightly discount any promise made now that they would be allowed to collect "windfall" profits later on. Instead, they would anticipate price controls (as on "old oil") and allocation schemes designed to eliminate the very profits that would otherwise make such accumulation worthwhile. When allocations were made, government officials would try to take supplies away from those users whose needs were judged relatively least urgent. Users who had built flexibility into their operations would not get the full benefits of having done so; for if they had arranged to be not so badly hurt, fuel would be taken away from them and given to less foresighted users.

For the short run, in other words, there is simply no hope for an optimal policy toward oil. On the one hand, it is perverse for the United States to use up its most accessible domestic oil in the supposed interest of security from foreign oil cutoffs and to lay on additional controls because past and present controls have eroded the credibility of any policy of allowing market processes to operate. But, on the other hand, the oil boycott and quadrupling of prices have imposed a relatively large cost on the United States and other oil-consuming countries that demands some remedy if one is available. Perhaps, at least in the short run, domestic production and consumption *are* inseparable, and a higher tariff on oil would yield benefits in terms of increased domestic production, storage, and proved reserves that would far exceed any costs due to the resulting accelerated depletion of total resources. Perhaps a policy of laissez-faire is literally too unbelievable to be tried now, when what we need is preparedness and not an experiment with government credibility. Perhaps, also, the appropriate government policy might hasten OPEC's collapse and thereby automatically solve much of the national security problem connected with oil.

So viewed, a tariff on oil is not a scandalous idea or even inconsistent, really, with what we have been saying all along. We shall argue below against any proliferation of "exceptions" to free trade. Yet the oil problem may provide a particularly plausible one.

Just what kind of exception should be made? Well, it might consist of two parts, the first being a willingness to buy available foreign oil, part of which would be stockpiled or used to replace the consumption of domestically produced oil. Another apparently sensible aspect of a second-best program would be a guaranteed price floor for domestic energy. Possibly the price floor should apply only to so-called exotic energy— energy from gasifying or pulverizing coal, from oil shale, from solar developments, and the like. The floor price should probably be lower than the equivalent current world price of oil; already, presumably, the artificially inflated world price gives plenty of incentives for development of domestic substitutes, or would give that incentive if it were expected to endure. A floor price, though set below the current price, could give assurance that the effective price would not utterly collapse and render domestic investment in substitutes worthless. It could also encourage price cutting by individual OPEC countries; the threat of cheaper alternative sources of energy in the future might induce oil exporters to cash in on their oil reserves now, before the price goes down.

If the import price (plus any tariff regularly in effect) should sink below the guaranteed floor, then the government could pay the domestic energy producers covered by the guarantee the difference between the price at which they could actually sell their energy and the guaranteed floor price. The scheme would be similar to the plan for farm products proposed by Charles Brannan, President Truman's Secretary of Agriculture. The revenue for these guarantee payments could come from an additional tariff on imports, which, in the contingency under consideration, would have become cheaper on the world market. The extra tariff would serve two purposes. Besides raising revenue, it would sustain the price of tariff-paid oil in the United States and so keep the market price closer than otherwise to the guaranteed floor, thus holding down the margin on which the Brannan Plan compensatory payments had to be paid. It might be desirable to set the tariff at such a level that, taking account of both its price-raising effect and the revenue it produced, the revenue would just cover the compensatory payments required under the guarantees. The guarantees would presumably contain, in the first place, some limitation on how long a time the compensatory payments, once initiated, would continue. The proposal might stipulate, for example, that after five years the floor price would begin to be lowered and eventually be removed. If OPEC should collapse, we would not want to have locked ourselves permanently into a program of orienting the American economy toward higher-cost energy than would otherwise have been available.

TRADING WITH THE ENEMY

In connection with national-security arguments for protection, we must face the question of policy towards socialized trade conducted by unfriendly governments in support of cold-war tactics or preparations for actual war. Individual American importers and exporters can hardly take accurate account of how their business decisions might affect some sort of power ratio between the United States and its adversaries. For this reason, some private trade may have a genuine cost for the country that escapes being fully considered, with the result that it expands trade too far from a national point of view. An intention to correct for this sort of divergence between private and national viewpoints presumably underlay the U.S. policy, during the 1950s and 1960s, of embargoing trade with Communist China, North Korea, and North Vietnam and of denying nondiscriminatory, most-favored-nation treatment to the goods of the Soviet Union and its European satellites.

The objections to uncontrolled trade with actual or potential enemies is not that they would send us their products; these, in themselves, could only be of benefit to us. Rather, unfriendly governments might manipulate trade deliberately to disrupt markets in our country or other countries friendly to us. More importantly, perhaps, our gain from trade with them, though real enough, might fall short of their gain and so make us worse off *relatively*. Though questions of relative gain or of power ratios are irrelevant in ordinary trade with friendly countries, it may be sensible to forgo any exchange with enemies that is not calculated to yield some net political-military-economic advantage to ourselves.

The debate over East-West trade has been dominated in the 1970s by efforts to achieve detente, by complaints about Soviet emigration policies (particularly as those policies affect Soviet Jews), and by the alleged effects on domestic food prices of U.S. grain sales to the Soviet Union. In 1972, the United States lifted its embargo on trade with Communist China and reached an agreement with the Soviet Union that would have made it eligible for "normal" (most-favored-nation) trade with the United States. Activation of this agreement was blocked, however, by Soviet objections to a section of the Trade Act of 1974 that denies most-favored-nation treatment to any country interfering with its citizens' "right or opportunity to emigrate." Complaints linking U.S.-Soviet trade with high food prices have failed to discourage the Nixon and Ford administrations from pursuing a policy of expanded trade in grains and other commodities.

Decisions regarding which countries are actual or potential "enemies" and which goods are of too "strategic" or "technical" a nature to be placed in international trade are a matter of political and military judgment. Nevertheless, we might offer the following judgments of our own about the debate as it now stands. First, the gain that an enemy might derive from its trade with the United States does give rise to a valid (but not necessarily conclusive) argument in favor of limiting trade to transactions judged particularly beneficial to the United States (and such limitation might go beyond merely barring exports of "strategic" and high-technology goods). In trade between two "enemies," gain to either country has political and military, as well as economic, dimensions. For example, we might well make the sale of some badly needed grain conditional upon a relaxation of Soviet barriers to emigration. However, there is not necessarily any direct connection between the question of free trade as such and that of the political-military goals that may loom up in our trade with actual or potential enemies. One way to get Soviet compliance on some issue such as emigration might be to give the President broad discretion to set the goals and conditions of trade with socialist countries. Through secret negotiations, he might offer a cold-war antagonist the opportunity to make political concessions without appearing to yield to U.S. interference in its internal policies. If trade is going to be restricted at all because of the special adversary relationship that exists between the United States and another country, then it is best made a part of the whole arsenal of weapons—political, military, and economic—that the executive branch has at its disposal for the purpose of dealing with that country.

On the matter of the inflationary effects of certain exports to disfavored countries, little must be added to what has already been said about the gains from trade and the causes of inflation. From a domestic and purely economic point of view, it hardly matters whether the possible upward pressure on the price of some finished good (such as bread) is due to the export of some intermediate good (such as grain) to a friendly or to an unfriendly country.

NOTES

1. Adam Smith, *The Wealth of Nations* (Modern Library ed., New York: Random House, 1937), p. 431.

2. Lewis E. Lloyd, *Tariffs: The Case for Protection* (New York: Devin-Adair, 1955), p. 10.

3. 1962 HW&M VI 4074 (see Chapter 1, note 9). Cf. the 1955 hearings before the same Committee, II, 2049.

4. 1970 HW&M XI 3111 (see Chapter 1, note 1).

5. Lionel Robbins, *The Balance of Payments* (Stamp Memorial Lecture, University of London; London: Athlone Press, 1951), pp. 25-26.

6. On the manner in which modern weapons and the world political situation have outmoded traditional pros and cons of trade barriers for defense, see Stephen Enke (pp. 102-4), Richard N. Gardner (pp. 503-4), and Klaus Knorr (pp. 649-61), in *Foreign Trade Policy* (1958). (See Chapter 1, note 5).

7. Percy W. Bidwell, *What The Tariff Means to American Industries* (New York: Harper, 1956), pp. 128-29, gives an apparently similar argument.

8. *Dialogue on World Oil,* ed. by Edward J. Mitchell (Washington: American Enterprise Institute, 1974), pp. 11-15.

9. Morris A. Adelman, "U.S. Energy Policy," in *No Time to Confuse* (San Francisco: Institute for Contemporary Studies, 1975), p. 41.

9

Importing cheap foreign goods raises rather than lowers a country's total real income, but it may affect the distribution of that income among the inhabitants in a conceivably undesirable way. A few tariff arguments depend upon this effect and its prevention. Some may have practical importance, while others are just intellectual exercises. Thinking especially of how tariffs may benefit particular producer interests and localities at the general expense, Professor Charles P. Kindleberger ranks distribution arguments as more important than any others in the United States today. "The tariff is a domestic, not an international issue."[1] Of course, affecting domestic distribution—taking from some to give to others—gets less than completely frank recognition in practical politics. Instead, those who gain from a tariff try to argue that their interest coincides with the general interest. They are inclined to suggest (committing the fallacy of composition) that since protection would benefit them individually, similar protection for all import-competing producers would benefit the country as a whole.

REDISTRIBUTION AMONG CONSUMERS

Tariffs could conceivably help redistribute real income from the rich to the poor. Tariffs or other restrictions on imports of so-called "luxuries" might lessen the importers' demand for foreign currency and so let the country maintain equilibrium in its balance of payments with its own currency worth more than otherwise in relation to foreign currencies. Supporting the foreign-exchange value of the home currency in this way

159

would tend to hold down the home-currency prices of imported "necessities." Their presumably rather poor consumers would find the purchasing
power of their money incomes bolstered at the expense of the presumably
rich consumers of imported but now restricted "luxuries." Similarly, tariffs
and import restrictions on "nonessential" consumer goods would bolster
the purchasing power of the home currency over "essential" imports of
machinery and raw materials. This argument, or something like it, is
tacitly accepted in many countries, notably in Latin America and Asia,
where import controls are used to ward off balance-of-payments deficits
or where multiple-exchange-rate systems apply different rates to different
imports according to their supposed essentiality. The argument also
influenced the trade policies of European countries for the first few years
after World War II. They postponed devaluing their currencies in realistic
correspondence with their having experienced more severe wartime infla-
tions than the United States. They used tariffs and import and exchange
controls and other measures of deliberate "austerity," instead, in planning
for balance-of-payments deficits no larger than what American aid would
cover. They apparently felt that at the exchange rates necessary for
equilibrium without drastic import and exchange controls, imports of
essential consumer goods and of materials for postwar reconstruction
would be ruinously expensive.

Several problems bedevil improving income distribution, especially
over the long run, by discriminating between essential and luxury imports.
The distinction is not a physical characteristic of the goods themselves. It
concerns the kinds of needs and wants served. One of the key propositions
of economics is that the satisfaction provided or dissatisfaction avoided
by an additional amount of a good depends on how abundantly its consumers are supplied with it. We can easily imagine circumstances in
which another dollar's worth or another ounce of penicillin would be less
satisfying or useful than another dollar's worth or another ounce of
orchids. A tariff increase on a supposed luxury might harm poor consumers
even more than a tariff increase on a supposed essential. In short, goods
and the wants they satisfy cannot sensibly be classified as essential or
frivolous on a broad philosophical basis. The relevant comparisons are
between small additional quantities of or expenditures on the different
goods. The task of the controllers is not simply to restrict luxury imports
and freely admit essentials; the logic of the redistribution argument
requires them to decide, somehow, how stringently to tax or restrict
imports of each thing in view of how much people's satisfactions would be
affected by their having a little bit more or a little bit less of it.

Import- and exchange-control systems often try to discriminate
against imports destined for "mere" consumption and in favor of imported

materials and machinery that contribute to production, especially the production of export goods. Unless practiced with improbable cleverness and precision to compensate for known specific distortions in the price system, this discrimination has little in logic to recommend it. Since the entire purpose of production, including export production, is ultimately to yield consumer satisfactions, discriminating against imports of consumer goods amounts to favoring indirect over direct attainment of consumer satisfactions merely because it is indirect. Steel production is no more inherently worthy an activity than importing perfume or singing in a nightclub; it is simply at a more remote stage from the final consumer.

Discriminating against luxury imports is a particularly wasteful way to redistribute real income if taxes and controls do not also apply to substitutes produced at home. So far as domestic production expands to replace the restricted imports, the supposedly frivolous wants still are satisfied, though satisfied less efficiently than before. (The country presumably has a comparative *disadvantage* in the domestic luxuries if their production depends on import controls.) It would be especially ironic if favored imports of raw materials and machinery went into producing the import-controlled luxuries at home, or if they helped divert home resources into luxury production. If a northern country limits its citizens' spending for Mediterranean cruises, this saving in foreign exchange may be partly matched by larger spending on imported fuel and other materials to operate vacation resorts at home, as well as by loss of foreign earnings as resources indirectly shift from export production into operating resorts and otherwise providing recreation. People might still get their recreation, though in a less desired and less efficiently supplied form than they would without the controls, and while still putting a drain on the country's foreign-exchange position. The thoroughgoing interdependence of economic sectors in many direct and indirect ways makes great demands on the knowledge and ingenuity of the controllers if they are to achieve their purposes. Just one of the additional things the controllers ought to know, ideally, is how price-sensitive the foreigners are in supplying various goods. If foreign sellers of necessities but not of luxuries happened to be quite dependent on their market in the importing country (which would give the controllers an opportunity to beat down the prices paid the foreigners for necessities but not for luxuries), then levying heavier duties on imports of necessities would theoretically be sensible. (This qualification refers to the terms-of-trade argument explained in Chapter 11.) Any desired discrimination against luxuries would better concentrate on burdening their domestic production.

The possibilities of redistribution by controlling imports have parallels on the export side. Duties or other controls on the export of necessities could help hold down their cost to their presumably relatively poor domestic consumers. Greater emphasis on exporting luxuries would force their presumably rich domestic consumers to pay higher prices in competition with foreign buyers.

Besides the practical and conceptual difficulties already mentioned, we must note that the correspondence is loose at best, anyway, between consumers of luxuries or necessities and the rich or poor between whom the authorities presumably desire to redistribute income. (This statement seems more completely true of developed than of backward countries.) Differentially rigging the purchasing power of the home currency by pinching and twisting the foreign trade sector of the economy is a crude and inefficient makeshift.

REDISTRIBUTION AMONG FACTORS OF PRODUCTION

A more direct approach to redistributing real purchasing power works on the money incomes that people receive in the first place. The clearest example would be a tariff to benefit a specific narrow group of people, the businessmen, employees, investors, and natural-resource owners in a particular company or industry. But if policy-makers want to assist some particular producers struggling against import competition or other troubles and frankly recognize the redistribution involved, more precise means than a tariff are available. Outright cash payments could be given with whatever "strings" seemed appropriate, and only to the persons deemed most deserving; they wouldn't have to go also to producers in no need of aid.

Academic economists have imagined certain situations in which the distribution of income even among broad economic groups might be better under judicious protection than under free trade. The free-trade distribution might be deemed less desirable on the basis of plausible value judgments. If labor were scarce and capital abundant, goods with a high labor content would supposedly be imported in exchange for exports with a high capital content. Free trade would tend in effect to lessen both the scarcity of labor and the abundance of capital, relative to the demands for them. Labor could conceivably receive a smaller absolute share of a larger total income than under protection. Tariffs might preserve labor's scarcity value, laying the costs of protection on the capitalists, presumed wealthy enough to bear them with ease. The cheap-foreign-labor argument may thus seem to have a grain of truth in it after all, but its relation to the present distribution argument is slight and subtle—too subtle to be understood by anyone who thinks that cheap imports harm a country as a whole. The cheap-labor argument that carries weight in actual policy discussions remains as disreputable as Chapter 7 showed it to be.*

The foregoing oversimplified example provides only a feeble case for tariffs in the real world. Before seeing why, we may note how another theoretical curiosity limits the relevance of this one. In the most clear-cut example of this other curiosity, foreigners are extremely dependent on our country both as a supplier of what they buy from us and as a market for what they sell to us; even our manipulating prices greatly to their disadvantage would only slightly reduce the volume of trade with us that they desire. We have a good opportunity to use tariffs to beat down our import prices in relation to our export prices. In the most extreme case, a reduced physical volume of exports buys an increased physical volume of imports. Even with the tariff added into their prices, imports become producers, the tariff is the reverse of protective. The demand for labor slumps and so do wages, since the shrunken import-competing industries were assumed to be especially labor-intensive. Labor loses despite the country's total gain at foreign expense. By spending enough of its tariff revenue on imports or import-competing goods, however, the government could prevent the relative fall in their prices and so prevent the fall in labor's share of income. Alternatively, the government might distribute much of its tariff revenue to labor either directly or in the form of services or tax abatement. But labor still would not be benefiting from the effect of *tariffs* on income distribution; rather, the harm from them would be more than outweighed by *domestic* measures to distribute to labor in particular the gain reaped at foreign expense. To express the point of this example briefly though technically, to the extent that economic conditions make the terms-of-trade argument for tariffs highly relevant, they reduce the relevance of the income-distribution argument.[2]

INTERNATIONAL LEVELING OF INCOMES?

Our example of how free trade could conceivably affect income distribution to the disadvantage of a scarce factor of production is a very

---

*The theoretically respectable distribution argument has had some slight influence in policy discussions. An early version of it received attention, for example, in the report published by the Brigden Committee in Australia in 1929 (J. B. Brigden and others, *The Australian Tariff—An Economic Inquiry,* Melbourne University Press). The Committee consisted of scholars, however, not politicians.

simple special case of what theorists have generalized into the so-called factor-price-equalization theorem. For some years this highly abstract topic "held the same fascination for trade theorists as scrabble or rock-and-roll for the populace at large."[3] It concerns whether free trade could conceivably make not only each commodity but also each factor of production have the same price at home as abroad. If factor prices were *not* everywhere the same, commodity costs and prices could not be equal. But, under certain conditions, free trade would ensure international equality of commodity prices, implying equality of costs as well. Hence factor prices could not differ among countries. International movement of labor and capital would not be necessary for this result. The necessary conditions relate to costless transport, pure competition, internationally identical constant-returns-to-scale production functions, full employment, incomplete specialization, substitutability among factors, fewness of factors relative to traded goods, and so forth. Most of these words refer to conceivable extreme conditions that reality seldom even comes close to, conditions "so restrictive and so unrepresentative of actual reality that the theory can be said to prove the opposite of what it seems to purport to say—namely, that there is no chance whatsoever that factor prices will ever be equalized by free commodity trade."[4]

Yet the factor-price equalization theorem has some disturbing implications. Stressing how unrealistic its assumptions are hardly makes a satisfying answer; for if American workers are saved from the plight of oriental coolies only by transportation costs, imperfect competition, and other realistic departures from a simplified theoretical world, the case for further departures in the form of tariffs may not look so bad after all. It is therefore worthwhile to consider the equalization theorem on its own simplified grounds first. Most disturbingly, the theorem seems to supply the hitherto missing theoretical rationale for mere appeals to intuition such as the following:

> These people are not exporting pipe fittings or nuts and bolts. They are exporting man hours of labor in one form or another. We had not compunctions of conscience in setting rather low quotas on immigration to this country when our labor market became glutted.
>
> Ellis Island became a decaying monument to that period in our history. Why should we shy away from setting quotas on the products of this same labor which we prohibit from entering as such?. . .
>
> Unless the American manufacturer receives fair and just treatment in this consideration, we can promise you that every port in the United States will become an Ellis Island of the late

1800's and early 1900's, overflowing with foreign labor in one
form or another. So who cares about our immigration quotas?
How inconsistent can we be?[5]

Given the unrealistic assumptions of the factor-price-equalization
theorem, free trade would seem to be "a complete and not merely a
partial substitution for free international mobility of labor and other
factors of production."[6] The traditional analysis of the gains from international trade seems to contain a contradiction. (1) According to this
analysis, trade raises a country's standard of living. (2) Immigration
makes natural resources less abundant in relation to population and so
worsens the standard of living of a country whose population has reached
or passed its "optimum"—the level at which real income per person is
highest. (3) Yet trade, in tending to equalize wages at home and abroad,
resembles immigration. If goods made by poorly paid foreigners flood a
country's markets, what difference does it make whether those foreigners
have immigrated or are still living and working in their home countries?

The answer is that *trade and migration may conceivably be similar
in promoting international equalization of factor prices but not of average
real incomes per person.* Equalization of wage rates is not equalization of
average output or income per person. Trade does not lower average
output per person in the way that immigration might. Immigration makes
the country share its advantages among more people; it worsens the ratio
of labor to natural resources and other nonlabor factors, so total output
may rise less than in proportion to population. Trade, in contrast,
increases a country's total real income without increasing the number of
people sharing it. It enhances rather than lessens the good fortune of a
country where natural resources, capital, and business ability are especially
abundant in relation to population. International equalization of factor
prices in no way implies equalization of how abundant or scarce the
different factors of production are in relation to each other, nor equalization
of the average per person of the total income earned by all of the various
factors.

We can see this difference between trade and ordinary immigration
by imagining how immigration of foreign laborers might indeed resemble
trade in raising the standard of living of the native population. When
immigration worsens overpopulation, it pulls down average production per
worker. But for the average to be pulled down, the marginal product of
labor—roughly speaking, how much an additional worker adds to total
production—must be below the average. Under realistic conditions, this
marginal product, as well as the average product, declines as the labor
force grows, other things being equal. Under competition, each worker
tends to receive a wage rate equal to his actual marginal product (i.e., what

he adds to total value produced). This wage rate, however, is below what his marginal product *would have been* if a smaller volume of immigration had left the labor force smaller than it has actually become. It follows that if each immigrant worker is kept from receiving any kind of income other than wages in line with his actual marginal product, then the total income of all immigrant workers is less than the total amount they add to national production. The difference remains as additional real income for the native population. True, the natives do not receive it as additional *labor* income; in fact, the competition of immigrants beats down their wage rates too. It is as landowners, capitalists, and businessmen that the natives benefit.

Immigration is sure to raise the standard of living of the native population only if the immigrants are discriminated against and kept from receiving any nonlabor income, even in the form of government services and welfare payments, charity, gifts, and inheritances. Under these circumstances, being able to hire immigrant labor at bargain rates would be just as advantageous to the native population as being able to buy bargain imports made by cheap foreign labor. Maintaining the necessary discrimination against immigrants and their descendants would be impractical, however, and the caste system involved would be repugnant. Importing only the *products* of the foreign workers but keeping out the workers themselves is a more practical way of discriminating against them and taking advantage of the bargains they offer. (Of course, this is not at all to say that the foreigners are worse off when we do this than when we do not allow them to sell their bargain labor or products to us in any manner.)

Whatever similarity between trade and immigration the factor-price-equalization theorem demonstrates, in short, concerns the distribution but not the level of income. Importing goods made by cheap foreign labor could, like immigration, change the distribution of income to the disadvantage of native labor.

DISTRIBUTION THEORY AND ACTUAL POLICY

We have considered this abstract possibility for two reasons only: to be honest in mentioning everything that might even seem to salvage something out of the cheap-foreign-labor argument for tariffs, and to illustrate why conscientious economic theorists may feel unable to give an unqualified endorsement to free trade under all *conceivable* circumstances. Now we shall consider what the income-distribution analysis means for policy in the real world. This abstract analysis is valuable in its own right, and we intend no disparagement by listing why it has so little practical relevance.

First: as applied to actual tariff policy, references to overseas factor endowments and conditions of production are a red herring. True, they might help *explain* the world price pattern; but it is only this pattern and its relation to domestic prices, not its possible explanation, that counts for our well-being. When unconnected with the question of relative prices, descriptions of foreign standards of living are irrelevant; it is misleading to suggest that free trade would drag our own workers even part way down to the miserable conditions prevailing in some countries. What really concerns us is how imports affect our own economy. Imports selling at a certain price affect our economy as they do regardless of what explains their price. Imports competing with a high-labor-content domestic product tend to lessen the effective scarcity of labor at home regardless of how they were made and regardless of what wages were paid to the foreign workers who made them. To attempt calculations of the distributional effects of free trade, we would need to know how our export industries would expand and import-competing industries contract if exposed to the world price pattern, but not what caused that pattern to exist (and respond to trade) as it does.

Second: theories of factor-price equalization and related distributional effects apply only on very special and unrealistic assumptions. "Production functions"—relations between inputs of ingredients and outputs of products—can be identical in all countries, for example, only if the physical, social, political, and intellectual "atmospheres" or "climates," as well as other more obvious circumstances, are everywhere the same. Reality also fails to satisfy the assumption of incomplete specialization: each country does not continue under trade producing some of each product that it would have produced in isolation. In reality, furthermore, factors of production cannot be classified into a relatively small number of kinds, each made up of units that are identical within and between countries. As mentioned in Chapter four, moreover, making a definite product does not inherently require the use of land, labor, materials, machinery, and so forth in fixed proportions; the proportions used may depend on factor prices. One of two products could have the higher labor content at one set of factor prices and the other the higher labor content at another set of prices.[7] This possibility qualifies the proposition that a country exports products containing relatively large amounts of its abundant factors of production and imports products containing relatively large amounts of its scarce factors. The effect of imports on the income shares of scarce factors becomes correspondingly vague; so, in particular, does the idea of a tariff protecting the scarcity value of scarce labor. Several other assumptions of the income-distribution and factor-price-equalization theories are just as questionable, but enough has been said already to illustrate the unrealities involved. Under not at all implausible departures from the extreme conditions necessary for factor-price equalization, trade may even make wage rates and other factor prices in different countries more unequal rather than less, while still tending to raise average real incomes.

Third: hypothetical examples typically make labor the scarce factor that free trade harms and protection benefits. It is just as possible, though, to concoct examples in which free trade expands rather than shrinks labor's share in an increased total real income.*

Fourth: using duties on trade to affect income distribution is especially difficult when several factors of production exist, not just the two of simple examples. Even three factors pose difficulties. Suppose that import-competing domestic watch production uses not only much labor but also much capital relative to land, while wheat production, the export industry, uses not only little labor but also little capital relative to land. What trade policy could shift income to labor from capitalists and landowners both? This difficulty might be overcome if some third commodity, say chemicals, used much capital relative to land and labor both. Taxing exports or subsidizing imports of chemicals might then restrict the demand for home-produced chemicals and so for the capital entering into them.[8] The more numerous the traded commodities are relative to factors and the

---

*A well-known statistical study by Professor Leontief of Harvard might even be interpreted as suggesting that actual American conditions come closer to those in which free trade would affect not merely the size but even the distribution of total income to the special *advantage* of labor. Surprisingly enough, Leontief apparently found that in the United States the ratio of labor to capital was lower in the production of goods that substitute for imports than in export production. This would seem to imply that a switch from import-competing lines to export lines would increase the relative scarcity and hence the real income of labor. Of course, his results have caused much puzzlement and brought forth several conflicting interpretations, showing the genuine uncertainty prevailing among experts. Wassily Leontief, "Domestic Production and Foreign Trade: The American Capital Position Re-examined," *Proceedings of the American Philosophical Society,* September 1953, pp. 332-349. See also Robert A. Cornell, "Trade of Multinational Firms and Nations' Comparative Advantage," in *Multinational Corporations and Governments,* ed. Patrick M. Boarman and Hans Schollhammer (New York: Praeger Publishers, 1975). Cornell's findings support Leontief's, for trade as a whole. For "new" trade, however, Cornell finds an increase in the capital intensity of exports relative to imports.

more varied the proportions are in which different factors enter into different commodities, the more things policy makers have to work with in trying to affect income distribution as they wish. But the whole approach is obviously complicated, clumsy, and unsure—and basically just a theoretical toy. This is especially true in a country where foreign trade is small, anyway, in relation to domestic production and consumption. The practical difficulties of knowledge and so forth hardly need belaboring.

Fifth: the approach is clumsy for still another reason. The aim is presumably to redistribute from rich to poor persons, not among factors of production as such; yet by no means all persons receiving income primarily from the nonlabor factors from which the policy would take income are richer than the average worker. Some landlords and capitalists (retired persons and "widows and orphans," for example) are poor, just as some workers are rich.*

Sixth: even if other effects of free trade might conceivably tend to shift income distribution from labor, its antimonopoly effects presumably tend to shift the distribution towards labor.

Seventh: even if the gain from free trade does in the short run go fully or more than fully to nonlabor factors of production, the higher total real income provides the opportunity for increased saving and capital formation. In the long run, then, the average worker can gain both absolutely and relatively, since the increased amounts of machinery and other capital equipment that he has to work with raise his productivity.†

---

*Furthermore, tariffs can hardly shift much income away from private owners of natural resources, since this income is only a small fraction of national income anyway. And when a significant proportion of the returns from resource ownership accrues to the government, a decline in this income falls on taxpayers in general, including workers. (Cf. J. H. Young, *Canadian Commercial Policy,* (Ottawa: Royal Commission on Canada's Economic Prospects, 1957), p. 91. Referring to Canada in particular, Young sees more reason to suppose that the tariff has lowered than that it has raised labor incomes.)

†A theoretical case of sorts can be made not only for complacency about spontaneous shifts of income distribution away from labor in the short run but even for tariff policy to reinforce such shifts. The idea is that the shift in distribution might be in favor of higher-saving groups, benefiting capital formation and productivity in the longer run. (Cf. Richard E. Caves, *Trade and Economic Structure,* pp. 252-253, who refers to such suggestions made by Alvin Johnson in 1908 and by Frank D. Graham in 1923.)

Eighth: inventions and trade are similar not only in providing benefits but also in conceivably affecting distribution. An invention of a particularly labor-saving type could conceivably shrink labor's share in an increased total income. Years ago Professor A. C. Pigou noted how "exactly the same analysis" applies to an ordinary invention and to a country's opportunity "to obtain some commodity more cheaply than before by making something else with which to purchase it from elsewhere, instead of making the commodity itself." In both cases, "more of what people want is made available; and . . . the proportionate parts played by labour and capital in production may be changed."[9] The result will almost always be a rise in labor's real income, as well as in the national total. The reverse is possible but "decidedly improbable." "Nobody would seriously propose to interfere with, or to obstruct, inventions in order to provide a safeguard against it."[10]* Pigou's judgment seems just as applicable to trade, and for the same reasons.

Ninth: the effects of trade and tariffs on income distribution have great theoretical importance in any attempt at a complete survey of how intellectually respectable the free-trade case is. But the topic is complicated quite out of proportion to its practical importance, and the space it takes up should not give the impression that it somehow disproves the gains from trade after all. No one denies that free trade could harm certain narrow groups, such as lead-mine owners or glove workers, in the short run; but harm to broadly defined groups such as "labor" in general is much more of a theoretical than a practical possibility. Because it is such a non-specialized, versatile factor of production in the long run and because in reality it receives such a large share of total national income anyway, labor as a whole is almost certain to gain rather than lose from free trade. Also, the returns to labor and capital hardly accrue to two distinct groups of people. Almost everyone who earns an income by selling his services as labor owns some capital in the form of a bank account, life insurance policy, stocks, or bonds. A fall in the real incomes of some narrowly defined factors signals people to switch their efforts into other, more productive, lines and in that way to share in the higher national income made possible by free trade.

---

*One still might insist on a difference between protecting labor against trade and against inventions: the latter protection does and the former does not frustrate technological progress itself. But is this a real difference? Except as it may contribute to the growth of pure scientific knowledge, quite apart from any applications, we do not want technological progress any more than we want trade solely for its own sake; we want each, rather, for the economic gains it offers.

Tenth: if we insist on how judiciously designed tariffs could theoretically affect income distribution in a desired way, we must recognize that domestic tax policy could do a better job because it has more scope to work with; it works at the core rather than on the fringes of the national economy. Conceptually, domestic tax policy could preserve the gains from free trade and offset and more than offset any unwanted effects on distribution. With this alternative, policy makers can come closer to identifying what groups benefit and what groups pay. As Professor Kindleberger warned Congress, the tariff as a means of redistribution "is highly arbitrary in its incidence on consumers, having no systematic relation to ability to pay or to the nature of consumption, on the one hand, and is fairly erratic in the distribution of its benefits, on the other." Import restriction designed to benefit a particular group frequently masquerades as promoting national defense and so forth "without the check of any political Federal Trade Commission which can halt misrepresentation."[11] Governmental price-rigging in response to the political effectiveness of various groups saps political morality and subverts our economic system.

NOTES

1. Charles P. Kindleberger, in *Foreign Trade Policy* (1958), p. 81. (See Chapter 1, note 5.)

2. The possible conflict between these two theoretical possibilities was explained by Lloyd Metzler in "Tariffs, the Terms of Trade, and the Distribution of National Income," *Journal of Political Economy,* February 1949, pp. 1-29. (Chapter 11 below deals with the terms-of-trade argument.)

A further refinement takes into consideration nontraded goods, whose presence renders less stringent Metzler's conditions for failure of a tariff to protect the import-competing industry. The tariff may cause the prices of nontraded goods to rise relative to the prices of traded goods, overriding any stimulus otherwise conferred on import-competing domestic production. See I. A. McDougall, "Non-Traded Commodities and the Pure Theory of International Trade," in McDougall and R. H. Snape, eds., *Studies in International Economics* (Amsterdam: North-Holland Publishing Co., 1970), esp. pp. 159, 181-82.

3. Richard E. Caves, *Trade and Economic Structure* (Cambridge: Harvard University Press, 1960), p. 76.

4. Gottfried Haberler, *A Survey of International Trade Theory,* revised edition. (International Finance Section, Princeton University, 1961), p. 18.

5. J. Wiley Perry, Chairman, Import Study Committee, Cast Iron Soil Pipe Institute, 1970 HW&M VI 1815 (see Chapter 1, note 1).

6. Haberler, op. cit., p. 17.

7. See Bagicha S. Minhas, "The Homohypallagic Production Function, Factor-Intensity Reversals, and the Heckscher-Ohlin Theorem," *Journal of Political Economy,* April 1962, pp. 138-56. The empirical likelihood of such factor-intensity reversals is disputed, however,

by Jagdish Bhagwati, *Trade, Tariffs and Growth* (Cambridge, Mass.: MIT Press, 1969), pp. 100-2, 104-5.

8. Cf. J. E. Meade, *Trade and Welfare* (London: Oxford University Press, 1955), pp. 309-11.

9. A. C. Pigou, *The Economics of Welfare,* 4th ed. (London: Macmillan, 1950), pp. 671-72.

10. Ibid., p. 680.

11. Kindleberger, op. cit., pp. 82-83.

10

TRADE, TARIFFS, AND CAPITAL MOVEMENTS

The preceding chapter dealt with worries that unrestricted imports would have bad effects similar to those of unrestricted immigration. This chapter also deals with movements of factors of production. It considers the worry that unrestricted imports not merely cause effects similar to those of losing capital from the country but actually promote such loss. The argument fits in conveniently here, before we get too far beyond the cheap-foreign-labor argument, because it uses similar rhetoric.

RUNAWAY CAPITAL AND THE MULTINATIONAL CORPORATION

An old worry about capital movements contains some truth, mixed with fallacy: If allowed to bring their products freely into the United States, American companies would send capital and managerial talent abroad to take advantage of lower production costs there. The London *Economist* predicted over twenty years ago that tariff removal might spur American companies "to set up subsidiaries in Europe, to take advantage of low labor costs there, and export their product to the United States."[1] Similar warnings were given during the trade-policy debates of the early 1970's. Worry about runaway capital has been a principal consideration behind the Burke-Hartke proposals to eliminate the foreign tax credit and tax-deferral features of U.S. policy. Under this policy, income taxes paid by foreign subsidiaries of a U.S.-based corporation are deductible from the corporation's U.S. tax liability, and profits are not taxable until repatriated to the United States.

The Burke-Hartke proposals were directed in large measure against U.S.-based multinational corporations—MNCs—firms like General Motors or IBM, with head offices in the United States and operations throughout the world. It was the rise of the MNC during the 1960s and early 1970s that, in many minds, rendered the free-market system a hopelessly fanciful ideal. "Some will make the charge that we are putting on the cloak of protectionism," said Jacob Clayman of the AFL-CIO. "Those who do so fail to recognize that old concepts and labels of 'free-trade' and 'protectionism' have become obsolete. They have been outdated in this new world of managed national economies, international technocracy, multinational corporations and record U.S. investment overseas."[2]

Speaking on behalf of Nathaniel Goldfinger, also of the AFL-CIO and a strong Burke-Hartke supporter, Andrew Biemiller explained to the House Ways and Means Committee that

> The choice is not between free trade and protectionist theories. Free, competitive trade relations hardly exist any longer in this world of managed national economies of large-scale operations of foreign subsidiaries of U.S. companies. It is neither possible for the American economy to hide behind high-tariff walls nor to pretend that free, competitive trade relations are possible.[3]

Mr. Biemiller went on to list his own proposals for managing the world economy: elimination of U.S. tax deferrals, the development of "regulations covering U.S.-based multinational companies," and "the establishment of international fair labor standards in world trade," among others.[4]

According to its critics, the MNC is a stateless monolith that undermines not only the market economy but also the protective policies of national governments. Richard Barnet and Ronald Muller have scored "the ability of global companies to shift production from one facility to another perhaps thousands of miles away" to the detriment of labor and without discipline from market or government.[5] MNCs are bad for being big enough to cover the losses incurred in one country with the profits earned in another, to borrow and lend in the Eurodollar market, to manipulate exchange markets, to divert capital from infrastructure projects in underdeveloped countries to the selfish purposes of the corporation, and to bribe foreign bureaucrats. The bigness of the MNCs, combined with the scope of their operations in underdeveloped countries (at least those in which their assets have not been confiscated) and the continued existence of poverty in those countries, prompt some commentators to question the very logic of a free market. "What is 'freedom,' 'justice,' or 'need' in a world in which 4 billion inhabitants are struggling for food, water, and air?" ask Barnet and Muller. "What does 'efficiency' or 'growth' or 'rationality' mean in such a world?"[6]

Defenders of the MNC often question the *factual* basis of such criticisms. According to the National Association of Manufacturers, U.S. investments in foreign countries have increased most in relatively high-wage and high-material-cost areas like Canada and Europe, proving that cheap wages are not the only incentive for producing abroad. U.S. corporations supposedly invest abroad in self defense; curtailing their foreign activities would let hard-won foreign markets go by default to foreign competitors whose activities are not similarly curtailed. U.S. direct investment abroad tends to be concentrated in industry groups supplying relatively low volumes of imports to the United States. Conversely, product groups with the highest imports, such as shoes and textiles, are among the industry groups with the lowest direct investment abroad. Although the U.S. electronics industry has, by exception, been characterized by heavy imports of goods made by foreign affiliates, that industry simply *had* to invest abroad or lose even the American market to competitors taking advantage of cheap labor.[7]

While probably correct, such assertions miss the point. What difference does it make whether there are one or one hundred exceptions to the rule that MNCs are typically not heavy importers or that the goods they import do not typically embody cheap labor? The case for free trade (temporarily ignoring the question of capital movements) does not hinge on debatable or changeable facts about the size or factor content of commodity trade. The cheap-foreign-labor argument is wrong even if the goods alleged to contain such labor happen to be produced by the foreign affiliates of U.S. corporations. The correct response is to question not the facts asserted about MNCs but their relevance. If sympathy for U.S. electronics workers is a matter of overriding national concern, then the appropriate solution, short of a special welfare program, is to restrict the import of electronics products, whether or not they are imported from American-owned affiliates abroad and embody cheap labor.

Neither the advent of the MNC nor any other fashionably alarming development has rendered efficiency or rationality obsolete. The United States cannot be blamed for all the world's problems. The United States would be making quite a contribution to the world in preserving an efficient economic system at home and a liberal trade policy. The growth of U.S. direct investment abroad is no mere manifestation of some dialectical tendency of the free market to destroy itself. That growth is partly due to deliberate foreign efforts to attract U.S. capital into "tariff factories" (as discussed below).

The nihilistic view that free markets are impossible stands on two legs; it presupposes "government" success as well as "market" failure. The widespread existence of government interference or "management" is always asserted or implied. Yet it is never conceded that such management might continue to worsen what it has so conspicuously failed to correct in the past. Only market failure is expected to occur with continued regularity.

Perhaps the critics of the MNCs and of big business in general believe that the shortcomings of market and government are the fault of the general citizenry for not voting them or their views into power. These shortcomings would disappear if only the public powers were used to protect starving peasants from Coca-Cola, for example, and to prevent corporate treasurers from hedging against currency fluctuations.

What difference would it make to the United States if U.S.-based MNCs had come, in some sense, to dominate foreign production? It is not enough to proclaim an enlightened self-interest in the conduct of American business abroad. The regulation of capital flows is a slippery rock on which to base diplomacy. Even if Americans believe that it harms a foreign country to absorb certain kinds of U.S. investment, the country itself may not. To "protect" a foreigner against his own wish for American-owned plant and equipment may be regarded as gratuitous interference rather than as a benign act.

Apart from any national-security issues that may be involved and certain points noted later in this chapter, whether a U.S. firm should invest abroad is essentially the business of that firm and the host country. If a U.S. firm commits its capital to a foreign site with the acquiescence of the host country, the U.S. government cannot rationally be held responsible for the actions of either the firm or that country. Neither the firm nor the U.S. government can be blamed if bribery is an accepted way of doing business there.

Critics of the MNC might well turn their attention to those public institutions that deliberately or accidentally encourage foreign investment. It is legitimate to ask why the U.S. government should insure approved foreign investments against expropriation, as it does through the Overseas Private Investment Corporation. One answer invokes an externalities argument: capital is needed for foreign development, and since that development is a goal of U.S. foreign policy, U.S. foreign investment may be said to confer social benefits on the United States beyond the return to private investors. Since private incentives are not strong enough to assure an optimal flow of capital to the underdeveloped countries, the U.S. government should strengthen those incentives by offering investors insurance against political risks.

The appropriate response is that if a genuine externality of this kind exists, it is best eliminated by subsidizing development itself rather than by providing insurance against confiscation. We shall discuss the development issue at greater length below. Here it suffices to consider its bearing on U.S. policy toward capital movements. By insuring investments against political risks, the U.S. government dulls foreign incentives to reduce the risk of confiscation. Foreign governments do not have to give the Overseas Private Investment Corporation the same assurances that they would have to give a private insurance company in order to attract U.S. capital. Therefore, the OPIC subsidy goes in part to support the unwillingness of foreign governments to reduce the risk of confiscation. A better policy would gear the entire U.S. subsidy to those developmental efforts from which the external economies to the United States were supposed to emanate.

It is sometimes argued, in effect, that U.S. foreign investment imposes an external *diseconomy* on foreigners and Americans alike by providing a cover or incentive for CIA activities or by exploiting the foreigners' innocence of the threat such investment poses to their sovereignty. This argument merits no extended comment. What the CIA does is the responsibility of Congress and the President, not ITT. The fact that a host country *can* expropriate foreign-owned assets fixed to its own soil would seem to offer adequate protection against misbehavior by the guest investor. This, by the way, goes for the United States as well as any other country that may be concerned about foreign takeovers of its businesses.

CAPITAL EXPORTS AND THE NATIONAL INTEREST

If we set aside the effects of U.S. foreign investment on the host countries, we can explore the effects of that investment on the United States from a purely nationalistic point of view. The incentives operating in free markets tend to steer capital and other resources into the uses where they can contribute most to the value of output; strictly speaking, the tendency is to allocate resources in such a way that no opportunity remains unused to gain more in one line of production than is lost in another by shifting a unit of any resource. Getting the greatest total value by such an allocation does not depend on whether two alternative uses of a resource differ in technology, in consumer tastes, or in location. The income on domestically-owned capital is part of national income, not foreign income, regardless of what industry the capital serves in at home or whether it serves at home or abroad. If the capital contributes more to the value of production and so earns more for its owners when employed abroad than when employed at home, its employment abroad makes for a bigger domestic national income.

One rather sophisticated counterargument supports the Burke-Hartke objections to the foreign tax credit. Defenders of the credit claim that its elimination would subject U.S.-based corporations to "double taxation" of their foreign earnings, once by the foreign government and again by the

U.S. government. The United States follows common practice among other nations by avoiding this unfairness.[8] Yet doing so creates a divergence between private and national incentives for capital to flow abroad. Although, for equal rates of taxation, the U.S. corporation is indifferent between earning an extra dollar at home and earning one abroad, the dollar earned at home yields tax revenue to the government that the dollar earned abroad does not.

> . . . private foreign investment offers the recipient country, as a result of double-taxation arrangements, the considerable advantage of being able to tax profits on foreign capital at the direct expense of the government of the country from which the capital comes.[9]

More fundamental than the question of the foreign tax credit are questions about the corporation income tax itself and the domestic double taxation of corporate earnings that it involves (for profits distributed to stockholders are taxed again as personal income). Another difficulty with the corporation income tax is that no one knows how its burden is accidentally divided among consumers, investors, employees, and other suppliers of productive services. These difficulties join with complaints about the foreign tax credit in raising the question of whether the corporation income tax should not be abolished and replaced by taxes of more straightforward kinds.

A final worry about outflows of capital concerns how they affect the distribution of income. When capital is invested abroad because it earns more there than at home, this gain to its owners is partly offset by loss to domestic land and labor. Having less capital to work with reduces their productivity and income-earning ability. In other words, land and labor lose some of their scarcity value because they become less scarce relative to capital. If perfect commodity mobility (under free trade) implies a tendency toward factor-price equalization, perfect factor mobility does so at least as much.[10]

To this point we may apply the reservations expressed in the preceding chapter about the factor-price-equalization theorem. In particular, the emigration of capital is less disturbing from a nationalistic point of view than the immigration of labor. A policy of permitting free labor as well as capital movements would make it impossible to prevent some of the immigrant labor from getting some nonlabor as well as labor income and from eventually blending in with and receiving the same treatment as the native population.

TRADE POLICY AND CAPITAL FLOWS

Simply assuming for the sake of argument that capital exports are undesirable for distributional or other reasons, let us turn back to their possible connection with free trade.

In the first place, the only bearing that *trade* policy may have on U.S. policy toward capital flows concerns those capital flows that may or may not take place in the future. Past capital flows and their possible contribution to the existing pattern of comparative advantage are irrelevant. Unhappily for protectionists, the MNC issue does not turn out to be a handy way to exorcise the law of comparative advantage.

Second, the factor-price-equalization theory, as applied to capital movements, is a two-edged sword. Just as a reduction of trade barriers may expand commodity trade and thereby create a tendency toward factor-price equality, a rise in such barriers may expand capital flows and so preserve the same tendency. If we grant all the extreme assumptions upon which the factor-price-equalization theory rests, a rise in U.S. trade barriers would cause U.S. wages and foreign interest rates to rise and U.S. interest rates and foreign wages to fall. This would in turn stimulate capital exports from the United States to the rest of the world and reverse the tendency initially set in motion by the rise in trade barriers. In short, factor movements tend to substitute for commodity movements. Controls aimed only at the latter are self-defeating.

In returning to the question of how freer commodity imports might promote capital outflows, we must again beware of the fallacy of composition. Quite conceivably, removing a tariff on one particular product could lead its domestic producers gradually to transfer their capital and operations abroad. But it is a fallacy to infer that complete free trade will cause a general migration of industry to supply its former home market from foreign bases. After all, increased exports of goods and services will more or less match the increased imports if a balance-of-payments balancing mechanism is allowed to operate. There seems to be no general presumption that expanded opportunities in export production will be either more or less attractive to domestic capitalists than expanded opportunities in overseas production of imports. Anyway, we must not overlook this expanded export production as an inducement to capital to stay home. If imports, swollen by overseas output of domestic firms, *did* happen to exceed exports, exchange-rate depreciation of the home currency would tend to restrict imports (and investment opportunities in their overseas production) and expand exports (and investment opportunities in their home production). In fact, an outward transfer of capital would itself influence the exchange rate in the direction of restraining imports, promoting exports, and probably also restraining the capital transfer itself. With a free exchange rate assuring overall balance-of-payments equilibrium, an actual outward transfer of capital requires a *surplus of exports* over imports of goods and services. (This is an answer, incidentally, to balance-of-payments worries over capital exports, provided that the government does not interfere with the automatic balancing mechanism). In short, the process that the commodity-import-and-capital-export argument worries about is a self-restraining process.

Our conclusion is certainly not that capital outflows will never occur but that they mainly depend on other things than domestic tariff policy. While tariffs on some particular products may influence whether or not domestic firms invest in producing them abroad for import into the United States, American tariffs must be just a fringe influence on the total outflow of capital. The outflow could be restricted more effectively, if restriction really is desirable, by removal of existing government encouragements to it and by changes in tax policy. Probably still more important to investment at home rather than abroad is the general state of prosperity and profit opportunities in the home economy. The argument we have been considering is circular in tacitly taking it for granted that free trade is bad for prosperity and profits.

"TARIFF FACTORIES"

According to the "tariff-factories" argument, a country, by erecting import barriers, might prod some of its suppliers of imports into establishing local branches or subsidiaries to supply the protected market from the inside. Abundant anecdotal evidence suggests that the trick can indeed work. But how sweeping a conclusion follows from individual cases? Is such a policy in the real interest of underdeveloped countries? It must be a delicate task to choose the right products and the right duty rates or other import restrictions to get the desired results rather than simply ward off useful imports without attracting much capital. Furthermore, the fallacy of composition looms. Because of trade-balancing tendencies, reduced imports of some products entail either larger imports of others or smaller exports, so that while some industries invite investment more strongly than before, others invite it less strongly. After all, not only import-competing industries but also export industries may be important fields of foreign investment.

An appeal to irreversibilities may strengthen the argument. Disinvestment in industries that a change in the tariff structure makes relatively less attractive than before will not promptly and fully offset any new investment drawn in by the change. Gaining this new investment depends on whether or not a tariff can aid the birth or growth of infant industries. (Here some things become relevant that the chapter on economic development discusses more fully.) Foreign capital and enterprise are likely to prove especially valuable to an underdeveloped country—if it can win them—for they bring business skills with them, provide training for local workers and managers, and in general demonstrate by their own example the approach to business, the attitudes, and the freedom from inhibiting old customs that characterize economically more advanced countries. It is for precisely these reasons that many underdeveloped countries have encouraged investment by multinational firms.

The tariff is itself only a "second-best" way to attract foreign capital. (On second-best tariff arguments in general, see pp. 203-04 below.) What is wanted is capital and the entrepreneurship associated with it, not the attraction, *as such,* of capital into industries in which the country has a comparative disadvantage. Even if the tariff does attract foreign capital, it imposes the usual production and consumption costs. A better policy might be to subsidize foreign capital without the string that it associate itself with a particular industry (unless it can be shown that the particular industry radiates external economies, in which case we have the usual externality argument).[11]

In some ways commodity import barriers are likely to hinder rather than encourage capital inflows. If the barrier causes export industries to shrink and these are more capital-intensive than the protected import-competing industries, capital might actually flow out of the country.[12] For the financial side of a capital inflow to have a real counterpart that adds to the country's currently available real resources, imports of goods and services must exceed exports. There is more room for this import surplus when trade is not restricted than when it is. A large unrestricted two-way flow of trade, furthermore, probably gives prospective foreign investors more reassurance than a small restricted flow does about their being able to take their earnings and capital home if they should care to do so in the future. A large two-way trade volume presumably means less danger of a balance-of-payments crisis that could bring restrictions on repatriation of earnings and capital; for one thing, active trade offers corresponding scope for cutting imports if necessary to deal with a future balance-of-payments crisis without restrictions on re-export of capital. Continuous operation of an automatic payments-balancing mechanism would be even more reassuring. Also, the prospective investor can realize that the larger the volume of trade, the easier it should be (especially with an automatic balancing mechanism) to generate a goods-and-services export surplus accomplishing a net capital repatriation of a definite size, in case he and other foreign investors should some day desire to withdraw their funds.

In attracting foreign capital as in retaining domestic capital, the main influences are profit opportunities, prosperity, and the general "investment climate." Compared to these, government manipulations of trade can be only marginally helpful. On balance they may even be harmful if they symptomize a distrust of the price system and the profit motive, a suspicion of business and especially foreign business, and a general government meddlesomeness.*

EXPORTS OF NATURAL CAPITAL

The title of this section is an artifice for squeezing in consideration of a hard-to-classify emotional argument against free trade. It centers on export of goods embodying large amounts of a country's exhaustible natural resources. The country draws down its irreplaceable natural endowment for the sake of foreigners—so the argument goes—in exchange for goods that may well have no comparable natural resource content.[13]

Tariffs on *imports* would be a crude way of dealing with this supposed problem, however, since their repercussions would tend only to shrink exports in general instead of selectively deterring the particularly worrisome ones. A more fundamental comment is that embodying resources

---

*A more general and sophisticated but admittedly less realistic version of the tariffs-to-attract-investment argument than the version just considered invokes the theory that commodity and factor movements are substitutes for each other. A tariff on a capital-intensive product will raise its relative price and may attract both foreign capital and domestic factors of production into its expanded domestic production. The shift of domestic factors associated with this expansion will tend to make capital scarcer than before relative to labor in each of various industries, with the result that the productivity and real wages of labor will fall. The inflow of foreign capital will not entirely prevent this result, since the new capital will largely go into expanding the output of the protected capital-intensive product. Only certain restrictive assumptions would guarantee a more clearly desirable outcome, as well as the inflow of the foreign capital. (See Gerald M. Meier, *International Trade and Development* (New York: Harper, 1963), pp. 122-23, and R. A. Mundell, "International Trade and Factor Mobility," *American Economic Review,* June 1957, pp. 331-35.)

in export goods is an indirect way of using the resources to "produce" the imports obtained in exchange, and a more efficient way, presumably, than producing such goods at home. The distinction between embodying exhaustible resources in exports traded away for imports and embodying them in goods both produced and used at home is empty. The genuine issue concerns, rather, the total rate of exhaustion of natural resources in production for export and for direct domestic use alike. The correct answer can hardly be never to use exhaustible resources at all, for this would be equivalent to not having them. Properly formulated, the issue is whether unregulated private profit and saving incentives lead to "too high" a rate of exploitation of exhaustible resources, as compared with some "socially optimum" rate. Too many subtle and peripheral points are involved for further discussion here, except to assert that the prevalent naive conservationist arguments are fallacious, and that a more sophisticated worry turns on the adequacy of private incentives for saving in general rather than for saving of natural resources in particular.[14] The issue is not basically one of international trade policy.

NOTES

1. *The Economist*, February 20, 1954, quoted in Lewis E. Lloyd, *Tariffs: The Case for Protection* (New York: Devin-Adair, 1955), p. 90.

2. 1970 HW&M VI 1779 (see Chapter 1, note 1).

3. HW&M IV 1010.

4. Ibid.

5. Richard J. Barnet and Ronald Muller, *Global Reach* (New York: Simon and Schuster, 1974), p. 30.

6. Ibid., p. 25.

7. National Association of Manufacturers, *U.S. Stake in World Trade and Investment: The Role of the Multinational Corporation,* (undated; c. 1971).

8. Ibid., p. 61.

9. Harry G. Johnson, *Economic Policies Toward Less Developed Countries* (Washington: Brookings Institution, 1967), p. 61.

10. Cf. Robert Mundell, *International Economics* (New York: The Macmillan Company, 1968), p. 85.

11. S. N. H. Naqvi, "Protection and Economic Development," *Kyklos,* 1969, no. 1, pp. 143-45.

12. Ibid.

13. An example of this worry occurs in Thomas Roy Jones's footnote to Committee for Economic Development, *Japan in the Free World Economy* (New York: Committee for Economic Development, 1963), p. 53.

14. For an excellent refutation of the naive conservationist arguments, see Anthony Scott, *Natural Resources: The Economics of Conservation* (University of Toronto Press, 1955). Also see p. 36n.

11

TAX REVENUE AND
THE TERMS OF TRADE

This chapter considers three interrelated possible uses of tariffs: (1) to raise revenue for the government from the home population; (2) to correct for a supposed distortion involving the income tax under free trade; and (3) to raise revenue at foreign expense.

RAISING REVENUE

Are tariffs a good source of tax revenue? Well, the higher an import duty is (beyond a certain point) and the more goods it keeps out, the less revenue it brings in. A tariff to provide both protection and revenue necessarily does each job incompletely. A fully protective tariff yields no revenue at all. On mass-consumed articles, furthermore, tariffs burden poor people more heavily than the rich. Middlemen between the foreign producer and the home consumer pay an import duty to the government before passing it along to the consumer; and to justify tying up their capital, they must figure their markups not on the wholesale price of the article alone but on the price plus duty. As a result, the duty raises the price to the final consumer by more than its own amount (unless enough of the duty is shifted back to the foreign suppliers, a possibility considered later in this chapter). This "pyramiding" occurs with domestic excise taxes also, which is a reason for levying commodity taxes close to the final consumer. Since all taxes have some bad effects, however, condemning one kind is not sensible without considering how else to raise revenue.

If some domestically produced commodity bears a selective excise tax, there may be good reason (but not necessarily a conclusive reason) for a similar tax on competing imports. Otherwise, the discrimination in favor of imports would be the same in kind, though opposite in direction, as the discrimination and falsification of price signals that condemn ordinary tariffs. The false price signals could lead consumers to buy the imports, even though the exports paying for them cost more in other production sacrificed than would domestic production of the import-type goods. A respected economist sympathetic to free trade put the matter this way:

> The fathers of free trade made special exceptions for such cases; where a domestic industry is taxed in a discriminating fashion, and its inability to compete successfully with imports is a result of such discriminatory taxation, and if it is not politically practicable to abolish such taxes, that industry has a valid claim, within the logic of the free-trade doctrine, to protection by an import duty. I would call that a free-trade import duty. If we impose artificial costs on an American industry, we owe it artificial protection against imports. The two would balance out as far as trade was concerned.[1]

The same argument for a compensatory import duty does not hold when the "artificial costs" fall on domestic production generally. If domestic sales or turnover taxes fall on commodities uniformly, prices do *not* misrepresent how much producing each one costs in terms of others sacrificed. As for selective domestic excise taxes, while the case for matching them with import duties is theoretically sound, it is not conclusive in the face of other considerations. The issue is not of right and wrong but of weighing pros and cons.

If a particular domestic commodity and the competing import are both to be taxed, should the rate be the same on both? Our earlier reasoning might seem to say yes; only if the costs of the commodity coming from home and foreign sources alike are boosted by the same percentage will there be no misrepresentation in the prices that tell consumers whether it is cheaper to buy the commodity produced directly at home or "produced" indirectly through exports to pay for the import.* But this answer overlooks one remaining distortion: the taxed commodity appears more expensive from the private point of view than it actually is

---

*More precisely, the earlier reasoning would seem to call for an import duty corresponding to the *excess* taxation of the domestic commodity beyond whatever domestic taxation may apply uniformly. Terms-of-trade considerations that might call for a higher tax on the import are postponed until later in this chapter.

from the national point of view in terms of nontaxed commodities forgone. As a result, its total consumption is "too small," and too few resources are devoted to obtaining it either directly by home production or indirectly by trade. This distortion would be absent only if consumption were completely unresponsive; consumers would have to be so stuck in the market for the commodity that they would buy a fixed amount regardless of price. Only then would the simple reasoning in favor of equal domestic and import tax rates be persuasive. In general, consumption will be distorted downward, and unequal tax rates might usefully avoid part of this effect. The idea is to raise the desired amount of revenue with the best possible compromise between avoiding two distortions, that of total consumption and that of the choice between home and foreign sources.

An example will help clarify the issue.[2] Our country produces some widgets at home and also imports some. We start with a pure production tax: domestic widgets pay it but imports are exempt. Now we begin to cut the domestic tax and recoup the lost revenue with an import tax. When the rate is the same on both domestic and imported widgets, the tax has become a consumption tax. Further adjustment in the same direction could result in a pure import tax (though it might not be possible to maintain the desired total tax revenue). How far from a production to a consumption to an import tax is it wise to move? No answer is generally valid, but two considerations are relevant. One weak presumption runs in favor of taxing consumption from both sources rather than only domestic production or only imports. The idea is that the broadest tax base permits a lower rate of tax and therefore a lesser degree of price-signal falsification (a smaller divergence between price paid by consumers and net price received by some producers). A second presumption favors the heavier tax on whichever activities it will least cause to shrivel up or things it will least cause to disappear. This is an old general maxim of taxation (and forms a familiar argument for such taxes as on land or cigarettes); taxation of the opposite kind would especially affect economic activity and, in so doing, prove inefficient in raising revenue. The idea follows to tax imports more or less heavily than domestic production, depending on whether their amount would shrivel less or more sensitively. The shriveling of each depends on the price-sensitivity of consumers and suppliers both, since the tax wedges itself between the effective prices for the two groups. Domestic supply is presumably (though not necessarily) less price-sensitive than import supply; its responsiveness depends only on how easily producers can shift into other lines to escape the tax. Import-supply responsiveness depends not only on such shifts of production abroad but also on possible diversion abroad from export sales to increased local consumption. (It also depends on foreigners' opportunities to divert their sales to other countries where import duties are absent or lower, a point considered more fully later in this chapter.) By and large, then, import supply has more scope than domestic supply to respond to a tax, which tells in favor of taxing imports *less* heavily. An ideal pattern of selective tax rates on various domestic and imported commodities is, of course, more easily described in the abstract than achieved in reality.

A tax that badly shrivels what it tries to raise revenue on is inefficient. If the tax is selective rather than general, some people will manage to escape it by changing their affected consumption or production. These responses can ordinarily be more complete in the long run than in the short run, so that a tax rate ideal for revenue purposes at first will prove too high later on.

One escape from high import duties is smuggling. Some protectionists will say, "So what? Murder also is hard to stamp out; yet this is no argument for making it legal." The difference is that importing things duty-free is not *inherently* wicked; and on grounds both of maintaining respect for law and of allocating police forces to where the need for them is most urgent, a presumption runs against illegalizing activities that are neither inherently wicked nor easy to suppress.

Besides possibly being inefficient in raising revenue, import duties cast away the gains that people could have reaped on the shriveled two-way import and export trade. This dead loss occurs over and above the revenue transferred to the government, as explained in Chapter 4. While other forms of taxation also cause comparable losses, tariffs seem worse in this respect than some other ways of raising revenue.

Turning from abstract analysis to actual American conditions, we now ask how strongly revenue requirements demand keeping our tariffs. Before World War I customs duties did provide the bulk of Federal revenue, but in recent years they have been providing less than 1.5 percent. Even this small contribution to revenue is partly offset by the burdens that the tariff system puts on the government and the public: the costs of running the customs "service," the extra paper work and legal expense imposed on business, the expenses to business of keeping informed on tariff issues and of lobbying, the costs of Congressional and International Trade Commission hearings, debates, and investigations, the costs of the customs courts, the costs of international trade negotiations, the losses from delays in the availability of imported goods and from uncertainty about their tariff-inclusive prices, the costs of time lost and irritation experienced by travelers waiting to be searched, and so on, not to mention the lost benefits of the trade destroyed. Even Malone of Nevada, in his day the most vocal protectionist in the United States Senate, used to agree that "the revenue collected on imports is not particularly important." One further point is minor, we admit: additional income-tax revenue from the increase in real income due to free trade would replace some part of the lost customs revenue.

Clear-cut free trade, unmarred even by a revenue tariff, would have still other advantages. A duty discriminating against imports of something also produced at home gives at least incidental protection and leaves a foot in the door for outright protection. Also, as a sign of understanding the logic of the price system and as an example to foreign countries, free trade is clearer than even a moderate revenue tariff. People would be justly skeptical about free trade "with minor exceptions." It would be more convincing to show the world that the United States had adopted free trade with no strings.

TARIFFS AND THE INCOME TAX

We have already recognized a theoretically sound though not conclusive argument for a duty on a particular import to match a selective tax on the corresponding domestic article. Sometimes this is generalized into an argument for matching domestic income taxes with across-the-board import duties (or an equivalent burdening of imports, such as "Buy-American" practices in government procurement). In a fable published by the American Tariff League, a newspaper reporter asked the hero whether the government order he had received wouldn't cost the American taxpayer more money.

"Let's look at it this way," Rufus said. "British octane injectors are $10 per $100 cheaper than ours. In addition, the government collects $12 per $100 import duty on British injectors."

"So the government really saved $22 by buying British octane injectors," the reporter said.

"That's what it looks like," said Rufus. "But on every $100 worth of octane injectors we sell to the government, the government collects $26 taxes from us and our workers. If you match this tax loss of $26 against the apparent saving of $22, you see that the government really loses $4 per $100 worth of octane injectors if the government buys from the British."[3]

A Westinghouse vice president furnished a real-world example of this argument in complaining about a government purchase of a large power-dam transformer from the English Electric Company. Westinghouse employees and officers lost $1 million in wages and salaries, stockholders lost prospective dividends, and the government lost $600,000 in taxes that Westinghouse would have paid if it had won the contract. By buying the cheaper foreign equipment, the government allegedly inflicted a net loss on itself and on the whole American economy.[4]

The executive vice president of the National Lumber Manufacturers Association appeared before the House Ways and Means Committee not "to seek any unfair advantage" over foreign competitors but only to ask Congress "to equalize the competitive factors" with which his industry must contend. Among these factors he cited domestic taxes, and he stressed how corporation and personal income taxes were less favorable to business in the United States than in Germany.[5]

In other words, according to this argument, the U.S. government does not tax the company profits and personal incomes of the foreign producers of goods imported into the United States (except to the extent that foreign companies become liable to tax because of branch offices and the like in the United States). American producers do pay such taxes. By failing to take this difference into account, private buyers and sometimes even the government itself impair Federal tax revenues and thus harm the country as a whole when they choose a foreign over an American product. Besides this, ailing businesses pay less state and local taxes and give less generously to charity. "All in all, most of the apparent saving is merely shifted to other products or persons."[6] Import duties are therefore needed to keep buyers from finding imports deceptively attractive and to preserve the domestic tax revenue lost when buyers do turn away from domestic producers.

The fallacy here is our old friend the fallacy of composition, the fallacy of drawing conclusions from too narrow a view. It is not enough to consider only the import-competing sectors of the economy. When tariff protection lures labor, capital, business ability, and natural resources into these sectors, or holds them there, is it simply saving them from perpetual idleness? Or would the labor and so forth have been active in other lines of production instead, earning profits and incomes there and paying taxes on them? The tariff does not spell the difference between full employment and underemployment. Whatever might be said about employment difficulties in a *transition* from protection to free trade, free trade does not cause permanent unemployment or any distortion involving income taxes. The protectionist fallacy would be blatant if Bastiat's candlemakers argued for protection against sunlight on the grounds that the sun paid no income taxes while everyone connected with the artificial lighting industry did pay them (see Chapter 7, pp. 142-43).

As we know, the reason why some foreign goods are cheaper than American goods does not affect the advantage of buying them—not even when the reason is less burdensome taxation abroad. A discriminatory tax on a particular domestic product or industry does invite correction, but only because it is an *internal* distortion shunting resources out of the especially taxed line of production and disrupting the presumably more efficient allocation of domestic resources that would have emerged at unrigged prices. A general income tax does not cause such distortion. *Unevenness* of taxation *at home* is what may call for a remedy. The pattern of taxes abroad is just one of the many influences on foreign prices that the home country need not worry about, since only those foreign prices themselves matter to it. Theorizing about how to offset a domestic distortion with an opposite distortion in the form of an import duty is respectable, but the naive income-tax argument fails to see that the issue is what industries domestic incomes get earned in rather than whether or not the incomes get earned at all.

The domestic economic sectors yielding more incomes and tax revenues under free trade than under protection include, of course, the export industries. But suppose, implausibly, that exports somehow fail to balance bigger imports and that the foreigners simply accept more and more claims on the United States in payment for their surplus sales to us. Far from being a calamity, this gives us the use of foreign capital, and cheaply, too. The possible dim side of this picture—problems of the balance of payments and exchange-rate pegging discussed in Chapter 6—is quite different from the question of total employment, production, income, and tax revenues in the United States. Getting imports temporarily free, as they are when they exceed exports, or getting them permanently free, as in the fable about sunlight, does not erode Americans' capacity to pay taxes. On the contrary, the more cheaply Americans can get imports in relation to exports and the more efficiently they allocate their resources, the greater their real incomes are at full employment and the more total taxes they pay at given rates.

THE TERMS OF TRADE

Any idea that a tariff raises revenue from foreigners *instead of* from a country's own citizens is naive. The consumer pays in tariff-boosted prices. Any chance of shifting part of the burden onto foreigners leads into the academic argument that a tariff may improve a country's terms of trade. Though it has little importance in American practical politics, it deserves close attention as one of the few most intellectually respectable reasons why, in theory, free trade may not be the best conceivable policy.

A tariff might push down the prices paid for imports relative to the prices received for exports, giving the country a bigger quantity of imports per unit of exports sent out in payment. In contrast with more politically influential tariff arguments, this one recognizes that cheap imports are good, not bad. It also partially clashes with the idea of protecting home producers. Full protection would keep out imports rather than increase the gain from them. And insofar as foreign suppliers did absorb import duties in lower net prices and did continue shipping in their goods, competing home producers would find their protection incomplete. (The hypothetical curiosity noted on p. 163 is an extreme case of this effect.) Awareness of this possibility may perhaps explain the increasing protectionist clamor in the United States for quotas to limit imports rigidly by quantity rather than just to discourage them with duties.[7]

An extreme example, to start with, will show how tariffs might work. Suppose that foreigners are very dependent on us as a market for their goods. They and their factories and farms and natural resources are highly specialized in making the things we import from them, and they have no good opportunities to switch into making other things. Neither do the foreigners have much chance to switch their sales from us to other countries; the world market just does not allow it. Finally, the foreigners could not satisfactorily readjust to shrunken trade by consuming more of their export-type goods themselves to replace lost imports. In short, the foreigners are "stuck" in our market. If necessary to hold it, they would take large price cuts without much reducing the quantity of their goods offered. In conditions as favorable as possible for us, furthermore, we are not at all dependent on the foreigners. We could easily do without our imports from them. We could switch our consumption to close substitutes produced at home, easily diverting the necessary resources from export production, directly or indirectly. Because we care so much less about trade than the foreigners do, it is they rather than we who would endure "exploitation" if necessary to keep it flowing.

If so, why hadn't we, all along, beaten down the prices paid to foreigners? The answer is that "we" have not been acting as a unit; we have not been ganging up on the foreigners to exploit our bargaining power. Instead, our separate importers have been competing against each other in buying the foreign goods. A tariff can in effect restrain this competition and make our country act more nearly as a single buyer. The tariff wedges itself between the prices our consumers pay and the prices the foreign sellers get. Under the assumed extreme conditions, the wedge mostly presses the foreigners' prices down rather than our consumers' prices up. The foreigners have to absorb the tariff almost entirely.

Even in less extreme conditions, a tariff can yield us some gain. A gain is not even theoretically possible only if the foreign supply of imports to us is completely price-sensitive, that is, only if the slightest cut in the price we would pay would make the foreigners completely stop selling to us. But as long as foreigners *would* absorb any part of a tariff in lower prices rather than completely stop selling to us, the tariff could correct for a divergence between our national and private views of import prices. Strictly speaking, the divergence occurs between the two views of how much we would have to spend extra for a small increase (or would save by a small decrease) in our imports. (1) The individual competitive importer simply looks at the ordinary price of imports to see this; he can buy as many or as few units of imports as he wants at the going price; he alone is too small in relation to the whole market to consider that his reduced buying would beat down the price. (2) Yet all importers, taken together, *are* more than a drop in the bucket; their increased or reduced purchases, in the aggregate, do bid up or beat down the price paid to foreigners. From our national point of view, therefore, additional imports add more to our total expenditures than their price times quantity; and a cutback in imports saves more than price times quantity.

Additional imports add more to total expenditure than their own price-times-quantity because buying them bids up not only their own price but also the price of the same imports already being bought; a cutback in imports saves more than their own price-times-quantity because the cutback also beats down the price of the imports still being bought. This change in total expenditure per one-unit change in imports is called *marginal expenditure.* Marginal expenditure is higher than price in the ordinary sense for a buyer or group of buyers so large in relation to the total market that any increase or cutback in its own purchases would appreciably bid up or beat down the price. The only exception would be the extreme case of completely price-sensitive foreign supply; for then not even all importers taken together could bid up or beat down the foreign price by buying more or less of the import. The foreigners would respond entirely in the quantity supplied and not at all by changing the price.

Marginal expenditure is important because it measures the extra cost of an extra unit of imports from the national point of view. A tariff designed in accordance with the terms-of-trade argument would raise the price paid by individual importers up to the level of the country's marginal expenditure. This would make importers see prices and decide on purchases as if they were acting together and were taking account of their aggregate influence on the price paid to foreigners.

An intuitive way of realizing that there must be some ideal or "optimum" rate of duty which does this is to note that a duty increases the gain *per unit of trade* by beating down the price paid to foreigners but also shrinks the volume of trade. (It will shrink trade except on the import side in the extreme theoretical case mentioned on p. 163.) For the country imposing it, the duty affects price beneficially and trade volume harmfully. A duty of zero would not affect the volume of trade but would not beat down the price, either. A prohibitively high duty, at the other extreme, would kill off trade and destroy rather than increase the gain from it. Hence, some in-between rate of duty would yield the greatest *total* gain.

Here we should explain why the volume of imports that in some sense is ideal for the country depends on the marginal expenditure, which is what the import price plus the ideal tariff equals (by definition of the ideal tariff). When consumers must pay this corrected price, they buy just so many or so few imports per time period that the "last" unit bought is just barely worth the price to them, and thus worth the other goods they might have had instead for the same price. (Necessary qualifications about transportation costs, costs of running import businesses, including normal profit, and the like are too obvious to justify complicating our argument by spelling them out.) By not buying these other goods, consumers are directly or indirectly freeing productive resources to produce exports worth enough to cover the country's marginal expenditure on imports. In effect, consumers are neatly balancing the worth to them of the "last" unit of imports against the worth to them of what they must give up to get this last unit. The volume of imports is then just right, with the last unit of imports worth neither more nor less to consumers than what they must sacrifice to have it. Now suppose, in contrast, that the divergence between national and private views has gone uncorrected; no tariff raises the price to consumers up to the level of marginal expenditure. Deciding on purchases in view of this uncorrected price, consumers carry their import consumption too far. The "last" unit of imports bought is not really worth as much to consumers as the other goods the country must forgo to permit production of the additional exports to pay for it, since the marginal expenditure to be covered exceeds the ordinary import price that consumers pay. In short, this uncorrected price is a false indicator of opportunities from the national point of view; it fails to make consumers take account of how restraint in importing could beat down the price paid to foreigners.

The rate of the ideally corrective tariff depends on how much greater the marginal expenditure is than the price at which the foreigners supply the imports. This in turn depends on how slightly the foreign supply responds to price or, in other words, on how sharply the foreign supply price would be bid up or beaten down by increased or decreased purchases. With foreign supply completely price-sensitive and our country thus lacking any influence over the supply price, the ideal tariff is zero; we have no divergence between private and national viewpoints to correct for. At the opposite extreme, with foreigners ready to take a price cut almost to zero rather than see their sales to us shrink appreciably, the ideal tariff would amount to almost the entire amount of the price previously paid. As a percentage of the new beaten-down price paid to foreigners, it would be immense. With the foreign price-sensitivity in between these extremes, the optimum rate of duty, expressed as a fraction of the beaten-down price, is $1/e$. The e stands for "elasticity" and expresses how sensitively the supply of imports to us depends on price the foreigners receive.*

The terms-of-trade argument theoretically justifies export as well as import duties (which helps explain why the argument is not used by people who feel that imports are bad, somehow, but exports good). Suppose that foreigners depend on our country as a source of supply of some product they can hardly do without, while we have such attractive alternative uses for our resources that we hardly care about exporting it. An export duty, wedged between the price received by our exporters and the price paid by foreign buyers, would then fall almost entirely on the foreigners. A less extreme example considers any less than completely price-sensitive foreign demand for our export product: a price increase would not stop foreign purchases, and some price cut would be necessary to expand them. Here, as in the import example, private and national viewpoints diverge. An individual competitive supplier simply looks at the ordinary price he can get (as well as at his costs) in deciding how much of the export product to supply. He is too small a part of the market to consider how he might push the price down or up by selling more or less. The extra receipts from an extra unit of exports are called *marginal revenue*. For an individual competitive supplier, marginal revenue coincides with the ordinary price received. From the national point of view, however, it must be something less, since increased exports push down the price not only of the *additional* units sold but also of those *already* being sold. The ideal export tax corrects for this divergence of viewpoints. It takes enough out of the gross price the individual exporter receives so that what he has left, net of the tax, equals marginal revenue from the national point of view. The tax thus induces exporters to act as if they were taking account of their aggregate influence on the price paid by foreigners.

Intuition agrees that there must be some ideal rate of export duty, in between the zero rate that has no effect and the rate so high that it stops

---

*More precisely, the supply elasticity is the ratio of percentage change in quantity supplied to a small percentage change in price. Zero elasticity means no responsiveness of quantity to price; infinity means complete responsiveness, or, in other words, that changes in quantity leave the supply price unaffected. An elasticity of 2 means that a 1 percent price change calls forth a 2 percent change in quantity supplied per time period. The article cited in the next footnote reviews the derivation of the familiar expression for an optimum import duty, $1/e$, as well as the corresponding expression, to be mentioned below, for an optimum export duty.

foreign purchases entirely. This ideal rate depends on the size of divergence to be corrected for between the national viewpoint and the viewpoint of competitive exporters—on how far marginal revenue falls short of the ordinary export price. As the parallel with the import-duty case suggests, the ideal rate of export duty depends on how price-sensitive foreign buyers are. Expressed as a proportion of the duty-inclusive price paid by foreigners, this rate is $1/E$, where E is the elasticity of foreign demand. (This elasticity is the ratio of the proportionate decrease in purchases of our exports to the proportionate increase in price that foreigners pay because of the duty.)

THE SIZE OF NET GAIN

The ideal rates of import or export duty we have explained are those that maximize the *net* gain at foreign expense. "Net gain" refers to the fact that the tax revenue collected from foreigners through lower import or higher export prices is not all clear gain to us; from it must be subtracted the dead loss due to the shrinkage of trade. This dead loss does not include that part of the government's tax revenue paid by domestic consumers of imports or producers of exports rather than by foreigners, since this part of the revenue is considered a mere transfer within the home economy. Rather, the dead loss is the waste from trade shrinkage already described in Chapter four.

Subtracting this dead loss from the revenue collected from foreigners leaves—to repeat—the *net* gain for the home country. Its maximum size can conveniently be expressed as a percentage of the value under free trade of the import or export trade on which the ideal duty is imposed. In the most favorable cases of infinitely elastic home demand (in the import-duty case) or infinitely elastic home supply (in the export-duty case), the dead loss is zero. Even so, the maximum net gain as a proportion of the value of trade when free of duty is only 25 percent when the foreign elasticity is as advantageously low as 1 (for supply of our imports) or 2 (for demand for our exports). This proportionate net gain shrinks to 15 percent for foreign elasticities of 2 (for supply) or 3 (for demand). It shrinks to less than 7 percent for foreign elasticities of 5 or 6. Less than infinite home import demand or export supply elasticities also shrink the proportionate net gain. An optimum import duty yields a gain, net of dead loss, amounting to about 15 percent of the free-trade value of imports when home demand and foreign supply elasticities are both 1, under 9 percent when both elasticities are 2, and under 4 percent when both are 5. An optimum export duty yields about 14 percent when home and foreign elasticities are both 2, about 8 percent when both are 3, and under 5 percent when both are 5.[8] The elasticities mentioned in these illustrative computations are by no means unrealistically high, considering all the conditions making for considerable price-sensitivity of supplies and demands in international trade, especially in the long run. Incidentally, the percentages given express net gain in relation to *trade;* net gain is even smaller, of course, in relation to national income.

Any reader puzzled by the last two paragraphs is invited to accept their main point on faith for the time being: the size of the net gain a country is likely to be able to reap by putting the terms-of-trade argument into practice is small—surprisingly small in relation to the amounts of time, paper, and ink used up on the terms-of-trade argument in the academic literature. The smallness of the net gain from a terms-of-trade tariff parallels, in a loose way, the smallness of the allocational damage otherwise done by a tariff, explained in Chapter four.

Even the small percentages of gain in our illustrative calculations presuppose *optimum* (ideal) duties. If the rates are not optimum, the net gains are smaller and may well be negative. Even apart from the important problem of foreign retaliation, the practical difficulties of setting and maintaining optimum rates are immense.* It is not easy to make reliable numerical estimates of how price-sensitive foreign supplies and demands are. The elasticities differ from product to product. Also, they are likely to increase as time passes. At first, an adverse price change may leave people selling or buying nearly as much as before. They need time to shift resources around, to readjust patterns of production and consumption, to develop new markets and new sources of supply. Eventually, though, people see and act on these possibilities. Changes in tastes, technology, and the competition of buyers and sellers in other countries also change supply and demand elasticities. Even experts, free from political influence, would have trouble getting the detailed and changing information needed and using it accurately to readjust import and export duties continually on hundreds of separate items. In practice, it is politicians and other nonexperts who set rates of duty.

---

*Even apart from net loss through excessive terms-of-trade improvement, an import duty might conceivably *worsen* a country's terms of trade because of complicated interdependence among industries through their employment of factors of production. (See F. H. Gruen and W. M. Corden, "A Tariff That Worsens the Terms of Trade," in I. A. McDougall and R. H. Snape, eds., *Studies in International Economics* (Amsterdam: North-Holland Publishing Company, 1970), pp. 55-58.)

Policy-makers tend to set rates above any theoretically ideal level. One reason is the influence of protectionist beliefs and pressures. Another is that the supplies of imports to an individual country and the foreign demands for its exports are likely to be rather highly price-sensitive, making the ideal duty rates correspondingly low. The foreign businessmen, capital, labor, and other resources supplying some import product are unlikely all to be trapped in a particular country's market or even in their current line of production despite a serious drop in price. In the long run, at least, they can shift into other activities. Some mineral or farm products to which a country's natural resources or climate more or less irrevocably commit it suggest the most plausible partial exceptions. Even so, though especially with products produced in a more diversified economy, export supply is more responsive than production. A fall in the price paid supplier countries will lead them to shrink the quantity they offer not merely by cutting their production but also by increasing their own consumption of the cheapened product. Even if a country trying to improve its terms of trade with import duties does restrain buying competition among its own importers, they will still be competing with buyers in other countries. Even if unusual circumstances do make the total foreign supply rather insensitive to price, the supply to the particular importing country trying to take advantage of the foreigners will be sensitive if they can shift their sales to the competing buyers in other countries.

Similar considerations suggest that high foreign demand elasticities for one country's exports will limit the advantages of export duties. First, the foreign importing countries may already have some local production of competing products, or might develop it if prices rose enough. The foreigners' demand for the exports of the duty-levying country is therefore more price-sensitive than their total consumption demand for such goods; yet possibilities of switching some consumption to other goods may make even this total demand rather responsive. Probably still more important is the competition on the world market that one country's exporters face from producers in other countries. (Compare the reason why the demand for the wheat grown by an individual farmer would be almost completely responsive to the price he tried to charge, even though the total demand for wheat might be very insensitive to price.) Furthermore, the full extent of world competition with a single country's exports depends on more than how many other countries are already important exporters of the same goods. Potential as well as actual competition counts. If export duties did raise the world-market price of some product, competitive supplies might grow not merely as countries already exporting responded with greater production and reduced home consumption but also as new countries joined the list of exporters. Breakdowns of coffee and rubber price-support schemes, even though several exporting countries were trying to act together, furnish historical examples of this real possibility.

AN INDIRECT APPROACH TO EXPLOITING
EXPORT MONOPOLY

Still, we must not exaggerate. A cleverly set export duty could reap some gain at the foreigners' expense; it would not dry up their purchases entirely. Although foreign demand elasticities of realistic size would ordinarily hold the net national gain to a small fraction of the previous export value, there may be exceptions. If a country is specialized in supplying the great bulk of the total world supply of some agricultural or mineral product for which very few other places have the needed climate or resources, and if the total demand for the product is inherently quite inelastic, then the country has a usable monopoly position. Several countries do in fact dominate the world markets for their major export products, though whether their near-monopoly positions could survive long-run attempts to exploit them is less clear. Furthermore, the highly specialized resources that enable a country to dominate the world market for its major export product also tend to make its own supply of the product, as well as the foreign demand, rather inelastic. An export duty would therefore fall on domestic suppliers as well as on foreign buyers, and the dead loss from shrunken trade would make the net national gain smaller than the revenue squeezed from foreigners.

Realistically, a near-monopoly in selling exports is more plausible than a near-monopoly in buying imports. Ironically, then, one of the few academically respectable arguments for duties on trade comes closer to having practical relevance on the export side than on the import side. (The oil price increases imposed by the OPEC cartel are analytically very similar to export duties levied by agreement among the cartel members.) Yet export duties are politically less popular, as illustrated by their being prohibited in the U.S. Constitution.

Even when a country's near-monopoly position lies on its export side, an argument of sorts can be made for *import* duties as a crude substitute for export duties ruled out by political or other obstacles. Restricting import tends, indirectly, to restrict exports as well as so to raise their prices on the world market. By restraining import demand, tariffs keep the exchange rate of the home currency stronger and thus the foreign-currency prices of exports higher than they would otherwise be. (Under a system of fixed exchange rates but with automatic import-and-export-balancing tendencies allowed to work, the country's export prices would likewise be

higher than under free trade because the import restraint would make its
money supply larger and its general price level higher.) Some advantages
can even be claimed for this roundabout way of exploiting an export
monopoly: (1) The political popularity of import duties would help out-
flank opposition to export duties. (2) To some extent terms-of-trade improvement might be combined with protection of import-competing
industries to promote economic development—if the latter really were a
sound idea. (3) Although direct collaboration on export duties among
several countries exporting the same product might break down, politically
popular import duties might achieve a near-equivalent of this collaboration.

There are some obstacles to this indirect approach to exploiting an
export monopoly. The way that import duties affect export prices through
the exchange rate (or through the money supply and the general price
level) depends on the price-sensitivity of various import demands. A
rather low price-sensitivity of import demand, for example, would ordinarily
lessen the exchange-rate strengthening through which the indirect process
works. Anyway, an ideal program of exploiting an export position must
take account of home import demand as well as foreign export demand
elasticities. Actually, this complication bedevils the direct as well as
indirect approach; it is just more obvious with the latter, which has all the
complexities and impracticalities of the direct approach, and then some.
Its chief *distinctive* difficulty is its lack of selectivity. The most thorough
exploitation of foreigners would involve different rates of export duty on
different products and on sales to different foreign markets according to
different elasticities of foreign demand (just as import duties would
ideally differ by products and sources of supply). Yet the indirect approach,
using import duties, amounts to imposing some sort of average rate of
duty on all exports. This failure to discriminate among exports is probably
not important, however, for a country specialized in just one or two
products.* Still, just as there would have been some ideal rate of export
duty, so there would be some ideal degree of exchange rate strengthening
(or increase in the general price level) to be achieved through import
duties. In fact, some definite *pattern* of different duties on different
imports, taking account of their different supply and demand elasticities,
would theoretically be the best one, even though hardly attainable in

---

*And it is for such countries that something like the scheme outlined
here has been proposed. (See Raul Prebisch, "Commercial Policy in the
Underdeveloped Countries," *American Economic Review,* May 1959, pp.
251-73. While drawing on Prebisch's hints, the present discussion does not
pretend to be a faithful account of his proposals.)

practice. Still another difficulty with the indirect approach is that it gives obvious shelter against import competition and breeds vested interests that might well limit the controllers' freedom of maneuver.

TERMS OF TRADE: A CONCLUDING APPRAISAL

Besides noting the practical difficulties of both direct and indirect approaches to exploiting partial monopoly positions in importing and exporting, and besides noting the relatively small size of the gain theoretically attainable, we should ask who, exactly, stands to receive this gain. The consumers of imports and producers of exports, as such, certainly do not get it; the duties raise the prices they pay and lower the prices they receive. Instead, it is the government that gains by collecting taxes that in effect fall partly onto foreigners. The hope is that the government will use this revenue either to provide more public services than otherwise or else to set home taxes lower. Its citizens thus benefit in a rather indirect and uncertain way. (The particular uses made of the revenue would in principle affect what duty rates would most thoroughly exploit the foreigners. See pp. 142-43n. of Leland B. Yeager, "The Size of Gain from an Optimum Tariff," cited in note 8 above.)

Perhaps the closest approach to use of the terms-of-trade argument in actual policy discussions is the idea that a country might use tariffs or other controls to *resist a worsening* of its terms of trade when something unfavorable happens, such as a loss of export markets or an increase in import demand because of damage to production at home. This idea apparently was influential in European countries maintaining drastic trade and exchange controls in the first few years after World War II. But even for a country fallen on hard times, there is some optimum level or pattern of duties or controls; and still higher duties or tighter controls would do more harm than good. A country able to keep hard times from worsening its terms of trade could presumably have improved them in the first place; one wonders why it didn't. The most nearly plausible answer is that hard times give its government added incentive to pursue an optimum tariff policy. Anyway, there is little presumption that tariff increases remain a sensible response to recurrent difficulties, since each increase raises the chance that the tariff will be above the theoretically optimum level.

The terms-of-trade argument is a strictly nationalistic one. It tells how one country can gain, theoretically and probably only temporarily, at the expense of foreigners. Given the unrealistic assumption that one country's officials have the detailed facts and the nonpolitical tariff system needed to apply the theory, one should suppose that foreigners also know how to play the game. The outcome of retaliation and counterretaliation would be an all-around shrinkage of trade and probably a loss to most or even to all countries. Everyone cannot exploit everyone else. We may have some sympathy when poor countries specialized in primary products grasp at straws in attempts to exploit their rich overseas customers. The United States, though, would be inconsistent if it tried to exploit foreigners while at the same time spending billions of dollars a year to help them and even sympathizing with the questionable price-propping schemes of primary-producing countries. For reasons besides difficulties in practice and limited possibilities even in theory, trying to shape tariff policy according to the terms-of-trade argument would be especially inappropriate for the United States, which has particular responsibilities to set a good example.

Our unenthusiastic verdict does not mean that the space spent on the terms-of-trade argument has been wasted. We had to justify, not merely assert, our verdict, especially since the argument enjoys a prominent place in the academic literature. Economic theorists are fascinated by this and the few other tariff arguments that are formally valid, even though on a highly abstract plane. This one has even been described as "the only valid argument for protection as a means of maximizing economic welfare. . . ." The other arguments, to the extent that they are valid at all, are really arguments for government intervention in the domestic economy rather than in trade.* Tariff protection in such cases would conceivably be a second-best expedient when for some reason the appropriate domestic intervention could not be put into effect.[9] This assertion about other arguments is one we shall have to justify in the chapters that follow.

---

*The only exception we can think of to this assertion would be the argument that importation of certain foreign goods is undesirable as such, perhaps for "noneconomic" reasons (cf. Harry G. Johnson, "Optimal Trade Intervention in the Presence of Economic Distortions," pp. 32-24, cited in note 9).

NOTES

1. Jacob Viner, in *Foreign Economic Policy,* hearing before a subcommittee of the Joint Economic Committee (Washington, D.C.: Government Printing Office, 1962), p. 26.

2. The following is adapted from J. E. Meade, *Trade and Welfare* (London: Oxford University Press, 1955), pp. 190-96. See also Ch. 5 of Meade's separate *Mathematical Supplement,* (London: Oxford University Press, 1955).

3. *Innocence Abroad* (New York: American Tariff League, 1955), pp. 22-23. It is not clear how the example arrives at the $26 figure; it must depend not only on tax rates but also on tacit assumptions about profit margins and wage payments.

4. Letter introduced by Senator Malone into the *Congressional Record* of May 18, 1954, cited in Bidwell, *What the Tariff Means to American Industries* (New York: Harper, 1956), p. 250.

5. 1962 HW&M IV 2092 (see Chapter 1, note 9).

6. Lewis E. Lloyd, *Tariffs: The Case for Protection* (New York: Devin-Adair, 1955), pp. 28-29.

7. Cf. C. P. Kindleberger in *Foreign Trade Policy* (1958), p. 74. (See Chapter 1, note 5.)

8. For the formulas used in calculating these numbers, as well as the derivations of the formulas and the underlying assumptions, see Leland B. Yeager, "The Size of Gain from an Optimum Tariff," *Southern Economic Journal,* October 1964, pp. 140-48.

9. Harry G. Johnson, "Optimal Trade Intervention in the Presence of Domestic Distortions," in Robert E. Baldwin et al., *Trade, Growth, and the Balance of Payments* (Chicago: Rand-McNally, 1965), p. 5.

12

"SECOND-BEST" POLICY

CORRECTING DIVERGENCES

This chapter considers a range of problems of which at least three examples have appeared in earlier chapters. The first concerned an industry supporting national security by providing a "service of availability" not salable on the market; the second, a selective domestic tax possibly justifying an import duty to match; and the third, an opportunity to exploit a degree of buying or selling monopoly on the world market. In all these examples, the domestic price system is distorted: prices do not tell private decision-makers what the true terms of choice are from the national point of view. The third example might seem to involve an external, not an internal, distortion, since it concerns the country's position on the world market. Still, it has a domestic-distortion aspect: the national and private points of view diverge in decisions about trade. In that sense the domestic price signals are false.

It would be convenient if we could debate international trade policy on the assumption of a distortion-free home economy with a "correct" distribution of income. Since this "first-best" situation is unattainable, however, we must seek a "second-best" alternative. To lessen the damage caused by false prices, some new distortions may be appropriate as a partial offset to irremovable ones. A tariff or other trade barrier may be introduced in the hope that the damage it does will be less than damage it undoes. This is all quite abstract, but it goes far toward explaining why few economists endorse free trade without qualification. A careful student of trade policy realizes what assumptions underlie the standard demonstration of the gains from free trade and of what leads businessmen to reap this gain for their country. An airtight demonstration presupposes that money prices and costs of things produced correctly measure their real costs in other things forgone. If they do not, the demonstration loses its definiteness; and tariffs or quotas may seem useful to make the best of a less-than-ideal situation.

Suppose, for example, that a definite quantity of clothing costs more money on the home market than a definite quantity of wheat but that the two goods are worth the same on the world market. (For simplicity we assume that these are the only two tradable goods.) Our businessmen have a profit incentive to export wheat and import clothing, which seems to be in the national interest also. But suppose the home-market prices are false ones: instead of costing more per unit than wheat, clothing really costs less in other production sacrificed. Private and national viewpoints diverge.* In producing higher-actual-cost wheat to trade for clothing on the world market, our country's businessmen are throwing resources away. Costs, prices, and profits *in money* make trade flow perversely, unless the government somehow compensates for the falsity of price signals, as by putting a tariff on clothing. (There is no presumption, of course, that price falsities are generally of kinds that motivate too much trade; they might just as well motivate too little.)

TAXES AND TARIFFS

Probably the most easily understandable source of price falsity is a selective domestic excise tax of the kind mentioned in the last chapter. To put the matter in a way that will be convenient in describing other distortions, the tax makes domestic clothing production less attractive from the private producer's point of view than from the national point of view. The clothing manufacturer collects only part of the total value of his output; the rest goes to the government as tax revenue. Or, in other words, the private cost of clothing exceeds the social cost, since what the government collects is a cost to private parties but not to the country as a whole. The divergence between private and social values or private and social costs makes domestic clothing production too small and imports too large in comparison with what would happen at unfalsified prices.

One apparently paradoxical application of the "second-best" argument shows that if something blocks the removal of *all* import duties, it might

---

*The reader should appreciate the crucial difference between this example and the one given on p. 141. There, the distortion occurred in the foreign economy; here, it occurs in the home economy.

not be desirable to remove all of the others that could be removed; retaining some of these, or even imposing some new duties afresh, might compensate for the irremovable ones. Suppose, for example, that our imaginary country levies an import duty on butter but not on oleomargarine. As a result, the cost ratio of imported butter to imported oleo is higher from the private than from the national point of view, skewing choices in favor of oleo. Putting a duty on oleo as well might be a useful corrective. Of course, this would further falsify the prices that had been skewing choices between both of the imports on the one hand and domestic substitutes on the other hand; but if there was little of this substitutability anyway and thus little scope for wrong skewing of any choice other than the choice between the imported butter and imported oleo, the correction achieved by adding an oleo import duty might conceivably outweigh any damage done.

A similar example involves one product imported from more than one foreign source. A duty on widgets from Ruritania but not from Graustark makes importers favor the latter source, even though, we assume, Ruritanian widgets are actually cheaper, not counting the duty (and the duty does *not* count from our *national* point of view, since our government and not the foreigners would collect it). A duty on Graustarkian widgets would help correct for the skewing of importers' choices. Of course, it would unfortunately tend to skew choices still further in favor of still-higher-cost home widgets; but if the scope for this skewing was slight, the case for the new duty would be quite the same as for the oleo duty in the last example. Consider the matter from the other end; we start with uniform duties on widgets from all sources and contemplate adopting free trade with Graustark only. The benefits of the widget trade created through lowering the price to our private consumers might quite conceivably be outweighed by the loss from diverting trade from a lower-cost to a higher-cost foreign source.

A case is even conceivable in which our avoiding free trade would benefit foreigners. Suppose that the tariffs of Ruritania and Graustark are irremovable for some reason and that they particularly hamper trade between those two countries. Their tariffs spread costs to producers and values to consumers apart, leaving private merchants no incentive to expand trade beyond its actual volume. Yet an expansion would be beneficial from the national viewpoints of the two countries because the excess of value over cost on the additional trade would accrue to the two governments as tariff revenue. How might we, a third country, improve this situation? By levying duties on our imports and thus shrinking Ruritania's and Graustark's trade with us, we might cause them to expand their trade between themselves. Conceivably their benefit on this expansion might outweigh the combined loss that we and they felt from the shrinkage of trade between them and us.

This happy result is least unlikely if very low duties on our imports, constituting only slight value-over-cost divergence on our trade with the foreigners, would nevertheless lead the foreigners greatly to expand their trade between themselves. Since their duties on their mutual trade are assumed to be high, making value greatly exceed cost, their expansion of this trade could add more to world welfare than was lost by the shrinkage of the low-excess-of-value-over-cost trade between them and us.

Various commodity interrelations might expand trade between the foreigners even in items besides those we imported or exported less of than before. For example, our reduced imports of blankets from Ruritania might promote sales not only of blankets but also of beds from Ruritania to Graustark; and a fall in our sales of apples to Ruritania (because of the tendency of an export shrinkage to match our import shrinkage) might stimulate Ruritanian imports of pears as well as of apples from Graustark. Our cut in shoe imports from Graustark might cause Graustark to sell more socks as well as shoes to Ruritania, and our trade-balancing decline in fish exports might cause some of the foreigners to import more meat from the others. For any definite pattern of adjustment in trade volumes, the higher are the tariff-caused excesses of value over cost on the foreigners' expanding trade and the smaller are the newly tariff-caused excesses of value over cost on our shrinking import trade, the more plausibly could the overall result turn out favorable from some sort of world viewpoint.[1]

Possibilities like these are of great theoretical interest, for they rob the case for free trade by one country (unilateral free trade, if necessary) of any *general* validity it might have been thought to have. The case is not necessarily valid even from the standpoint of *world* welfare. Yet we need not belabor why the abstract possibilities we have imagined are hardly to be taken as serious policy advice in the real world.

PRICE FLOORS AND SUPPORTS

Price floors or supports provide other examples of how governments may falsify prices. Suppose the government simply decrees an artificially high minimum legal price for some commodity. Consumers accordingly restrict their consumption to the amount per time period at which the "last" unit they consume does have a value to them as high as the artificial price. Although domestic producers could expand their output at a cost below this price, they do not do so because they are forbidden to cut their price to sell the additional output. Yet this suppressed additional output would be worth more to consumers than its actual cost. Since domestic production is in this sense already too small, it might seem reasonable not to worsen this problem due to the price floor by letting competing imports come in duty-free.

Instead of simply decreeing a floor price, the government might support the price by buying up the commodity, thereby stimulating domestic production as well as restraining consumption. The government's accumulation of troublesome surpluses would show that the social value of the commodity was not as high as the artificial price. It would only make matters worse to let the supported price attract duty-free imports, since this price—paid ultimately in export products—would exceed the commodity's social value. Allowing consumers to buy imports free of duty would also increase the share of domestic production that the government would have to stockpile to maintain the support price.

Price support of a raw material is a particularly interesting case. The falsely high money cost of clothing in our example on p. 204 might be due to price support of the cotton that goes into it. Until August 1964 the U.S. government supported the price of cotton, subsidizing exports by up to 8.5 cents a pound to make American cotton competitive on the world market, yet withholding any subsidy from domestic cotton textile mills as an offset to the supported price they had to pay. Since subsidized exports probably made the world cotton price somewhat lower than it otherwise would have been, the government was not only burdening American textile manufacturers by making their raw material artificially expensive but also actually aiding their foreign competitors. In the absence of any other remedy, this created a formally valid case for a further intervention.

Professor Jacob Viner, who described himself as a 98 percent free-trader, was one of many economists who recognized the case for a compensatory duty on cotton-textile imports:

I would not say that cotton costs the American textile manufacturer all of the export subsidy on the amount of cotton in each yard of cloth he produces, but the export subsidy is undoubtedly a handicap to him in his competition with foreign textiles. I would see nothing wrong in principle in some kind of an adjustment for that. Abandonment of the export duty [subsidy] on the cotton would be my preferred solution. But I am again assuming that politics will continue to be a necessary and desirable ingredient of American life, and that such things as export subsidies on cotton are an inevitable by-product. I would then certainly sympathetically examine whether it isn't in the interest of the national economy that the textile industry should in some way be relieved of the burden of an artificial cheapening for its foreign competitors of one of its ingredients.[2]

In other words, American cotton-textile production perhaps deserved protection against import competition. The social cost of that production was less than its private cost, to phrase essentially the same point in another way. Every pound of cotton used at home instead of dumped abroad saved the United States the export subsidy; yet private American producers and consumers of textiles could hardly have taken this national saving into account in their own decisions. Textile import restrictions could achieve some of this saving, however, by expanding the domestic manufacture of cotton goods, thus reducing the amount of cotton left over to be exported with the government subsidy.

American textile producers complained about the "unnatural" or "unfair" cost advantage that their foreign competitors enjoyed. Ordinarily, such complaints are pointless, since the reason for low costs abroad is irrelevant. But the cotton subsidy posed an exception: foreigners enjoyed their cost advantage at the expense of American taxpayers, and the more of this advantage they took, the greater was the American expense. Any cost saving in buying foreign rather than American textiles was not as great for the United States as a whole as it was for the private buyer, since the U.S. government was indirectly paying part of what the private buyer saved by choosing the import. The case for import restrictions to correct for this divergence of viewpoints had some formal validity.*

The "voluntary" restrictions on cotton textile exports to the United States negotiated under the Long-Term Arrangement of 1962 may therefore have had a degree of legitimacy on economic grounds. If the damage introduced by these restrictions was more than outweighed by the amount by which they reduced the damage attributable to cotton price supports, the LTA would have yielded a net economic gain for the United States. We reflect at greater length below on the question whether, in fact, it is likely to have done so.

---

*It is instructive to ponder this exception to our much-emphasized scorn of the *reason* why foreign goods are cheap. The reason does not matter to us when it is something entirely internal to the foreign economy—"exploitation" of labor, other foreign price distortions, or whatnot. The present case is an exception because the reason for the foreign cheapness, instead of being entirely internal to the foreign economy, involved conditions inside the American economy as well—in this case, taxing and spending by the U.S. government.

MONOPOLY

Monopoly causes a distortion much as if the monopolist himself, rather than the government, were imposing a tax or a price floor on an otherwise competitive industry. The monopolistically high price misrepresents the true domestic cost of the product in alternatives sacrificed; not all of what consumers pay to the monopolist represents the withdrawal of labor and other resources from other lines of production. Since the "last" unit bought per time period is worth as much to consumers as the padded price they pay, the value of additional domestic output would still exceed its cost in terms of other kinds of output sacrificed. In this sense the domestic industry is too small; and since imports divert some purchases away from it, they are too large.* Something can be said for a partial corrective in the form of an import duty.

> If apparent costs only equal true costs under conditions of perfect competition, and competition hardly ever is perfect, the bottom seems to drop out of the Free Trade argument. This is in fact a fair description of the state of mind which quite a number of economic students seem to have reached.[3]

It is noteworthy that the foregoing comparisons of social value and cost and of true and apparent costs do not count the monopoly profit transferred from consumers to the monopolist as part of social cost. The monopolist is part of the national economy or society, and what he gets is not lost to it. (To society defined as not counting him, however, his monopoly profit *would* be a genuine cost.)

The tariff "remedy" for the monopoly distortion is a rather odd one. The tariff raises the price of competing imports, shunts demand toward the domestic monopolist, and allows him to raise his price further, even though it already was too high in comparison with genuine costs. Even though the remedy does improve the efficiency of the country's pattern of production

---

*There is no contradiction in talking of a *monopoly* product facing *competition* from imports, for "monopoly" never realistically means complete absence of competition. Here, "monopoly" simply means that competition at home is weak enough to leave the monopolist considerable room to set his price as he sees fit in the light of demand, without having to pass on to consumers all or most of any cost advantage he may have over foreign producers.

and resource use, it is the monopolist, not consumers, who reaps the gain from this improvement. In fact, he gets all the gain and then some (unless some clever tax accompanies the tariff to recapture some of the monopolist's gain for the government). Consumers as such lose. They not only turn from imports to the domestic product but also, because of the boosted price, cut their total consumption from the two sources combined. The worsened falsity of the price from the consumers' point of view makes the pattern of consumption even less efficient than before. Furthermore, the case for the tariff on grounds of production efficiency seems to depend on a questionable tacit assumption that the degree of monopoly is fixed and unalterable. Yet one argument for free trade is that it tends to prevent or break down monopoly, whereas a tariff promotes it. If import restriction has reduced competition to a degree now questionably taken for granted, the argument seems to justify further protection, even though it would not have justified its original introduction. Such an argument surely is suspect, especially considering that protection probably lessens the degree of competition.[4] The case for tariffs that it provides is only a theoretical curiosity, and is hardly ever used in practical politics.*

RIGIDITIES

Another source of distortion, loosely akin to taxes, price supports, and monopoly, is cost and price rigidities due to such things as minimum-wage laws, union pressure, or even just a strong feeling that wage cuts are wicked. Returning to our earlier example of clothing, let us suppose that real costs are below money costs because some unemployed labor and other idle resources are "attached" to the industry: additional clothing production would cost the money spent to hire these idle resources but would cost no diversion of resources from other industries nor any production cutbacks there. Businessmen in the clothing industry must decide on production and employment in view of money prices and costs. They cannot afford to consider how low the costs may be in production cutbacks forced elsewhere, even though this is what counts from the national point of view.

---

*The marketing director of the California Almond Growers Exchange came close to using the argument, apparently without realizing it. His testimony suggested that his industry required continued tariff protection to shelter the pricing practices it followed under a government-fostered cartel. (See 1962 HW&M III 1640-48.)

The specific trouble in this case is not that resources attached to the clothing industry could transfer into other lines of production only with great difficulty. Whether or not the transfer is difficult, the discrepancy between money and real costs is due, instead, to inflexibility in wage rates and other resource prices.

With true flexibility, no obstacles would keep the price of a resource from adjusting to make its supply and demand equal. Flexibility means lack of obstacles to this adjustment; it does not mean that clothing wages would necessarily fall sharply in the face of intensified import competition. This would not happen if clothing workers saw good opportunities to transfer easily into other jobs. Or it would not happen if the labor supply were very price-sensitive—for example, if many women cared little about having a job and would stay home rather than accept appreciably lower wages. (Housework or leisure are themselves valuable, like other goods besides clothing that labor can produce.) But perhaps clothing workers have little usefulness in other lines of production, or could transfer only with great difficulty and unpleasantness, and also have little desire for or cannot afford additional leisure. These realities about the supply of labor would reflect themselves in a flexible wage rate. The money cost of employing labor from the private viewpoint of clothing firms would then correctly reflect how abundant such labor was and how small the other production opportunities sacrificed were. It would be regrettable if the opportunities open to clothing workers were so extremely poor and narrow, but regrettable realities are not the same thing as a distortion of the price system out of line with reality. Incidentally, flexibility of wages would benefit rather than harm the clothing workers to whom it gave the choice between a low-paying job and no job at all, instead of just leaving them with no job and no choice.

If rigidities are distorting money costs but we reject the idea of allowing import competition to help break them down, we can make a theoretical case for a tariff against imports so that the domestic industry will expand more nearly as its lower real costs recommend.

EXTERNALITIES

The "external" costs and benefits discussed in Chapter 3 (with examples of smoky chimneys, apple nectar for bees, saxophones, and lawn care) admittedly seem farfetched in tariff arguments; yet they do illustrate additional kinds of divergence between private and social viewpoints that block unqualified endorsement of free trade. The theory of externalities and of possible correctives for them is very important for understanding theoretical discussions of economic policy. A remarkable number of apparently distinct arguments for government operation or control of particular activities turn out, on examination, to be hardly more than instances of the "externalities" case. Our interest in appraising these arguments, including tariff arguments, requires some attention to them. We would not be justified in skimming quickly over them just because we think they have been carried to farfetched extremes; that judgment is a conclusion into which our readers deserve some insight.

Simple examples such as we have already given usefully dramatize what the worry over externalities is all about. Less childish examples point to such things as the training of workers that certain manufacturing firms might incidentally provide, at a cost to themselves, without being able to count on full payment for the benefits created. Similarly, the benefits of research may become generally available and not remain under the control of the firms that bore the expense. Research might develop production methods particularly suited to the home country and distinct from methods used abroad to produce the same products under different conditions. An industry or firm might generate other nonsalable benefits in the form of general familiarity with industrial affairs. Its growth might help provide a market for transportation, communications, information, research, and other services; it might help provide scope for large-scale economies in producing such things as electricity. In doing so, it would lower the costs of other industries or firms. External benefits of these kinds, including the one involving worker training, will deserve broader and fuller consideration in the sections on infant industries and general economic development in the next chapter.

What does all this have to do with trade policy? The point is that a domestic firm may provide any of numerous side benefits by producing certain goods or by employing certain factors of production. Though valuable to society, these side benefits do not command a price for the firm generating them. Since, in deciding how much to produce, the firm compares the cost of an additional unit of output only with the additional money to be received for that unit, its output or its employment of factors will be too small from the national point of view—if, indeed, the firm even comes into existence to produce anything at all. Protection against imports, among other measures, could expand its activity.

Even here, though, in advance of appraising second-best tariff arguments generally, a warning is in order against the fallacy of composition. Protection might be sensible for a particular firm or narrowly defined industry known to provide external benefits in an especially high degree, but not indiscriminate protection. Selectivity is needed—assuming the necessary theoretical acumen, factual knowledge, and freedom from political distortion. Since resources are scarce, a policy of expanding some lines of production means shrinking others. The shrunken others might have provided equally or more important external benefits than the lines of production artificially aided. The need for selectivity is increased by tariffs or quota restrictions on foreign inputs entering into the favored lines of production. The appropriate degree of "effective protection" (see above, pp. 62-65) must somehow be provided for those domestic activities from which the coveted external benefits are sought.

External *costs* are still more farfetched in tariff arguments. Export industries might spew out smoke, might cut timber in a way that caused erosion on other people's land, and so forth. Since these social costs would not enter as money costs into their own profit calculations, the export industries would produce at a higher-than-ideal level. If no direct remedy could be applied, a crude substitute would be to tax imports so as indirectly to restrain exports and export production. This is just a possible argument, for there is no general presumption that export industries are more likely than others to inflict external costs.

Another farfetched case supposes external costs in non-import-competing production generally rather than in export production especially. If these domestic industries produce at too high a level because they inflict social costs without counting them, it follows that the other industries, those competing with imports and assumed *not* to inflict uncounted costs, produce at too low a level from the social point of view. Restraining their import competition would allow them to draw resources away from the overexpanded socially costly industries.

External costs and benefits in consumption as well as in production could figure in tariff arguments. We have already recognized a possible case for taxing oil imports. But we need not stop there. One might want tariffs against cigarettes and saxophones—or even against furs because they make the friends of their wearers unhappily envious. Or perhaps the trouble with imports is not that they actually harm persons other than their own consumers but simply that they fail to benefit these other persons as some domestically produced consumer goods might. Education and educational materials are a supposed example; they not only benefit their own buyers but also help improve the general character of the society. Taxing imports, especially of things (like wine) that serve frivolous wants, might help divert consumer spending to the socially beneficial domestic goods. However legitimate or fanciful these examples may appear, they are properly regarded as externality arguments. Though some commentators might characterize them as "noneconomic" arguments, they share the premise that certain domestic activities competing with imports for the consumer's dollar deserve protection because they confer social benefits beyond their marketable benefits.

Externality arguments such as these clearly do not concern international trade *in particular*. They make an abstract case of sorts for government meddling generally, and international trade is just one of many aspects of life that supposedly should not go uncontrolled.

THE HEIGHT OF SECOND-BEST DUTIES

Though opposite distortions are just as easily conceivable, our examples have illustrated what might make domestic production of nontraded goods too small and both import consumption and export production too large. Dismissing the ideal removal of all distortions as impossible, can we say anything about how high corrective import duties (or equivalent quotas) should be to achieve a second-best solution? In approaching this question, it is helpful to see the distortion in a too-small industry as a "wedge" holding the social value of additional output per time period above its additional cost. Measures to expand output are worthwhile according to the size of this wedge. As output does expand, the wedge shrinks on both sides; its upper side comes down as still further additions to the supply of the product become less valuable to consumers, and its lower side rises as physical costs of production rise or at least as the sacrifice of other products from which resources are diverted becomes increasingly significant.

As for an import being restricted to divert demand to the otherwise too-small home industry, the duty on it is itself a wedge between social value and social cost; the duty-inclusive price measures the value of an additional unit to consumers, while the price without duty measures the cost to the country.* The task of the policy-maker is to balance the loss of the

---

*Trade restriction does not impose a national loss per unit of imports destroyed fully equal to the duty if it beats down the price to foreigners. Here, for the simplicity and tidiness of talking about one thing at a time, we assume a constant foreign supply price and neglect this possibility of terms-of-trade improvement. The interested reader may himself modify the analysis that follows. A duty adopted for both second-best and terms-of-trade reasons is presumably higher than one adopted for one reason only.

We feel obliged to put on record another qualification about the statement in the text. It is strictly true that "the duty-inclusive price measures the value of an additional unit to consumers, while the price without duty measures the cost to the country" only if all other kinds of production and consumption in the economy are free of uncorrected value-cost divergences. In reality, of course, they are not. The same sort of qualification has to be made about all examples of correcting particular distortions in accordance with the second-value-over-cost wedge on excluded imports against the gain of value-over-cost-wedge on expanded home production. The ideal duty is just this high: increasing it slightly would make the further wedge-times-quantity loss from further import shrinkage exceed the further wedge-times-quantity gain on further home expansion, whereas slightly cutting the duty would make the wedge-times-quantity gain from import expansion fall short of the wedge-times-quantity loss from shrinkage of home production. This ideal import duty rate is unlikely to be fully as high as the rate of domestic social-value-over-cost divergence that it is supposed to correct for.[5] The "last step" from a duty very nearly this high to a duty at the full equal-divergence rate would make the loss per unit on import shrinkage equal to the gain per unit on home output expansion; yet the further import shrinkage and its chunk of loss would exceed the further home expansion and its chunk of gain. Expanded home output would not fully match the cutback in imports, since the rise in price-plus-duty would shrink total consumption of the product. (One may ask what becomes of the resources freed from producing exports to pay for imports and not fully absorbed into the import-competing industry. The answer is that they go into other lines of production at home, including lines lacking any social-value-over-cost divergence that would make their expansion especially desirable.)

This explanation now permits the whole matter to be restated more simply. Starting with an import duty that is very small compared to the domestic divergence to be compensated for, a slight increase would add more to welfare than it took away. Although the duty increase shrank imports more than it expanded competing home output, the welfare loss per unit on import shrinkage would be smaller than the welfare gain per unit on home expansion. At the other extreme, with the duty fully equal to the domestic divergence, the loss per unit on import shrinkage does equal the gain per unit on domestic expansion; furthermore, the "last step" toward this level of duty has done net damage by causing more import shrinkage than domestic expansion. It follows that the "ideal" rate of compensatory import duty is somewhere in between zero and the rate of domestic divergence. (The conclusion in Chapter 11 about an import duty matching

---

best theory. The difficulty emphasizes how wide the gap may be between imagining formally valid cases for corrective interventions in the abstract and devising and applying beneficial interventions in the complex and changing real world. This gap looms all the larger when we recall how nominal tariff rates and effective rates of protection may diverge in degrees almost impossible in practice to measure.

a domestic excise tax turns out to be a particular application of this more general principle.) Even roughly estimating a specific figure for the ideal compensatory duty rate is just one of the many difficulties with putting the second-best case for tariffs into actual practice. Realizing that the unknown ideal rate is lower than the divergence to be compensated for, anyway, should further dampen enthusiasm for trying to apply the second-best case in practice.

AN APPRAISAL OF THE SECOND-BEST CASE

A few things remain to be said about second-best tariff arguments as a group. Most obviously, the remedy for domestic distortions provided by domestic measures is more precise and more direct than the remedy provided by external measures. Tariffs are, after all, "second best." While a tariff or equivalent quota may move the pattern of production in the direction of what would correspond to a distortion-free economy, it also introduces a new distortion of its own by depriving the consumer of an opportunity to adjust his consumption to his preferences in view of world-market prices. The tariff distorts those prices as he perceives them, thereby causing too little of the dutiable good to be imported. In short, the tariff achieves a more nearly ideal pattern of production at the cost of a less ideal pattern of consumption. There is no presumption that the production gain exceeds the consumption loss; the supposedly corrective tariff might do more harm than good. Subsidizing the favored industry out of taxes on less favored industries could ideally avoid this consumption cost.

Problems of distorted prices, of discrepancies between social value and social cost, and of second-best remedies provide abstract theoretical cases for all sorts of government interventions throughout the economic system; it is really "reaching" to use them as serious arguments for pinching and twisting the foreign-trade sector in particular. The issue of free trade versus controls applies more broadly than to imports alone.

Equally important, the whole topic of second-best solutions is largely a theoretical toy—or so we hope—though some distinctive applications of it do deserve to be taken seriously. Theoretical toys are not to be despised; there is no need to decree how economists should amuse themselves and how they should practice making delicate distinctions. Reviewing second-best cases is good preparation for coping with policy arguments that fatuously rely on mere theoretical curiosities. The review is also worth while as a reminder of how a moderately competent theorist can dredge up arguments, intellectually respectable and sound in abstract principle, for almost any policy plausible enough to enjoy political support.* Precisely this possibility of concocting plausible cases for all sorts of government interventions warns against overenthusiasm for any one of them. Each has repercussions on the pattern of other interventions that would be ideal. Adapting each one not only to the distortions of a free economy but also to the distortions caused by all other interventions is hardly practical. All economists might agree on the abstract proposition that some specific but unknowable pattern of taxes and controls and import duties would (temporarily) be superior to free trade at home and internationally. Yet because they could not know and agree on what specific actual pattern would be ideal, their abstract agreement would be empty. Furthermore, each intervention has political and administrative as well as purely economic repercussions. Any large fraction of the individually plausible interventions, if they were all attempted together, would change the whole character of the economy, the political system, and the society. It is necessary to be selective, adopting only the minority of interventions for which the case is most persuasive. Deciding on them ties in with a broader choice between types of economic system—the market economy and price system on the one hand or central planning on the other.

Some protectionists do call for what would amount to detailed government economic planning. This does not necessarily mean an economic system in which a central bureau makes and enforces all production and resource-allocation decisions; it might mean a price system subjected to detailed manipulation. To do a good job, the manipulators would need the same overview of the economy and the same detailed factual grasp of the interdependence of all its activities and sectors that outright planners would need. In that implausible case, a drift into outright central planning would be understandable. The Manufacturing Chemists' Association has provided an example of planning-minded protectionism. Referring to the tremendous variety of products its industry produces, it argued as follows for individual rates of duty set "selectively in accordance with need":

Obviously the broad spectrum of related products of mines, wells, fields, forests, streams, sea water and the atmosphere, permits of few hard and fast generalizations as to the need for tariff protection. Production ranges from millions of tons to a few milligrams. Processes vary from the simplest chemical reaction

---

*"There is no end to the variety of arguments which can be found to defend any given course of action by anybody who has once decided to pursue it." (John Black, *Oxford Economic Papers,* June 1959, p. 208.)

vessels to the most intricate complexes of multiple-stage equipment. Some lend themselves to a high degree of automation; others require vast amounts of skilled labor per unit of output. Some are continuous; many involve batch operations. Some products are inevitably produced in relatively fixed proportions as byproducts of other operations, yet must be used or marketed.

For these reasons, this association has consistently advocated appropriate measures to offset differences in the cost of producing chemicals at home and abroad. It believes that customs duties assessed on imports constitute the most efficacious means of providing such protection, and that rates of duty should be established selectively in accordance with need. Hence, it has opposed, and will continue to oppose, across-the-board chances— increases or reductions in tariff rates.[6]

The protectionist slogan that free trade may be right in theory but wrong in practice becomes more sensible (if the theory-versus-practice distinction were not itself nonsense) when the word "protectionism" replaces "free trade."* Drawing up tariff schedules in even rough accordance with the intellectually respectable protectionist theories would require knowing how sensitively production, consumption, and imports would respond to price changes caused by import duties, and how these responses would change over time, as well as how interference in the market for each particular thing would directly and indirectly affect the markets for all other things. It would involve adjusting tariff rates frequently to keep abreast of the changes continuously occurring in everything affecting supplies and demands and the sensitivity of responses to price changes. In addition, it would require the tariff-makers to have immunity from being pressured or misled by the clamor of special interests. Reality is different. "The result is, and always must be, the enactment of a tariff which resembles the theoretical protectionist's idea of what a protective tariff should be about as closely as a bucketful of paint thrown against a wall resembles the fresco of a Raphael. . . . Even a rough approximation to the protective theory is impossible. There never has been a protective tariff that satisfied protectionists, and there never can be."[7] It is no answer to say that it is good enough to apply respectable protectionist theory in a rough and ready way. Apart from the difficulty of even coming close to a second-best optimum, the obvious reply

---

*Professor Milton Friedman has turned the theory-versus-practice slogan against its users in pretty much the same way as is attempted here. (See *A Program for Monetary Stability* [New York: Fordham University Press, 1959], p. 98.)

remains open that the uncorrected free market, too, can do a rough and ready good job (for its imperfections are, by comparison, fringe ones), and without all the turmoil of trying to apply protectionist theory.

As Harry Johnson has mercilessly observed,

> The fundamental problem is that . . . determination of the conditions under which a second-best policy actually leads to an improvement of social welfare requires detailed theoretical and empirical investigation by a first-best economist. Unfortunately policy is generally formulated by fourth-best economists and administered by third-best economists; it is therefore very unlikely that a second-best welfare optimum will result from policies based on second-best arguments.[8]

A related difficulty centers on stability versus instability in policy. Tariff rates continually adjusted to changing conditions, as they would have to be in pursuit of a second-best optimum, would clash with the objective of having a reliable framework within which everyone can plan his own affairs. Changes in controls and taxes and other rules of the game are more disruptive than changes in prices and quantities, whose continuous free-market adaptations to wants, resources, and technology are part of the game itself. Economic policy is most constructive when it sets a broad framework of institutions and known rules and avoids continual fiddling with details.

Another reason why second-best arguments are "wrong in practice" even if "right in theory" centers around a dilemma. On the one horn, the case for a particular import duty or other intervention as part of a comprehensive program is stronger than the case for it alone. The last section of Chapter 4 suggests just how comprehensive an investigation of tariff rates is required for a determination of the rate at which a given activity is effectively protected. This point about effective protection is, however, just one indication of the general interdependence of each trade-policy measure with the others. Each intervention touches off repercussions to which, ideally, all others should be adapted; all, ideally, would have to be planned as interlocking parts of a consistent program.

On the other horn of the dilemma, the case for a particular intervention is strongest if it is to be the only one. Interventions themselves have external diseconomies: each additional one complicates the administrative, legislative, and electoral tasks of choosing, operating, and supervising all others.* Applying theoretical-curiosity remedies to more than a tiny fraction

---

*Milton Friedman has stressed the possible external diseconomies ("neighborhood effects," as he calls them) of government intervention,

of all departures from ideal conditions would require an extreme degree of theoretical and factual expertise and could hardly be done by parliamentary procedures. Experts would inevitably have a good deal of independence, if for no other reason than that others would have trouble keeping track of what they were doing and why. Legislators are not without influence over experts; but the influence is often likely to be piecemeal and capricious, based on incomplete information and responsive to lopsided political pressures.

An illustration of this dilemma is provided by the discussion above (pp. 4-5) of the cotton arrangement of 1962 and its eventual expansion into a comprehensive system of textile controls. The cotton-price-support system did create a theoretically plausible case for import restrictions on cotton textiles, as we recognized earlier in this chapter. It is most unlikely that voluntary restraints on foreign exporters of cotton textiles were imposed, in the first place, for any other reason than to accommodate a politically powerful special interest whose worsening economic condition was only marginally influenced by price support of its raw material. American textile producers were granted a 6.5¢ per pound subsidy in 1964 to make up for the price support, which was itself subsequently abandoned (along with the subsidy) for an "acreage-reduction" system. The latter system was abandoned in 1970 for still another price-support system, which nevertheless set the "target price" so low that no payments have been made under it since 1973. The Long-Term Arrangement of 1962 was not negotiated for second-best reasons; but even if it had been, the argument that would have given it some legitimacy has been made inapplicable by removal of the government-imposed price distortion in question. Meanwhile, the government has broadened the controls on textiles to keep imports from almost entirely displacing U.S.-made cotton goods.

In short, free trade can be put into practice; ideally compensatory second-best policy cannot. Free trade is a meaningful, specific, discussable policy proposal; ideal protectionism is not.

Economists should try to be clear about what bearing, if any, their theories have on policy-making in the real world. Discussing hypothetical policies may be fun. It may be good training. It may be an effective way of expounding some strands of theory. But it should not be allowed to generate a false, unintended impression of relevance to the real world. Serious writers have a responsibility to be clear, and this includes anticipating and so far as possible preventing any wrong inferences that their readers might otherwise make.

---

particularly in impairing freedom. See his *Capitalism and Freedom* (Chicago: University of Chicago Press, 1962), pp. 31-32.

NOTES

1. Our examples are of the same general type as J. E. Meade has made so familiar in his *Trade and Welfare* (London: Oxford University Press, 1955), pp. 200-25.

2. Jacob Viner, in *Foreign Economic Policy* (1962), p. 26. (SeeChapter 11, note 1.)

3. John R. Hicks, "Free Trade and Modern Economics," in *Essays in World Economics* (Oxford: Clarendon Press, 1959), p. 46.

4. Ibid., p. 47, and John Black, "Arguments for Tariffs," *Oxford University Papers,* June 1959, p. 203.

5. Cf. J. E. Meade, *Trade and Welfare,* op. cit., pp. 228-30.

6. In *Foreign Trade Policy* (1958), p. 1030. (See Chapter 1, note 5.)

7. Henry George, *Protection or Free Trade* (New York: Doubleday, Page, 1905) pp. 100, 101-02.

8. In McDougall and Snape, eds., *Studies in International Economics* (Amsterdam: North-Holland, 1970), p. 101.

13

DIVERSIFICATION
AND DEVELOPMENT

This chapter asks how good a case can be made for tariffs under conditions that hardly characterize the United States. It considers some ostensibly dynamic theories. The effects they envisage outweigh the static effects considered in earlier chapters. Suppose that adopting protection cuts 5 percent from the current level of real national income through misallocation of resources as explained by static theory. This initial loss would soon be amply repaid if protection helped change the character of the country's economy enough to raise the sustainable annual rate of growth by, say, 1 percentage point. Quite true; but the "if" is crucial. Can protection in fact yield any such marvelous result? If so, how? A respectable case for protection in underdeveloped countries almost necessarily appeals to some divergences between private and social viewpoints formally akin to those noted in Chapter 12.

DIVERSIFICATION

In one respect, the case for tariffs to promote diversification appears weak. Specialization in producing only one or a few major products for export presumably indicates a larger gain from trade than a widely diversified range of production and exports.[1] If a country were exporting only one product, the profit motive would see to its being the one that employed the country's resources most advantageously. It would be ideal for the country if supply and demand conditions enabled exports of this one most advantageous product to pay for all imports. If the country had to supplement its main export with other things as well, they would presumably be less advantageous ones.

For an analogy, consider an individual worker (and forget about any desire for variety in work). If he could get what he considered an adequate income from full-time work on the one job whose wages and conditions he found most attractive, he would be better off than if he had to piece together an adequate income from several part-time jobs. For the country, a different way to state the case is a bit more accurate. Assume it is exporting several things besides its main export. Under competitive conditions, the assortment of resources used in producing the "last" unit per time period of the main export would then be making the same contribution to value of output as an equal-valued assortment of resources in any other actual line of production. But if the country were exporting only *one* product, the resources used in producing even the "last" unit of it would be contributing not merely as much to output value as resources of the same value could contribute in any other line of potential export production, but more. That is why no other export goods would be produced.

This reasoning, like standard demonstrations of the gains from trade, presupposes known and stable demands and costs. A country then gains by specializing as fully as these conditions indicate, just as an investor gains most by putting his money in the one best stock. The difficulty for country and investor alike is in knowing the future. Diversification can be wise insurance for both; the gains sacrificed by not specializing more fully are a kind of insurance premium. In its strongest version, the case for artificially promoted diversification argues that no premium really need be paid after all; the insurance is free, so to speak. Any loss of efficiency in forgoing some trade might be outweighed by more stable costs and prices and levels of demand, permitting more accurate market appraisals, cost calculations, and investment decisions. This gain is something beyond stabler and fuller employment through a measure of insulation from the unstable world market.[2]

Some risks of extreme export specialization are obvious. Fluctuations in the world demand for the country's few exports require reallocating resources between export and home-market production; and if this is not easy, the frictions of readjustment spell unemployment, idling of specialized equipment, and perhaps what hindsight shows to have been waste in planting crops. A country exporting industrial raw materials is vulnerable to business recessions in industrial countries. Bad weather could shrivel up agricultural exports from time to time.

A policy of maintaining an official reserve of gold and foreign exchange, adding to it in good times and drawing it down in bad times, is no full answer. Theoretical dangers have sometimes proved real. When export trade is booming and export earnings exceed import spending, the country's central bank or other exchange-rate-stabilization agency buys up the surplus gold and foreign-exchange earnings and pays for them with newly created local money. This expansion of the money supply supports an inflationary process that is also fed by the swollen incomes of exporters and the chain reaction of increased spending and increased domestic money incomes that they touch off. When exports slump, export earnings fall short of import spending; and the central bank draws down its stockpile of gold and foreign exchange to support the exchange rate of the home currency. Sales of foreign exchange would shrink the home money supply, except that governments are inclined to resist domestic deflation and the unemployment it would involve. This resistance interferes with the fall in incomes and prices that would otherwise tend to pull imports down into line with exports. It worsens the danger that an import surplus will exhaust the gold and foreign exchange reserves, forcing resort either to import controls or tariffs or devaluation of the home currency. In short, a country heavily specialized in one or just a few exports subject to wide fluctuations in world demand or in its own supply has a bias toward inflation and currency devaluation.*

This inflation bias in an underdeveloped country with unstable export earnings has at least one further aspect. Government revenues are likely to come largely from taxes on exports or the profits of companies engaged in export production or trade. The government finds it easier and more tempting to expand its spending when an export boom is swelling tax revenues than to cut back its spending when exports and tax revenues slump. The result is a budget deficit financed by printing money or the equivalent. Furthermore, when the export slump is due to bad weather or other production difficulties at home, the decline in the physical efficiency of production and thus in real income tends to raise prices in general (unless deflationary policy

---

*Conceivably, of course, the central bank might undertake opposite open-market operations in domestic securities (assuming an adequate market existed) to neutralize the inflationary impact of its foreign-exchange purchases at times of balance-of-payments surplus as well as the deflationary impact of its foreign-exchange sales at times of balance-of-payments deficit. However, these operations would also tend to neutralize any automatic balance-of-payments correction and so would require the bank to stand ready for all the larger purchases and sales of foreign exchange.

If the central bank were not committed to stabilizing the exchange rate, it would not have to buy up any surplus earnings of foreign exchange in times of export boom nor make good any deficiency in times of export slump. It would then have a better chance to avoid alternate inflation and deflation of the home money supply. But while free exchange rates would do this much to simplify the domestic monetary problem, they would by no means sidestep all problems of overspecialization in exports.

causes a matching fall in money incomes). When the export slump is due to a drop in foreign demand, the country's export prices fall relative to its import prices, again amounting to a fall in real income and tending, in that respect, to be inflationary.

A less clear-cut supposed disadvantage of extreme specialization in raw materials is that the traditional export sectors may evolve as a sort of "enclave," attached geographically to the rest of the country but attached economically to overseas customer countries. This might happen if the export product grows on plantations or peasant holdings with little contact with the rest of the economy for supplies of materials and equipment and for processing of output or is a mineral product involving similarly sparse local contacts. The export enclave radiates few such constructive disturbances to the rut of tradition, few such obvious opportunities for new businesses and investments, and few such economic niches for varied kinds of personalities as more diversified production would cumulatively provide.

These conditions argue for distributing a country's economic eggs among many baskets. The policy question is whether private incentives for diversification are adequate. As far as instability in world demand or local production conditions for the main export crop is concerned, the individual businessman, worker, or investor does indeed have some incentive to weigh security against profitability. Instead of choosing the field with greatest expected earnings, he may choose another where probable earnings are lower but less uncertain. In this he is like the cautious stock-market investor. Still, the individual worker or farmer or businessman (or corporation, even) cannot be in more than one or a few occupations at once; he individually can hardly avoid having most of his eggs in one basket. He may not bother about diversification because he individually cannot achieve it. For the country as a whole, though, diversification is possible. Its policy-makers can see that the greater the fraction of the population producing one particular export product, the greater the risk for the country as a whole. Social and private views of risk diverge.

For an individual, much of this risk, as of living at all in an economy subject to inflation-biased monetary instability, exists almost regardless of what work he does. Even in producing the country's main export, the risks of unstable world demand and bad weather are also pretty much the same for the individual, regardless of how many of his fellow-countrymen are also producing the same thing. But doesn't the individual have an incentive to shy away from an overcrowded export field, just as travelers shy away from overcrowded coaches and distribute themselves evenly throughout a train? Doesn't overcrowding keep down the price of the product and encourage people to look for greener pastures? This would be true for a product or service sold mainly at home. But for a product sold on the world market in competition with larger supplies from other sources, the total world supply and the price obtainable would hardly be affected by one country's own degree of concentration in producing it. Rather perversely, having many of his fellow-countrymen in the same line of production may even encourage the individual to enter or stay in it. Trade connections, sources of technical information, and the like may be better in a large than in a small industry. Furthermore, the larger it is, the more effective political pressures are likely to be for the government to "do something" for it in hard times.

A more flexible economic structure could be a benefit of deliberate diversification. The national economic pattern appropriate to a world of change and uncertainty differs from what would be best under known and unchanging conditions. The process of economic development itself brings change in the country's pattern of comparative advantage (for example, an advantage based on cheap labor might sooner or later vanish). Allowing for change calls for not rigidly committing the country's economy to a traditional pattern of primary production for the world market.

In hinging on a divergence between private and social viewpoints—on an externality—the case for making the main export industry relatively less attractive resembles the case for measures against import dumping of the price-destabilizing kind. (The individual competitive merchant would seize import bargains when available, since he alone could not contribute to price stability, though government action conceivably could.) This is not to say that either case is conclusive.

Why doesn't the case for measures to discourage a country's overspecialization in exports also apply to a region within a country? Well, it may; but three differences make it less persuasive. First, monetary instability connected with fluctuations in trade threatens a region by itself less than it threatens a whole country, since the regional currency is the same as the national and is presumably managed by a national authority concerned with its stability. Second, labor and capital typically move more freely between regions than between countries, easing adjustments to changed demands or production conditions. Third, the national government's tax collections relative to its spending tend to go down in regions depressed by an unfavorable shift in demand and up in regions benefited by a favorable shift. In effect, the different regions belong to a mutual indemnity scheme.

What sort of measures might a country use to lessen overspecialization in exports? Tariffs on imports would reduce exports indirectly. Import restraint would permit a higher foreign-exchange value of the home currency; and the reduced home-currency equivalent of world-market export prices translated at the new exchange rate would discourage exports and export production. If the exchange rate were kept fixed, alternatively, the surplus of export earnings over restricted import spending would, while it lasted, expand the country's money supply and raise its price and money-income levels. With export prices mainly determined on the world market and failing to rise in step with domestic prices, costs, and money incomes, export production would become less attractive.

Discouraging exports indirectly, through import duties, permits the selective encouragement of particular import-competing industries; but we still have to consider whether this really is an advantage. It tends to shrivel exports generally rather than particularly promote diversification out of one or two overexpanded sectors. A more straightforward approach would discriminate against these particular exports. Unlike import duties, export duties can hardly invite special-interest political pressures in their support. The duties would prod some businessmen, labor, and capital into other lines of production. However, this approach might prove awkward for a government that had already been relying on export duties for a major part of its revenue; for if selective higher rates worked too well, they would reduce the total revenue brought in.

One partial reply to the diversification argument is that the more dependent on trade a country has become in the first place, the greater is the "insurance premium" to be paid in gains sacrificed. Perhaps this thought underlies Professor Haberler's judgment generally favoring active concentrated trade over shrunken diversified trade.[3] As for the specific problem of overimporting and foreign-exchange drain during export slumps, it is worth considering that the more nearly tariffs had restricted imports to practically indispensable ones in the first place, the less scope would remain for further import cuts. A country might do better to have a margin of nonessential imports in normal times so that cuts could be relatively painless in a balance-of-payments crisis.[4] (Ideally, the cuts might result from the "automatic" balancing operation of the exchange rate, forestalling any crisis, rather than from deliberate import-control policy.) Perhaps, however, this thought does not really face the issue. By adjusting to a lower level of trade, the country would reduce its exposure to export fluctuations and so reduce its need to respond by sometimes cutting imports.

On the other hand, promoting new exports seems a more constructive approach to diversification than merely restricting old ones. Admittedly, the question is how. (One possibility might be to subsidize new exports from tax revenue on old ones.) If diversification should expand total exports and so pay for additional imports, the country might enjoy a higher rate of development without inflation and balance-of-payments problems. A poor country would fare better in that way than by shackling its trade and so shunning some of the advantages the world market offers and the stimulus its export trade might give to its home economy.[5]

INFANT INDUSTRIES

The argument for diversification as insurance leads into the view of diversification as one aspect of economic development. Economists have long recognized the infant-industry argument as respectable in principle. Increasingly, though, they have come to see how special and implausible the circumstances are to which it applies.[6] A country might have a potential comparative advantage in a certain industry; yet that industry might never be born because its foreign competitors enjoyed a head start. Temporary protection, according to the argument, would let the infant industry find a wide enough market to support its becoming efficient. It could stand on its own feet after a while, and the tariff would be removed.

By itself, this prospect is no reason for a tariff. It is true that physical nature alone does not dictate a country's pattern of production; comparative advantage can be acquired. Yet though the foreigners' comparative advantage in an industry may indeed stem from historical accident, it may still be quite genuine. As Adam Smith recognized 200 years ago, "It is an acquired advantage only, which one artificer has over his neighbour, who exercises another trade; and yet they both find it more advantageous to buy of one another, than to make what does not belong to their particular trades."[7] And anyway—to repeat our familiar question—how does the source of a foreign cost advantage matter to us? If we can get a certain product more cheaply abroad than at home, why not? Not industries, but the products of industries, are what we really want. (Possible exceptions hinge on external benefits, explained in Chapters 3 and 8 and further considered in the pages ahead.)

History casts doubt on any great need to protect new industries for which a country or region is well suited. Manufacture of iron, hats, and other goods got a foothold in Colonial America despite British attempts at suppression. Manufacture of textiles, shoes, steel, machine tools, airplanes, and countless other goods has arisen and flourished in the American West and South despite competition under internal free trade with the established industries of the Northeast.

Protecting an industry during its infancy sacrifices some of the gains from international trade. This loss to the country, as well as diversion of resources into the artificially favored industry, burdens other industries, perhaps including potential new ones. Since these others might have had even brighter long-run prospects, the fact that the favored industry seems suitable for the country is not enough to justify protecting it; its prospects ought to be especially bright. But if they really are, why don't private investors see and act on them without special encouragement?

Of course the industry might have to run at a loss in its early years. Starting almost any business requires "losses" for some time as part of the initial investment. No reason is evident for distinguishing sharply between investment in material things like machinery and in immaterial things like building up a competent staff, gaining experience and knowledge, getting production running smoothly, and winning a foothold in the market. The investment is worth making only if the returns on it in the longer run, allowing for their uncertainty, are large enough at least to match the relevant rate of interest. From the social point of view, the costs to be justified in a valid case for protection include the deadweight losses imposed by the temporary tariff. The prospective benefits, stretching out longer in time, should be discounted more heavily than these costs. (It takes more than x dollars of remote benefits to justify x dollars of early costs.) Future benefits should be discounted not only because of this time or interest factor but also because of their uncertainty. They are particularly likely to be uncertain if they are "external" benefits of the kind considered later on. If prospective long-run profits do not meet the rate-of-return test well enough in the eyes of private investors to justify the industry's early losses, why should the government presume to know better and force consumers to pay for the gamble in tariff-raised prices?

This is not a rhetorical question; answers to it are conceivable. Some sort of case for protection can be made, for example, if policy makers really do know that the industry to be established will enjoy economies of large-scale production, that is, if larger and larger rates of output per time period within the range of domestically marketable output would permit lower and lower average costs per unit of product. Under free trade, import competition could deprive the prospective industry of the market necessary to give it the opportunity to get its costs down to a competitive level. Protection could give the industry its chance.

Apart from the uncertain empirical importance of this economies-of-scale case as applied to internationally traded goods, there are several difficulties. (1) The first one could be fully explained only at the cost of too much space and boredom and can only be mentioned here. In an industry whose average costs of production per unit decrease with expanded output, marginal cost is less than average cost. According to a certain strand of theory, ideal output and pricing require that price be equal to marginal cost. This would mean a price below average cost; the industry would be operating at a loss and would require subsidies to be able to do so. If this strand of theory were taken seriously as a rule for actual policy, protective tariffs could not achieve the ideal position; a complicated system of subsidies and taxes would be necessary.[8] This policy, furthermore, could not be a merely temporary one. The industry would not be an infant industry in the usual sense of requiring only temporary aid.

(2) If the proposed industry would enjoy mass-production economies in one country, it would presumably also be enjoying them in the other countries where it was already established. It seems paradoxical to use economies of scale as an argument for deliberately fragmenting the industry and spreading it around among countries. On the contrary, economies of scale offer gains from trade if the industry enjoying the economies is geographically concentrated and if most countries rely on importing its product.[9] One conceivable qualification to the case for undisturbed geographical concentration is that if only the industry got a protected start in its new home, it could develop a capacity for exporting as well as serving the domestic market. The world industry would then be relocated and would produce more cheaply than before. A more realistic qualification might be that the economies of scale make their full appearance while the industry is still small in relation to the market, so that establishing the industry in a new home would not scuttle economies of scale and raise costs abroad even if foreign production did decline somewhat.[10] This thought takes us back more nearly to the usual infant-industry argument.

(3) We are still left wondering why, if prospects of large-scale economies are so good, private investors do not see them and invest accordingly. Perhaps each potential investor group hesitates for fear that another will beat it to the punch, achieve economies of scale first, and so entrench itself in a position hard for latecomers to compete with. This worry seems particularly farfetched as a basis of trade policy. It is a kind of worry—still a farfetched one—that could apply to investment   in businesses not competing with imports.

(4) Perhaps the promised economies depend on the scale not of the individual firm but of the industry as a whole. Because they are "external" to the firm, prospective investors could not count on reaping those economies. But the postulated conditions would tend to give incentives for investment in one or a few firms constituting the entire industry or large segments of it. A firm could establish several factories. It is hard to imagine what sort of economies would be absent under unified ownership but present under fragmented ownership of the several factories. The very idea in question—economies of scale that are internal to the industry but external to the firm—verges on a contradiction in terms.[11]

(5) Less implausibly, perhaps, the supposed economies of scale hinge not on technical efficiencies in the industry's own production but on market and production opportunities that it would create for other industries by buying materials and services from them. Other customer industries of these supplier industries might also benefit. In Meade's words, the industry to be encouraged might promise "atmosphere-creating external . . . economies of conglomeration."[12]

Mention of external economies or benefits leads into the theoretically most respectable set of justifications for infant-industry protection. A more plausible case can be built around these than around scale economies lacking an externality aspect. An industry might promise benefits that would amply justify its early losses, except that not all of those benefits could enter into the calculations of profit-seeking investors. Firms generating them could not reserve all the benefits for their own use or else insist that other users pay for them. The earliest firms in the industry might have to experiment in modifying production methods used abroad to suit local physical and social conditions. They would be testing the market for the product and the usability of local labor and resources. Much of the knowledge developed could not be patented and would unavoidably be available free to latecomers.

Not all of it would be, of course. Some kinds of knowledge depend on each firm's own operating experience and cannot be spread to others. On the other hand, the very knowledge that a certain result can be obtained, even though the method is successfully kept secret, could be valuable but free to latecomers.

Latecomers might also benefit from the cheaper availability of ancillary services, such as specialized transportation and communications, for which the pioneer firms had had to pay dearly. Externalities of these kinds, like externalities involving knowledge, would provide incentives, however, for devising arrangements whereby the benefits could be reserved, after all, to the firms paying for them. Firms could make suitable agreements with each other, mergers could take place, or integrated firms could be established in the first place. The infant-industry argument points out, however, that not all externalities could be "internalized" in such ways. The industry could indeed promise greater advantages from the national point of view than from the private standpoint of prospective investors.

Knowledge acquired by labor provides a prominent example in the theoretical discussion. Early firms in the infant industry might be unable to reserve for themselves the entire value of the costly training and experience given to their workers and technicians. These men could reap the benefits themselves in higher wages obtained from new employers or as profits from self-employment. Competition on the labor market would force higher wages even for trained workers who stayed with their original employers. On the other hand, ways are conceivable in which firms could receive compensation for providing training and experience. Workers might in effect pay their employers for these expected benefits by accepting especially low wages during their first months or years on the job. But complete "internalization" is implausible. If relatively low wages were to be acceptable to them, particularly in a newly launched industry, workers would have to be able to foresee that the industry would survive to provide them with continued experience and make it valuable, foresee how well they individually could absorb it, and foresee what it would later be worth on the labor market. Workers might also need, yet be unable to get, loans to tide them over while accepting low wages as an investment in their own future earning power. Exercising foresight about new ventures and backing the gamble financially is more a function of business than of labor. Hence, to get the employees they needed, employers in a new industry would have to pay pretty nearly the going wage rates and stand the costs of training and experimentation themselves.

The infant-industry argument is defective without reference to benefits not fully capturable by the investors or firms that would have to bear their costs. These externalities deserve emphasis. And with reference to them, the infant-industry argument is not separate and distinct from some of the "second-best" arguments already reviewed. Its claim to distinctiveness is the hope that protection need only be temporary because the external benefits are "irreversible"; they—most obviously, the knowledge produced by experience—would remain generally available even after tariff removal lets output possibly slacken in the formerly protected enterprises.

Tariff protection could compensate investors or firms for creating benefits that they themselves could not fully reap. Or so the argument goes. But the tariff is only a crude corrective. Early entrants into the infant industry will realize that tariff protection will only heighten the incentives of late entrants to appear and share freely in any suitable knowledge developed in the meanwhile. Realizing this, early entrants will be hesitant about expenditures on research, experimentation, or training. Production encouraged by the tariff would be relatively inefficient.[13]

One traditional comment on infant-industry tariffs urges that subsidies are better. A subsidy can make explicit the costs of artificially influencing the country's pattern of production and can keep alive the question whether the results justify the costs. A more significant contrast applies not only to the infant-industry case but also to the other "externality" cases considered in the chapter on "second-best" policy. A tariff tries to correct for a discrepancy between privately and socially viewed benefits or costs by bringing a new distortion onto the scene: while conceivably promoting what counts as an improvement in the pattern of production when the externality is considered, it distorts the price relations confronting consumers away from those prevailing on the world market. In the language of Chapter 4, the tariff imposes a "consumption cost" that a subsidy could avoid. Instead of crudely encouraging the whole output of the domestic industry by restraining import competition, a subsidy can work more selectively by encouraging just those aspects of the industry's operations that are supposedly more beneficial from the national than from the private point of view. Research, experimentation, creation of knowledge, on-the-job training of labor, or whatever the externality-generating activity is can receive the subsidy. (In the opposite case of an external cost, such as pollution, similar reasoning might call for a tax on the activity to be discouraged.)

To state the contrast more informally, the tariff approach is negative; it restrains competition instead of giving positive encouragement. Henry George compared two approaches to developing air transportation, in his day still only a topic of science fiction. Subsidies would reward success with airships. Protection, instead, would impose deterrent taxes on existing methods of transportation, and the public would suffer inconveniences until—and whether or not—airships were developed. As for the interferences with other transportation, "we should never be able to tell how much they distorted industry and cost the people, or how much they stimulated the invention and building of air ships."[14]

Subsidies pose the problem of how to raise revenue to pay them. On the abstract theoretical level characteristic of so much of the infant-industry discussion, an answer is available. Artificial encouragement to some industries means relative discouragement to other sectors of the economy. The desired selective effect could be obtained by taxing those other sectors and subsidizing the favored activities with the revenue or even just favoring them with tax exemption.*

The merits of subsidies over tariffs seem just as real when the supposed distortion to be corrected for is that prospective investors in infant industries are not well enough informed about long-run profit opportunities or are too wary of taking risks. Tariff protection itself would increase the difficulties of learning from experience that business risks had been overestimated; one reason is that the tariff keeps up the price to consumers and so restricts their total purchases from domestic and foreign sources combined. Rather than enacting either tariffs or subsidies, the supposedly more knowledgeable government might better make its reassuring information freely available. However, prospective investors might not consider official assurances any substitute for demonstrated success. Early entrants into the industry who were to provide that experience would be

---

*Herbert Grubel has suggested a compromise between the tariff and subsidy approaches. Revenue solely from tariffs on competing imports could be used to subsidize the infant industry. The system would terminate itself as the protected infant grew up. As its costs and price fell, it would gradually crowd imports out of the market. If the protected industry did not grow up in that way, the scheme could be deliberately terminated. Meanwhile, at least the imported share of domestic consumption would have been obtained at the low foreign cost (from the national, though not the consumers', point of view). (*Weltwirtschaftliches Archiv,* December 1966, p. 340.) Analyzing the merits and shortcomings of this scheme can be an instructive exercise.

incurring costs and generating a kind of knowledge—the fact of profitability—whose benefits they could not fully reserve for themselves; hence entry might not occur in the first place. Again we meet a familiar theoretical problem.

Subsidies would also be preferable to tariffs when the problem was that capital-market imperfections were making the cost of finance too high, "especially if these industries require an initially large scale for economical production by the firm; in this case, subsidization of provision of capital would be the appropriate policy."[15]

In decisions on subsidies or tariffs alike, governmental assessment of profit prospects not apparent to businessmen, or governmental estimation of knowledge-creation and other future external benefits, "are processes which leave room for a lot of expensive mistakes."[16] Mistakes seem especially likely in underdeveloped countries. If a country lacks enough intelligent, perceptive, and bold businessmen and investors to take the risks of starting promising new industries that may not begin to pay off for some time, it also probably lacks enough intelligent, perceptive, and incorruptible government officials to make wise decisions about favoring some industries at the expense of others. Also likely to be in short supply are a true understanding of the relevant theoretical subtleties and the detailed factual information necessary for applying them in practice. Experience with hothouse forcing of supposedly prestigious industries such as steel and airlines in underdeveloped countries is hardly encouraging.

Some complacency about mistaken protection may perhaps be warranted if subsistence agriculture turns out to be the chief activity burdened for the sake of favored industrial infants. Perhaps agriculture is backward, overcrowded with workers really contributing little, and more in need of modern attitudes than of all the people and other resources it currently employs. Legislation, unionization, social pressures, or various market imperfections might require industrial employers to pay money wages higher than the value of agricultural output lost by the move of workers out of that sector. Similarly, wages in manufacturing might have to be high enough to outweigh workers' exaggerated ideas of the costs and unpleasantness of moving into urban occupations; yet the employers paying such high wages could not expect to reap the benefit of the knowledge eventually generated that the occupational switch was not so bad after all.*

------

*These strands of argument intertwine with the points about on-the-job training noted on p. 231 above. For analysis of a tariff argument by E. E. Hagen incorporating points like these, see Alexandre Kafka, "A New Argument for Protectionism?" (Quarterly Journal of Economics, February

Whether the assumed conditions prevail widely in the real world is doubtful: economists have increasingly questioned the concept of "disguised unemployment" in agriculture, while the prevalence of heavy urban unemployment in many underdeveloped countries, including unemployment among educated people, also casts doubt on the applicability of the argument. In the conditions of many underdeveloped countries, encouraging subsistence farmers to grow crops for sale on the market might contribute more towards developing the attitudes and skills required for material advance than could the protection of manufacturing.[17] Conditions are admittedly imaginable, however, in which any external benefits lost with the relative shrinkage of agriculture would be smaller than those expected from infant industries. The necessary provisos narrowly limit the scope of the argument. Costs must not be forgotten. Unfortunately, the benefits of an infant industry come to mind in a concentrated and obvious form, while the losses imposed elsewhere are scattered and hard to appreciate. The costs in danger of being overlooked include not only the diversion of scarce business talent and other resources but also the burdening of other existing or potential industries using imported ingredients and equipment now made more expensive by a protective tariff. The artificially high foreign-exchange value of the home currency resulting from or maintained in connection with import restrictions tends to hamper exports; yet the ability of the export industries to compete on the world market otherwise, under free trade, suggests that they may have been in the vanguard of economic development. It is hard enough to trace the far-flung repercussions of even a single protective duty, let alone the intertwining repercussions of a great many. (Compare what we have said about the concepts of effective protection and second-best policies on p. 219 above.) Yet taking account of repercussions is perhaps the essence of a sensible program of government interventions.

Mistakes in granting protection are hard to remedy even if recognized. Economic and political reasons combine. Weaning a former infant industry

---

1962, pp. 163-66). Under the conditions most favorable to the argument, tariff protection would still be inferior (as a subsidy to manufacturing output would also be inferior) to a scheme of taxing labor in agriculture and using the revenue to subsidize employment in or training for manufacturing. The reasons are broadly those we have suggested in appraising tariffs as "second-best" correctives for externalities and other distortions (See J. Bhagwati and V. K. Ramaswami, "Domestic Distortions, Tariffs, and the Theory of Optimum Subsidy," *Journal of Political Economy,* February 1963, pp. 44-50).

off protection is difficult: even though a solid core of the industry may have become well established and able to meet free import competition, not all firms will be secure. In most industries, typically, some firms have relatively low costs and are profitable; others have relatively high costs and are struggling. Removal of protection will menace firms that had been barely hanging on. Much the same holds for labor and other factors of production: some will have been just on the borderline between remaining in the industry and going elsewhere; removal of protection shifts the borderline and forces them out. Even if infant-industry protection works as intended for the bulk of the industry, it creates vested interests that will fight to keep it. Difficulties of ending temporary protection as the theory envisages count against putting the theory into practice in the first place.

GENERAL ECONOMIC DEVELOPMENT

The attempt to extend the infant-industry argument to the entire "infant economies" of backward countries is a confusion. "The infant industry argument, whatever its merits, envisages assistance to an infant sector of the economy at the expense of the rest of the economy. If the entire economy is regarded as an infant, there can be no fully grown sector to be taxed for the benefit of the infants."[18] Still, a sophisticated appeal to external benefits broader than we have yet emphasized can generalize the infant-industry argument and give it a new lease on life. If quite a few different manufacturing industries promise these broadly conceived benefits, policy makers need not exercise great and discerning selectivity after all. They might tax the domestic sector or sectors to be relatively discouraged—probably backward agriculture. Cash taxes on farm land could promote growing cash crops at the expense of subsistence farming. Import duties levied at a uniform rate on a broad range of manufactures could provide revenue to pay uniform subsidies on a broad range of competing domestic industries. The market would remain relatively free to choose the particular products most suited to the country's conditions.

This advice, however abstract, tacitly envisages attacks on old family ties and traditional living patterns, which may seem harsh. But development along Western lines does require social change; whether it really is worth its costs is an interesting question. At best, development shakes a backward country out of the rut of stultifying tradition. New industries promote general acquaintance with industrial goods and operations and contribute to a social atmosphere in which, for example, children grow up taking it for granted that employers expect promptness and dependability. Attitudes become more receptive to experimentation, change, and mobility of labor. With property rights defined and protected, people begin expecting to be able to reap the fruits of their own enterprise and thrift. Economic life becomes more diversified and affords constructive roles to a greater variety of personalities.

Even in more specific ways than these, a number of industries and investment projects, all developing in parallel, may support each other and make each more advantageous than it would have been alone. Some industries, in expanding and taking advantage of the economies of large-scale production, may lower the costs of others; electric power figures is a plausible example. Industries developing their efficiency and increasing the real incomes of their workers and owners may benefit others by increasing the demand for their products. Others may also benefit from an increased national capacity for saving and capital formation, or so the argument continues. Development theorists disagree on just what kinds of interindustry "linkages" to emphasize. Should linkages be sought "horizontally," in advance along a broad front, or should they be sought "vertically," in industries constituting successive stages in the processing of materials into final products? Should the government encourage industry "in breadth" or "in depth"? To pose a slightly different but related question, is economic diversification or economic specialization more likely to provide beneficial linkages? Different schools of thought on such questions agree, however, that an ideal judgment about what industries to encourage in line with prospective long-run comparative advantage involves somehow comparing the benefits of whole packages of industries and investment projects. The benefits of a package may be greater than the sum of the benefits of each of its parts, considered separately. On the other hand, the total benefit could be less than the sum of its apparent components, since some industries would get in each others' way in the competition for capital and other scarce resources or in the competition for customers or both. Private investors, without central guidance, would not see and take proper account, from the social point of view, of all such interrelations. In principle, then, a case can be made for governmental encouragements and discouragements.

This is a case, evidently, for central economic planning, not for tariff protection specifically. Tariffs would figure prominently, though, among the weapons wielded by the planners. In many countries striving for development since World War II, "what the planners used as the bedrock of all their efforts was the policy of import substitution. Import substitution seemed the easiest way of initiating industrialization...."[19] (Import substitution is the policy of restricting imports of many categories of goods, particularly manufactures, in the hope that the imports will be replaced by domestic substitutes.) Central planning implemented by tariffs, subsidies, licensing, and other interventions need not mean control in great detail of the input and output quantities and prices of each individual firm. Even so, that approach does require, after all, the kind of accurate selectivity which, as we have argued, cannot be realistically expected. Planning cannot work as intended unless government officials possess greater analytical powers, detailed factual knowledge, freedom from special-interest pressures, and selfless devotion than they are likely to have in reality. Furthermore, central planning and the measures employed to implement it not only do not promote the changes in attitudes necessary for economic development but even tend to reinforce unfavorable attitudes— submissiveness to authority as opposed to future-oriented self-reliance, a concern more for doing what one is told or expected to do than for obtaining actual results, a clinging to routine as opposed to curiosity and an experimental turn of mind, and an inclination more toward currying favor or wheedling privileges than toward *creating* wealth.[20] Central planning may look attractive on a very abstract level, yet be unsuitable for the complexities of the real world. A more practical approach leaves it to private businessmen and investors, spurred by more suitable incentives than those of bureaucrats and working through contracts and ownership arrangements, to reap as best they can the more obvious, at least, of the benefits of interindustry linkages.

Still, protectionists and planners need not wholly abandon their argument. They can admit the impossibility of carefully calculated "balance" among favored industries but insist on the merits even of *unbalanced* growth. Piecemeal development by fits and starts may well result, for example, in too little electricity relative to the demand for it or too much cement relative to other construction materials used along with it. Obvious gaps may develop in the supply of materials or equipment to certain industries, or in the further processing of their outputs, or in transportation. Obvious shortages of some things in relation to others will present investment opportunities that make few demands on the perceptiveness and boldness of investors. Then, if it is true that one of the scarcest resources in an underdeveloped country is the talent for seeing investment opportunities and making business decisions, conspicuous gaps are all to the good. Disproportionalities may usefully economize on this scarce decision-making ability and practically force investment decisions to make themselves. In this way, new industrial activities almost anywhere in the economy will serve as catalysts for others.[21] We say "almost" anywhere because some industries, in line with this argument, would seem worthier of protection than others. Oil refining might seem more attractive to private investors than shoe-manufacturing; yet the shoe industry would be more likely to mobilize entrepreneurs to supply its inputs of leather, laces, glue, and so forth, while oil-refining offers few such linkages.[22]

Static analysis would insist that refraining from special encouragement to some industries leaves resources available to others. Available, yes; but the question is whether they would be used, or used except in the old fruitless ways. Even capital or savings potential, that other notably scarce resource in backward countries, may become more effectively available if the developments just mentioned do economize on the decision-making ability that must be used along with it. Obvious opportunities for profitable industrial investments will make it relatively less attractive to sidetrack capital or savings potential into costly traditional ceremonies, jewelry, luxury housing, and gold and foreign securities and bank accounts. The important thing is to get the development process going, to touch off a chain reaction. Worrying about just what industries to start with may not be crucial.

One implication is already clear. If it is valid to emphasize a scarcity of decision-making talent, then siphoning off any great part of it into government bureaus seems a shame, particularly if the bureaus perform the negative function of prohibiting business ventures or subjecting them to screening and licensing. Even much of the talent and energy remaining in private business may run to waste in dealing with officials, trying to get projects approved, seeking licenses for desired imports, urging tighter restrictions on competing imports, and trying to circumvent regulations. As Lord Beveridge once wrote, the industrial development of a free-trade country is guided by men sticking to their business and seeking maximum results from available resources. Industries compete in economic efficiency. In a protectionist country, though, industrial development is guided by officials and politicians and by businessmen become politicians. Industries compete not just in productive efficiency but also in political wire-pulling. Bringing businessmen out of their factories and offices into politics misuses both business ability and political machinery.[23] Politicization of economic life raises the stakes in the struggle for political power and intensifies the struggle itself. It widens the range of activities in which attempts to satisfy or balance the claims of different racial and other groups affect the allocation of jobs and licenses. Formal or informal systems of racial or group quotas tend to arise on top of the quotas associated with import licensing and other economic controls. Political and group tensions sharpen.[24]

Such evils are less likely if a government avoids restrictive interventions and central planning. It still has plenty of work cut out for it in providing services that are relatively hard to sell on a business basis, such as basic education, public health measures, roads, research and advice on agricultural techniques, and, above all, a framework of law and security for persons and property.

TRADE AND DEVELOPMENT

The case for stimulating industries to get their broad dynamic repercussions cannot properly insist that this stimulus must come mainly from taxing or restricting imports. Imports can aid development in various ways. Imports of semifinished materials can create opportunities for their further processing into final form within the country. What Hirschman calls "import enclave industries" can create some of the gaps and disproportionalities whose constructive function he has emphasized. Imports can help modernize consumer habits and can test demand for local businessmen; rapidly increasing imports of some product show that the market exists and may attract investment into local production.[25] Diverting resources into import-competing sectors and so indirectly out of export production is counterproductive if the export sector is one of the least backward parts of the economy. Even agriculture may offer important external benefits, as agricultural exports stimulated railroad construction in the United States and Canada in the nineteenth century.[26] Export earnings play an obvious role in paying for imported materials, equipment, and technical assistance. Imported "incentive goods" like bicycles, known to be on sale for money, can encourage farmers to grow cash crops. In this and other ways, foreign trade can help orient subsistence farmers toward the market economy and, more broadly, can promote the adoption of new methods and ways of thinking. Trade gives businessmen experience in reconnoitering markets and sources of supply and in exercising business judgment.

Trade can help economic development by letting a region or country specialize in lines of production where it enjoys or can develop a comparative advantage without artificial support. Export and import opportunities make it unnecessary for local industries to grow in close step with each other so as to furnish each other with markets and supplies. Instead, the economy can *unbalance* itself along lines of comparative advantage. (This argument for unbalanced growth is admittedly different from and partly contradictory of Hirschman's.) An agricultural orientation as such is not what makes a country poor; the inefficient, tradition-bound character of its agriculture is more to blame. If agriculture becomes increasingly market-oriented and efficient as development proceeds, it may abundantly release resources into industrial production, as the postwar economic "miracles" of Japan and Italy illustrate. On the other hand, the determinants of comparative advantage may keep agriculture dominant, but with a strengthened export orientation. Countries need not be mainly industrial to be advanced and to enjoy standards of living among the highest in the world; witness the history of progressive agriculture in New Zealand, Denmark, and Iowa. More important than an early transfer of resources from agriculture to manufacturing is alertness to new ideas and opportunities in whatever productive activities people do undertake.

Protection against foreign manufactures ranks low, therefore, on the list of what a backward country needs for development. Locally produced manufactures sell poorly not so much because of import competition as because people are too poor to buy them either from local or from foreign producers; and so far as curbing international specialization and trade holds down real incomes, it impedes not only saving and investment but also the market for industrial goods.

One familiar argument does not necessarily deny the benefits from trade but suggests a supposedly different reason why the backward countries may sensibly control or tax imports: to save foreign exchange.[27] Discrimination against nonessential imports could divert scarce exchange to buying capital goods or other favored imports. This in turn could stimulate import-replacing industries considered essential to development. Total trade would not shrink, since the backward countries would still spend all the foreign exchange they could earn. Their trade would merely take on a more advantageous *pattern*.

We doubt that the "save-foreign-exchange" slogan really forms a separate argument for tariffs. If it makes sense, it must be as a catch-all term for several protectionist arguments already discussed. An apparent need to save foreign exchange implies actual or potential balance-of-payments trouble, which in turn implies lack of any automatic balancing mechanism working either through price and income levels or through the exchange rate. Logically, therefore, the "save-foreign-exchange" slogan presupposes some reason for not allowing a free exchange rate. One such reason might be that restrictions on some uses of foreign exchange could help hold its price down for other uses, which would encourage the favored industries pretty much as subsidies or tariffs do. Valid arguments for such favoritism must hinge, then, on such things as externalities or other distortions to be corrected for, or perhaps on income distribution. The logic of the policy requires favoring imports used by industries that create external benefits or have low genuine opportunity costs relative to money costs, or favoring imports consumed by relatively poor people. So justified, the policy might make sense, though not because saving foreign exchange would promote development in any distinct way not yet considered.

Attempts to keep a country's exchange rate pegged in the face of inflationary pressures commonly lead to balance-of-payments problems and policy responses likely to hamper development. Trying to "save foreign exchange," the authorities impose import controls on an ad hoc basis. The controls tend to spread over the whole range of imports. Haphazard price differentials arise between different types of imports. The suitably selective element in protection, if it existed at all, becomes eroded. For effective protection of a favored sector, nonprotected items should be importable freely and easily. The reason is obvious when the nonprotected items are inputs for the protected sector. The point also holds for consumer goods, since rises in their prices may draw resources away from and thus weaken the intended stimulus to the protected sector. More than ever, it is difficult to maintain an intended pattern of effective protection when inflationary pressure in the face of a fixed exchange rate is continually threatening to boil over into a new round of import restrictions.[28] Such difficulties are especially severe when, as is so common, the controls take the forms of quantitative restrictions, import licensing, and foreign-exchange rationing. Exchange-rate overvaluation hampers exports, restricting export earnings and thus the amount of foreign exchange available for allocation to importers. Within the country, imports are scarcer than they would be if a free market in foreign exchange prevailed. Their prices rise accordingly, giving import-competing industries a greater degree of protection than had probably been intended. Because of these high prices, importers favored with the scarce import privileges or foreign-exchange allocations receive a "quota profit" or scarcity rent corresponding to no constructive service on their part. Businessmen using imported materials and machinery, whose local-currency prices are artificially low to them at the pegged exchange rate, tend to apply for permits or foreign exchange to import even more than they could otherwise advantageously use. The system of controls unintentionally encourages purchases of new capital equipment over the maintenance of existing equipment and the selection of complex over simpler productive processes. The latter improves the prospects of fooling exchange-control officials with the overinvoicing of imported equipment, which, if successful, yields the culprits overallocations of artificially cheap foreign exchange.*

Scarce import privileges yield unearned profit, sheltered from competitive erosion. The favored importers, and the officials in a position to sell such favors under the counter, have a vested interest in such a system. Free trade would turn their talents and energies into more constructive lines. So would a system of protective tariffs honestly designed according to any of the plausible arguments we have been considering. Today's underdeveloped countries are not wondering, unfortunately, about a choice between free trade and tariffs. For many of them, any plausible tariff structure, though far from ideal, would represent an improvement over existing trade policies.

---

*Such consequences, predicted by standard economic theory, are actually observable in many underdeveloped countries. (See Derek Healey, *Journal of Economic Literature,* September 1972, especially pp. 781-83, and the studies cited there.)

Existing policies work against the main requirement for economic development—a general willingness to *create* wealth rather than keep trying to wrest it from others by power, privilege, influence, or trickery. The decisive conditions for development are intangible: a social and ideological climate favorable to business enterprise; a framework of law and order and stable property rights so people can count on reaping the rewards of their alertness and thrift; and freedom to make investments, adopt new methods, and market new products without clashing with strong traditions and without needing official permission at every turn.

The greater contribution of trade than of trade restrictions to economic development shows clearly in the experience of Japan, the only major country without a European background that has so far achieved industrialization along modern lines.[29] Starting a little before 1870 under a new government bent on modernizing the country rapidly to guard its independence, the Japanese deliberately imitated Western capitalism. Freedom of movement and occupation were established, internal tariff barriers removed, and property rights in land made freely transferable. A land tax replaced the old system of feudal dues; provided the bulk of government revenue, helped prod farmers into growing crops for the market, and helped prod former feudal lords and knights into more constructive business and government jobs. The government did take the lead in starting some industries, including railroads, ocean shipping, communications, cement, paper, glass, textiles, and iron and steel; but far from being committed to socialism, it was anxious to see private enterprise take over. Intangible factors connected with national traditions apparently contributed to a pervasive spread among large and small businessmen and farmers alike of a spirit of hard work, thrift and readiness to invest. The spread of education to all social classes helped make management and workers receptive to new ideas and methods. The government's role was positive rather than restrictive. Import barriers had little to do with getting development going; in fact, agreements with Western powers held the Japanese tariff at a level of only around 5 percent until 1899. The proceeds of exports, notably silk, helped pay for imports of machinery, textbooks, and educational equipment, for hiring foreign technical advisors, and for Japanese study in Western countries. Japan paid its own way during this period; it received no significant amounts of foreign aid and not even of foreign investment capital until economic development had been underway for several decades. Japan benefited from the liberal trade policies of Western countries, which enabled her to sell her exports on the world market, to buy goods and services embodying Western technology, and to gear herself into the international division of labor.

The more recent experience of Hong Kong suggests several interesting lessons. One is the value of law and order and stable, honest government.

The colony's light manufacturing industries have not only developed without depending on tariff protection but have become successful enough in exporting to alarm Western protectionists. Hong Kong's industrialization illustrates, incidentally, that poverty and agriculture, wealth and industrialization, do not necessarily go together. Low wages are due not to trade but to a great superabundance of labor and scarcity of other resources. Having an opportunity to work for low wages is better than having no job opportunities at all. Labor would be in a still worse position if the colony's overseas markets were even more restricted than they are. Even if the poor countries have scant advantages besides abundant labor, both they and the developed countries can still gain by trading with each other. This old argument is valid against barriers that would deny markets in the developed countries to the new manufactured exports of the developing countries.*

Unfortunately, not only the existence but even the structure of tariffs in developed countries tends toward that denial. In general, their tariffs tend to be escalated by stage of production.[30] Import duties tend to be zero or low on crude foodstuffs and raw materials of kinds not extensively produced in the importing countries, higher on foods and materials that have undergone substantial processing, and higher still on many types of finished consumer goods. Capital goods tend to bear lower duties than consumer goods. (The political reasons for such a tariff structure are fairly evident.) Such escalation gives a higher rate of effective protection to the processing of intermediate goods and the production of finished consumer goods in the industrialized countries than nominal or explicit duty rates would suggest, particularly if the domestic value added in those lines of production accounts for only a small share of the value of final output. Being highly protected in the industrialized countries, processing and manufacturing activities are discouraged in the underdeveloped countries. That discouragement is particularly significant for production of relatively unsophisticated, high-labor-content consumer goods such as the underdeveloped countries would be in a position to produce for export if markets were open to them. Yet tariff escalation and effective protection in richer countries tends to confine the poorer countries to their roles as primary producers, "hewers of wood and drawers of water." If better market opportunities were open, the poorer countries might produce simple manufactured goods for export; and industrialization would not have to await the emergence of adequate domestic markets.

---

*Gunnar Myrdal says that the underdeveloped countries "will have to bring Ricardo's old battery again to the firing line." *(An International Economy,* p. 258; cited in note 27.)

Progress of this sort has indeed taken place, and proposals abound for more. To be consistent with its own aid programs, the United States should allow developing countries to take full advantage of trade with it. Unhampered access to markets for their agricultural and mineral exports and their emerging high-labor-content manufactures will help them buy machinery and technical assistance. It would be a cruel trick indeed if Western countries were to penalize any success on the part of developing countries by raising barriers against their goods. A firm American commitment to free trade would provide valuable assurance. Allowing developing countries to trade without restriction on the world market would help promote their development along capitalist rather than socialist lines. The United States has an interest in seeing the uncommitted countries voluntarily choose peaceful and productive private business over governmental force in international relations. This interest no doubt overshadows the direct material advantage that free trade promises the United States.*

SUMMARY

The argument for promoting diversification has some merit in abstract theory, especially when it emphasizes encouraging new export industries rather than simply restricting imports. The infant-industry argument for tariffs can also be made intellectually respectable by careful appeal to external benefits. But then, apart from the hope that protection will be only temporary, the argument loses its distinctiveness and becomes just another abstract example of how policy might conceivably correct for divergences between private and social viewpoints. The argument can be saved, at least on paper, by turning it into a case for artificially encouraging a broad range of industries to shake the economy out of old ruts. It then

---

*While discounting America's self-interest, narrowly interpreted, in large-scale trade liberalization, Myrdal would find liberalization justified "as an act of international solidarity." (*An International Economy,* pp. 290-91.) William Penfield Travis (*The Theory of Trade and Protection* [Cambridge: Harvard University Press, 1964], p. 248), worries that if a country such as India unilaterally freed its trade, the advanced countries might block its specialization in labor-intensive manufactures with import restrictions. "The essential task of international economic cooperation will be, therefore, to make sure that countries which want free trade can have some opportunity to practice it."

blends in with the whole topic of economic development, about which a soundly based and unified theory remains to be worked out. Meanwhile, fascination with narrow, abstract theoretical justifications for all sorts of government interventions remains a real danger.* Actually, it appears that trade restrictions can at best make only a fringe contribution to development. Insofar as trade policy is important, it is largely in the hands of the advanced countries, which might allow today's developing countries the kind of opportunities that Japan enjoyed in the nineteenth century.

----

*"In much the same way as the governments of the underdeveloped countries succumb to the lure of the 'steel mills' embodying the most advanced and capital-intensive type of Western technology, many development economists have succumbed to the lure of the intellectual 'steel mills' represented by the latest and most sophisticated theoretical models. This," Hla Myint believes, "is where...the greatest mischief has been done." (*Economic Theory and Underdeveloped Countries,* p. 31; cited in note 18.)

NOTES

1. Cf. Frank D. Graham, *The Theory of International Values* (Princeton: Princeton University Press, 1948), especially pp. 209, 237-38.

2. John Black reports this argument without necessarily endorsing it (*Oxford Economic Papers,* June 1959, pp. 206-7).

3. Gottfried Haberler, *International Trade and Economic Development* (Cairo: National Bank of Egypt, 1959), p. 7.

4. John Black, *Oxford Economic Papers,* June 1959, p. 207.

5. Cf. Gerald M. Meier and Robert E. Baldwin, *Economic Development* (New York: Wiley, 1957), especially pp. 402, 409; and Gerald M. Meier, *International Trade and Development* (New York: Harper, 1963), especially p. 185.

6. See, for example, M. C. Kemp, "The Mill-Bastable Infant-Industry Dogma," *Journal of Political Economy,* February 1960, pp. 65-67; Harry G. Johnson, "Optimal Trade Intervention in the Presence of Domestic Distortions," in Robert E. Baldwin et al, *Trade, Growth, and the Balance of Payments* (essays in honor of Gottfried Haberler; Chicago: Rand McNally, 1965), esp. pp. 26-30; Harry G. Johnson, "A New View of the Infant Industry Argument," in I. A. McDougall and R. H. Snape, eds., *Studies in International Economics,* pp. 59-76; Herbert G. Grubel, "The Anatomy of Classical and Modern Infant Industry Arguments," *Weltwirtschaftliches Archiv,* December 1966, pp. 325-44; S. N. H. Naqvi, "Protection and Economic Development," *Kyklos,* 1969, No. 1, pp. 124-54; Robert E. Baldwin, "The Case against Infant-Industry Tariff Protection," *Journal of Political Economy,* May-June 1969, pp. 295-305; and Hla Myint, *Economic Theory and the Underdeveloped Countries* (New York: Oxford University Press, 1971), especially Chapter 6.

7. *The Wealth of Nations* (New York: Random House, 1937), p. 426.

8. Cf. Jan Tinbergen, *Selected Papers* (Amsterdam: North-Holland, 1959), pp. 143-44.

9. John Black, *Oxford Economic Papers,* June 1959, pp. 204-5.

10. Cf. J. E. Meade, *Trade and Welfare* (London: Oxford University Press, 1955), p. 260.

11. I. F. Pearce, *International Trade* (New York: Norton, 1970), p. 436.

12. Meade, op. cit., p. 258.

13. Robert Baldwin, *Journal of Political Economy,* May-June 1969, p. 298.

14. Henry George, *Protection or Free Trade* (New York: Doubleday, Page, 1905), p. 91.

15. Harry Johnson in Baldwin et al, *Trade, Growth, and the Balance of Payments,* p. 29.

16. John Black, *Oxford Economic Papers,* June 1959, p. 206.

17. Peter Bauer makes this last point in *Dissent on Development* (Cambridge, Mass.: Harvard University Press, 1972), p. 267.

18. Bauer, op. cit., p. 287n. Compare Myint, *Economic Theory and Underdeveloped Countries,* pp. 197-98.

19. Derek T. Healey, "Development Policy: New Thinking About an Interpretation," *Journal of Economic Literature,* September 1972, p. 761. Healey reviews many recent scholarly writings that document ample grounds for disillusionment about the central-planning and import-substitution approach to economic development.

20. See Bauer, op. cit., particularly pp. 78, 84, 101.

21. This is one of the main themes of Albert O. Hirschman, *The Strategy of Economic Development* (New Haven: Yale University Press, 1958).

22. This example is taken from Grubel *Weltwirtschaftliches Archiv,* December 1966, pp. 334-35. The "linkage" argument for protection or subsidy rests, obviously, on a supposed divergence between private and social points of view. In this respect it resembles the infant-industry argument.

23. William Beveridge and a Committee of Economists, *Tariffs: The Case Examined* (London: Longmans, 1931), p. 233.

24. Bauer, op. cit., p. 87.

25. Hirschman, op. cit., pp. 111-12, 120-25. Hirschman would be willing to consider protection of individual import-competing industries, once they approach a "threshold" of economic domestic production. But their reaching the threshold would not itself constitute a case for protection. The case would have to rest on specific arguments of the kinds we have reviewed.

26. Haberler, op. cit., p. 33.

27. See, for example, Gunnar Myrdal, *An International Economy* (New York: Harper, 1956), Chapter 13.

28. Myint, op. cit., pp. 167-69.

29. See William W. Lockwood, *The Economic Development of Japan* (Princeton University Press, 1954), especially Chapters 6 and 7 and, on early tariff policy, pp. 19, 326, 539.

30. For a review of empirical studies supporting this generalization, see Harry G. Johnson, *Economic Policies Toward Less Developed Countries,* (Washington: Brookings Institution, 1967). On the concept of effective protection mentioned in this paragraph, recall our pages 62-66 above.

Free trade would change the pattern of production in the United States; no supporter thinks otherwise. Shifts of labor and resources out of some industries into others are part of the process of reaping its benefits. Furthermore, precisely because comparative advantage and disadvantage are *comparative,* rapid technological progress in some home industries can throw adjustment burdens even onto others related to the most progressive ones no more directly than through the tendency for imports and exports to balance. A comprehensive program of protection against the need for change would be a program for economic stagnation. Industrial deaths as well as births are part of a progressive economy.

Still, we must ask whether the difficulties of adjustment to free trade might either make the change not worth while, after all, or require special measures to ease the troubles of some businessmen and workers. The pains of adjustment would not be due to free trade, as such, but to having adopted protection in the first place—which is something to consider in all decisions about adopting new government economic interventions.

THE EXTENT OF DISLOCATION

For perspective, we want an impression of how greatly a move to free trade would disturb the American economy. The size of necessary adjustments, however, does not really affect the free trade case. Great adjustments would suggest that tariffs had been greatly obstructing the efficient use of resources.

Robert Baldwin and John Mutti have estimated the benefits and adjustment costs of removing tariff protection from five U.S. industries—

textiles; chemicals; primary iron and steel; radio, T.V., and communications; and motor vehicles.[1] Using 1969 data, they estimated adjustment costs as the earnings that would be lost as the result of production cutbacks and related layoffs in each industry. (Average wages were multiplied by the quantity of labor that would be displaced for alternative lengths of time by production cutbacks attributable to the removal of tariff protection from each industry. The raw estimates of lost earnings were than adjusted for "personal characteristics" such as age, sex, race, and education.) The annual adjustment costs thus obtained and the annual allocative gains from the elimination of tariffs are cast by Baldwin and Mutti in present-value terms: the annual gains and losses are both discounted at an annual rate of 10 percent for a ten-year period and compared with each other as "present values" of the expected stream of gains and losses over that period.

The authors find that the present value of the gains from tariff removal is greater for each of the five industries than the present value of the costs of labor displacement, assuming an average eleven-week layoff period. Estimated benefits are greater than costs for four of the five industries (the exception being motor vehicles) for a 24-week layoff period. If we add the present-value figures for all five industries, we obtain an estimated total gain from tariff removal of $1,146.2 million. Total adjustment costs calculated in this way come to $283.5 million for the eleven-week-layoff scenario and $577.5 million for the 24-week-layoff scenario.

These estimates and our aggregation of them into total gain and loss for the five industries must be tempered by the assumptions that explicitly and implicitly underlie their calculation. In the first place, the Baldwin-Mutti estimate of gain and loss for each industry assumes that tariff protection is removed from that industry alone, while protection for each of the other four industries remains intact. Our adding the individual industry gains and losses to obtain a group total may therefore misrepresent the actual effects of simultaneous removal of tariff protection from all five. Also, the authors explicitly omit from their calculations any unfavorable effects that unemployment in the industries directly affected by trade liberalization may have on those firms and industries which depend on the directly-affected industries for customers or business. Similarly omitted are the employment *gains* that could be expected from the greater exports that would indirectly result from the expansion of imports, as well as all the other repercussions, good and bad, that might be indirectly attributable to the elimination of tariffs.*

---

*More fundamentally, all calculations of gain and loss attributing changes in employment and production in particular industries to the whole

Stephen Magee combines some additional calculations with the methodology and estimates developed by Baldwin and Mutti. The "costs of job changes per year" that would have been imposed by the elimination of all U.S. tariffs in 1971 are, in his analysis, $330 million, or about 0.04 percent of national income for that year.[2] Like Baldwin and Mutti, Magee does not calculate the adjustment-cost-reducing effects (or any of the other imaginable repercussions) of tariff removal. Still, his estimate of total adjustment costs is small even in comparison to the also-small allocative gains.

Adjustment costs are, by their very nature, temporary. Even if such costs did happen to exceed the various gains from trade liberalization for one or two or ten years, they would eventually disappear. Any suggestion that long-lasting adjustment costs constitute an argument against trade liberalization for one or two or ten years, they would eventually disappear. Any suggestion that long-lasting adjustment costs constitute an argument against trade liberalization is off target. The inability of labor to shift from a declining industry to other places of employment is due more to rigidities and structural difficulties in the domestic economy than to whatever it is that may be causing the industry to decline.

SOME FURTHER REASSURANCE

Growth of total demand in line with potential total output, thanks to suitably steady monetary policy, would help provide job opportunities for new entrants to the labor force and for workers released from their old jobs by rising productivity and by freer trade alike. Readjustment can be even less painful if the economy as a whole grows rapidly in relation to the rate of import liberalization; for then some import-competing industries need not shrink absolutely, but only in their shares of the market. Even absolute shrinkage can be almost painless to individual employees and businessmen

---

economy must rest on tacit assumptions about wage and price inflexibility. With perfect flexibility, removal of protectionism, like any other economic change, would bring about mere shifts in resource allocation and income distribution, without causing overall involuntary unemployment. Perfect flexibility is impossible, of course, but departure from it in the real world is a matter of degree and duration, and so, therefore, are the gains and losses due to specific changes. Estimates of them are rough not merely in practice but even in principle.

if it occurs through mere nonreplacement of people who retire, die, or leave voluntarily for better opportunities elsewhere.

Import liberalization on a broad front gives groups harmed by direct import competition a chance to gain from cheapening of things they consume or use in their own production; the general benefit partially smothers the harm to particular producers. Piecemeal, selective liberalization, in contrast, widens the discrepancy between effects on the average citizen and on particular producers. Liberalization done flexibly and tentatively, with a willingness to see how things turn out and to modify or retrace steps already taken, lets import-competing producers hope that the threatened liberalization will be abandoned after all, or postponed. Naturally they will strive to make their hopes come true, diverting energy into seeking political influence and away from adjusting to reality in a businesslike manner. In the end the delayed adjustments are likely to prove more painful than they need have been. The president of the Braided Rug Manufacturers Association unintentionally illustrated some of these points in Congressional testimony:

> Many mills are presently operating at a loss and continue so only because of the hope that some relief will be forthcoming shortly. Without a doubt, a considerable number of these mills will have to permanently close their doors unless steps are taken to restore at least a part of the market they contributed to building.
>
> For several years now, experiencing shrinking markets, dwindling profits, stagnated growth, and unemployment and insecurity among our workers, promises from the Government that domestic industry would be afforded relief from the throttling effects of unfair foreign competition fanned the industry's hope for survival.[3]

But if businessmen know that import liberalization will take place on schedule and irreversibly, even if the scheduled liberalization stretches well into the future, they will plan accordingly and escape some of the agony of uncertainty and procrastination. This, reports Professor Irving Kravis, is the most important single lesson of the nearly painless liberalization of European trade during the 1950s and the early years of the Common Market.

> Once businessmen become convinced that tariff barriers, trade barriers, are going to come down, European experience suggests that businessmen will take prompt and vigorous action to stay in business, and meet the new situation.
>
> ... certainty with respect to future tariff and trade policy is of critical importance. Once American businessmen are certain that

trade barriers are eventually going to be eliminated, they will have the necessary incentive to meet foreign competition through increased efficiency or to sidestep foreign competition by switching to new lines of production. Adjustment to changing market conditions is, after all, one of the responsibilities of entrepreneurship and the main social justification for the high rewards which characterize successful business leadership.[4]

Several American businessmen have seen this view justified in their own experience. The president of the Union Tank Car Company cited the example of a Belgian firm regenerated with his own company's assistance. To cope with freer competition, it had to break with the past, scrap its old plant for a modern new one, develop better operating methods, and retrain its employees. As a result, it could count on producing more than its old output with fewer than one-fourth as many workers as before; yet those displaced were rapidly being absorbed into new jobs in other types of business attracted by the company's new plant and new outlook. This, the witness reported, was no isolated instance; thousands of plants in Western Europe were making similar transformations. Representative European businessmen told him that an intensified competitive challenge was just what they needed to find forgotten resources within themselves and begin accomplishing things they never knew they could.[5] The president of International Telephone and Telegraph Company, which long has had plants and subsidiaries throughout Europe, noted that growing demand in a growing market was affording the best possible protection to local businesses there:

> ... one reason why this has been so is that the decision of the Six to establish the Common Market even in the face of real sacrifice was clean cut and firm. Therefore, there was no holding back, no investment in backfires, no encouragement to anyone to sit still in hope of saying, "I told you so."
>
> Because the experiment was boldly conceived and boldly undertaken, businessmen in the six countries could boldly plan, invest, and build for the future. Rather than waste resources opposing a change that was inevitable, most Common Market producers have invested their resources in making the best answer they can—going forward.[6]

Several further considerations help explain why adjustments can be fairly painless if import liberalization occurs against a background of adequate monetary and real growth and with certainty, even though by gradual stages. Only partial transfers of resources will be necessary out of most import-competing industries. Industries, factories, and farms making several products may be able to switch to producing more of some and less of others without going out of business or even drastically overhauling their general lines of production.* Most of the impact of change falls on owners of land or machinery or other resources that happen to be firmly specialized in import-competing production. Versatile and mobile factors of production, such as labor tends to be in the long run, have less to fear from increased imports. As for mobility, it is a well-known characteristic of the American population, which import competition calls into play far less than other economic changes do. Mobility, of course, has no special moral qualities; and wanting to stay in familiar surroundings need not be condemned. But the possibility of changing jobs without changing residence is still effectively greater than it once was, not only because population and economic activity have grown denser in relation to space but also because commuter transportation has become more available and rapid. "Triangular" transfer possibilities make it unnecessary for a man leaving a shrinking industry to move directly into one of the most rapidly expanding ones. Transfers can be indirect and minor at each stage: the lumbermill worker may become a construction worker, replacing a man who has moved into an airplane factory. Some workers, like machinists, construction workers, and office workers, may shift between industries and still use their old skills.[7]

Anyway, trade restrictions are themselves hardly a painless remedy for the misfortunes of workers displaced by imports. Imports and exports are interrelated not only by the mechanisms of the balance of payments but also by any excuse that U.S. trade restrictions provide for foreign restrictions and any impetus they give to formation of trading blocs abroad that discriminate against imports from nonmember countries. Such possibilities raise the question of which American industries should be allowed to shrink (absolutely or in relation to the whole economy)—import-competing industries or export industries. The question is not meant to suggest that exports are better for a country than imports. Exports are useful goods traded for quantities of imports that consumers value still more; getting rather than disposing of goods is the aim of economic activity. Neither does the question imply that export readjustments are especially painful and undesirable; to suppose so would be to verge on the protectionist

---

*Yet some years ago producers of glace cherries sought relief under the "escape clause," even though they had maintained their total production, employment, and profits by switching more heavily into the other glace fruits that they produced. (I. B. Kravis, in *Foreign Economic Policy* [1962], p. 318; cited in Chapter 11, note 1.)

save-an-industry fallacy. In fact, adjustment to declining exports probably would be easier than to increasing imports, since export industries typically are more rapidly growing, progressive, flexible, and versatile than import-competing industries, in which tariff cuts are likely to come on top of relative stagnation due to other causes. The only point of the question is this: in the responses our economic system always must make to inumerable sorts of change, would we rather see cutbacks in the relatively efficient or in the relatively inefficient uses of American labor and resources? Which would fit in better with a continuing rise in the American standard of living?

THE TRULY HARMED MINORITY

No amount of conjecture about exports, reassuring statistics, or actual examples of easy adjustments to imports can shake the fact that adopting free trade *would* harm a minority of persons, some badly.* These victims will find little consolation in the bright overall picture; misery loves company and may be worse for lack of it.

The fate of even a single person can take on a human-interest appeal that depends hardly at all on how many or few others are sharing the same fate; statistics like those of Magee and Baldwin and Mutti cannot answer emotional arguments. "We realize that the domestic scissor and shear industry with its 1,000-plus employees accounts for only a fraction of 1 percent of the gross national product," said its spokesman, "but we see this as no justification for letting the industry be completely destroyed by imports produced with low-cost labor."[8] Precisely because it is small, a damaged

---

*There is such a thing as overemphasizing even perfectly truthful examples of industries and firms that have responded easily and effectively to import competition. Free-traders are on shaky ground if they imply that practically all victims of import competition could achieve the same good results if only they tackled their problems in the proper spirit. This implied argument about the possibilities of defeating or sidestepping import competition all across the board has a subtle kinship with the protectionist cheap-labor fallacy. Actually, some industries will always progress less rapidly than others; and because comparative disadvantage is comparative and because imports do tend to balance exports, some industries, despite their best efforts, are bound to face trouble from import competition. Of course, imports are not the main source of troublesome competition. (Cf. Don D. Humphrey, *American Imports,* p. 485.)

group can plan on sympathy for the underdog.* The victims are definite, identifiable people; the freedom of foreign trade to which their interests are sacrificed seems an intangible goal. The economist's standard answer about the more productive reabsorption of resources "released" from import-competing industries, valid and crucial though it is in going beyond an excessively short-run and narrow view, seems hopelessly abstract and callous to actual victims. The economist cannot tell these people just where they will be reabsorbed, or how soon; his analysis deals with resources on the average or in general. It waves a red flag at the victims, who do not want to be "released." They are proud of their skill and work and do not know where they could be more productive. They will not listen patiently to any subtle explanation that their productivity appears as high as it does only because a tariff has been falsifying the prices at which their output is valued.

Comparisons with technical progress will hardly cheer up businessmen and workers in trouble from this source also and for whom import competition, even though a minor problem compared with others, may well prove a last straw. In fact, the combination of troubles from several sources wins sympathy among politicians and draws attention to the one trouble, marginal though it may be, that protectionist measures do seem able to remedy.

A few examples are worth noticing of the kind of heart-tugging appeals that free-traders must come to grips with if they can. The president of the Shears, Scissors & Manicure Implement Manufacturers Association, quoted just above, told the House Ways and Means Committee of talking

to an old German chap about in his sixties or seventies who came here many years ago because this country needed his skill— his scissor- and shear-making skill.

He came here, he worked hard, he built himself a little factory. He had a sizable mortgage. He raised a family. He built a business manufacturing scissors and shears to the point where he had 50 to 60 employees. The day that I visited him, he had himself, his wife and his two sons working. They were working on grinding wheels and his wife was packaging a few pair of scissors. With tears in his eyes he asked me what he was to do.

*See two hours of testimony and sympathetic interrogation of a spokesman for the wooden clothespin industry, which consisted at the time of 8 companies employing a total of approximately 650 people. (Senate Finance Committee Hearings, March 1955, I, 391-413.)

He said: "I came to this country because they needed me. It was the country of opportunity. After all these years, I am an old man. I trained my boys, I brought them along in this industry, and now we reach the point where this country does not want me anymore. What do you think I can do? Where can I go?" Unfortunately, in that period of 2 years since I last saw him, he died, so we do not have a problem with him anymore.[9]

A South Carolina newspaper reported interviews with employees of a carded gingham mill soon to be closed because of Japanese competition. "Older employees, who have worked at their jobs for 30 or more years and reared their children within the sound of the deep-throated mill whistle, accepted with mixed emotions yesterday the official announcement that they will have no jobs after this month." None of the employees had lined up new jobs. Few of the older ones had any hopes. Men who had "worked in the weave room for 21 years," had been "in charge of the dye department for 30 years," and had "worked in the card room and engine room for 35 years" outlined the tragedy facing their own and their friends' families. "Only one person, a gray haired woman who had worked in the winder room for 26 years, broke into tears when questioned by a newspaper reporter."[10]

Another newspaper reported the effect of glass imports on Arnold, Pennsylvania. "The giant glass manufacturing plant that has provided work here since the 1880s is now as silent as the distant green hills across the Allegheny River," said the paper:

The click-clack of machinery no longer is heard, and no work-men swarm about the yards.

Not a wisp of smoke comes from the rusting stacks that tower over this city of 10,000 residents.[11]

Workers who were left unemployed by the closing of the plant were, in the words of one local spokesman, "too young to retire" and "too old to get another job." The idea of going on relief was "bitter medicine" for a proud people "who never believed in taking a handout from anyone." "I never lose hope," said one fifty-year-old worker who had lost his job. "Maybe someone will buy the place and put us all back to work. After all, the best glass in the world always came from Arnold."[12]

"The American Schiffli industry is not seeking to impede United States foreign policy or efforts for greater trade among nations." Nor is it trying "to preserve an intrinsically uneconomic or useless industry through selfishness or chauvinism." But

if realistic import quotas are not imposed immediately, our industry will perish, and with its demise the book will be closed on the

economic future of the North Hudson area. We have no wish to
be a dimly remembered footnote in that book or have people ask:
    Is this how a grateful country showed its gratitude, its faith in
the so-called "little people?"[13]

Not all people who complain about import competition are preoccupied
with their own fate; some are more altruistic. This is true of the handbag
and leather-goods workers:

> . . . we are for more trade abroad and more aid for foreign countries
> in need of our help and appreciative of our help, but we are
> unalterably opposed to H. R. 1 [the trade-agreements bill], mainly
> and principally because the handbag and personal leather goods
> workers wish to be in a position to help others abroad. They can
> only do that if they are fully employed at home and not jobless
> and on relief rolls.[14]

Our using this quotation is rather sarcastic, but it stands undeleted to
suggest what kind of reply free-trade economists feel almost irresistibly
tempted to give to the overdrawn sentimentality so often used by
protectionists.

Sometimes free-traders slip from sarcasm into something worse. Few as
they are, genuine victims of tariff cuts are an annoying fact. We wish that
they and their plight did not exist, and from wishing so we drift into thinking
that they *ought not* to exist. We subconsciously *blame* them for existing,
or at least for letting their existence be known. They begin to seem less like
victims than culprits. They are special-pleading, whining, inefficient
vested interests, holding back progress and subverting the general welfare—
or so we come close to thinking.

Literally adding insult to injury in this way is a tactical mistake.* Sound
tactics and ordinary courtesy require trying to understand the position of
import victims. The businessman in a victimized industry has a responsibility
to do what he can for his stockholders, employees, suppliers, distributors,
and fellow-townsmen; the union leader has a similar responsibility towards
his members and neighbors. Men with special knowledge of the problems
of a particular industry or locality can hardly be expected to suppress this
knowledge and adopt an abstract, overall, national view instead. The

---

*And perhaps an analytical mistake as well. Victims of import competi-
tion are not necessarily less efficient, in an absolute sense, than their foreign
competitors. Recall pp. 50-54 above.

spokesman for an import-victimized industry is not necessarily doing something selfish and blameworthy; he is simply doing his job in reporting detailed, concrete facts that few people know as well as he does. Congressmen, for their part, welcome this information so that they can decide for themselves which facts really are relevant. Economists can insist on relevance while respecting the legitimate sympathy that one man can have for another man's plight. Nothing in the case for free trade opposes aid to innocent victims of poverty or unemployment, provided that aid is not preconditioned on misfortunes attributable to imports *in particular*.

THE ROLE OF FLEXIBLE COSTS

Although most points at issue between protectionists and free-traders hinge almost entirely on logic and facts, this is not true of the problem of adjustment difficulties. On this question, value judgments also are crucial. We cannot hope to settle the question, therefore, but only to clarify the dispute over value judgments.

Professor Yale Brozen once made an illuminating comment on a plea for a tariff to compensate for wage differentials and protect certain paper mills located in isolated small towns where people would be stranded if the mills were to close. Why, he asks, are wage rates so burdensomely high and would they remain so high even if paper prices were to fall? If the answer is competition from employers in other industries, the people are not really stranded. If other jobs are not available locally, yet workers want to stay where they are, a sufficient drop in wages could let the mills stay in business. Paper workers who value staying where they are despite a lack of job alternatives can stay, provided they themselves pay for this valued privilege by accepting low enough wages. Why should other Americans subsidize them, any more than they should have subsidized shipyard workers to keep on building unwanted ships after the end of World War II? Paper workers who do not value staying put strongly enough to accept the necessary low wages have the alternative of moving elsewhere.[15] One might add that given the drop in demand supposedly due to import competition, wage flexibility does not victimize paper workers. On the contrary, it gives them the third alternative of accepting lower wages in addition to the alternatives of becoming unemployed or moving elsewhere.

"There was a time in the past," says Mr. Abraham Weiss of the International Leather Goods, Plastics, and Novelties Workers Union, when efforts "to meet price competition in such a labor intensive product as handbags would take the form of cutting wages and speeding up workers. But the existence of strong and effective trade unionism in the handbag industry militates against such a possibility."[16]

In reply, one might question the desirability of the wage rigidities introduced by collective bargaining. Wage flexibility, on the other hand, would not keep workers from suffering an unfavorable redistribution of income when import competition grew more intense. This fact is close to the heart of the tariff controversy. Under a long-standing tariff, profits and wages in protected industries have become adjusted to the general level prevailing throughout the economy. A tariff cut might be just one of the many disturbances always occurring in a dynamic economy. To the victims, though, it "looks like a deliberately inflicted wound."[17]

ADJUSTMENT ASSISTANCE

Adjustment assistance was conceived of as an alternative to simply letting the victims of tariff cuts accept unemployment or wage cuts. This idea responds in part to the concern that some economists have expressed about a change in government policy, even a change from protection to free trade, that harms *anyone*. Endorsing such a change may imply the comparison or the adding and subtracting of changes in welfare of different people—a procedure considered incompatible both with sound economic theory and with a philosophy that respects each individual and recognizes no mystical social welfare above the welfare of individuals. Ideally, each person knows his own situation better than anyone else, and only everyone's consent could prove that a policy change harms no one.[18]

As embodied in recent trade legislation, the idea of adjustment assistance recognizes how impractical it would be to try to work out a program of compensation in advance to win the consent of almost everyone. Congress and the President and their tariff-negotiating agents must act for the good of the whole country as they see it, with no real hope of accurately assessing the gains and losses of particular groups. If some people then experience serious injury or face a clear threat, the government may step in to ease their adjustment to a more viable position in the economy.

The Trade Expansion Act of 1962 embodied this idea. In passing it, incidentally, Congress made its first formal admission that some of the tariff cuts to be permitted might indeed cause serious injury; earlier legislation pretended to seek the gains of freer trade at little cost to anyone. The act preserved the "escape-clause" feature of earlier legislation, whereby the President could raise or impose tariffs on imports found by the Tariff Commission to have been "the major factor in causing, or threatening to cause" injury to an import-competing industry and to have resulted "in major part" from "concessions granted under trade agreements."[19] This "tariff adjustment" feature presumably contradicted the spirit of the adjustment assistance provisions, which were intended in effect to compensate tariff cut victims without undoing the tariff cuts by which they had been victimized. Nevertheless, the President had the option, under the escape clause, of authorizing firms and workers in industries found to be "seriously" injured by past tariff cuts to apply directly to the Secretaries of Commerce and Labor for adjustment assistance. In those cases, therefore, firms and workers could obtain relief through adjustment assistance, in addition to or instead of relief through higher tariffs.

Individual firms and workers could also petition the Tariff Commission directly for adjustment assistance. The Commission determined whether the petitioner was suffering "serious injury" (in the case of a firm) or "significant" "unemployment or underemployment" (in the case of a group of workers) caused "in major part" by past trade concessions. Upon an affirmative determination by the Commission and a certification of eligibility by the President, the petitioner applied for assistance to the Secretary of Commerce or Labor, as appropriate.

The particular kind of relief offered, if any, depended in part on the judgment of the Secretary of Commerce or Labor. Workers laid off because of import competition could receive 65 percent of their earlier wages during up to a year of unemployment and up to a year and a half of approved retraining. (This program was in addition to government-financed retraining for workers displaced by automation or other technological change.) The Act also authorized some travel and relocation allowances. Injured companies could receive some slight tax relief, loans or guarantees of loans to finance modernization or conversion, and technical assistance (such as research aid, expert advice on improving efficiency, and information on markets for products they were already making or would switch into making). In industry cases, the President could raise tariffs to as much as 50 percent above the 1934 level (which could multiply the current rates on some products sevenfold).

As implemented, the adjustment assistance provisions of the Trade Expansion Act encountered criticism from supporters and opponents alike. One difficulty was attributed to the initial slowness of the Tariff Commission in certifying workers, firms, or industries for adjustment assistance or tariff adjustment. The Commission found unanimously against the petitioner in every one of the first 17 complaints submitted to it under the act (from May 1962 to August 1964). No petitions were submitted by a firm or group of workers until January 1963, and the Commission denied eligibility for adjustment assistance in the case of all fifteen petitions submitted by firms or workers through January 1968. Finally, in November 1969, it found that a group of "buttweld pipe and tubing" workers were eligible for such assistance, initiating a period of somewhat greater leniency toward petitioners.

This leniency was aided by the Commission's apparent discovery that a spurt in imports could be attributed "in major part" to trade concessions that had been made many years in the past. The idea was that, even though there were no past trade concessions that could have "caused" the troublesome imports, those imports would not have occurred "but for" past trade concessions.[20] Thus, in the 1975 case of "manufactured granite," the Commission found the petitioner firm eligible for assistance on the basis of trade concessions begun in 1935 that, by 1951, had reduced the applicable duty to one-fourth of its statutory level. Commissioner Will E. Leonard observed in dissent that manufactured granite imports had actually decreased in recent years and that "if imports are decreasing at a point in time when concession rates are at their lowest level, there is some question whether the import increases of earlier years were the result in major part of trade agreement concessions or of other factors."[21]

The Trade Act of 1974 relaxes considerably the statutory conditions for obtaining import relief and adjustment assistance. The Tariff Commission, renamed the International Trade Commission, is, as before, required to investigate industry complaints of injurious import competition. Under the new law, however, the industry is eligible for relief or assistance if increased imports are found to be "a substantial cause" (even if not the "major" cause) of its troubles, whether or not those imports are attributable to past trade concessions. "Substantial cause" is defined to mean "a cause which is important and not less than any other cause." Once it finds that imports are a substantial cause of "serious injury or the threat thereof" to a domestic industry, the Commission must recommend either import relief or adjustment assistance to the President. If it recommends import relief, the President must impose a corrective tariff or trade restriction of some kind (unless he deems such relief contrary to the national interest) and give consideration to the provision of adjustment assistance. If adjustment assistance is recommended, he must direct the Secretary of Labor or Commerce (depending on whether workers or firms are to be assisted) to give "expeditious consideration" to petitions for it.[22]

The import relief provisions of the new law are akin to the old "escape-clause" or "tariff-adjustment" idea: the government provides relief not by compensating import victims for their troubles but by curbing the imports on which their troubles are blamed. These provisions authorize the President to impose new duties or raise old ones by as much as 50 percent of their existing rates, to proclaim tariff quotas, to impose or modify quantitative restrictions, and to "negotiate orderly marketing agreements with foreign countries" in whatever combination he considers necessary to provide a remedy. If the President decides not to grant import relief recommended by the Commission, a majority of Congress can override his decision and compel him to implement the Commission's recommendation.

Under the Trade Act of 1974, as under the Trade Expansion Act of 1962, injured workers and firms can receive adjustment assistance by showing injury to themselves without having to show injury to the entire industry to which they belong. Under the new law, however, petitions filed by workers and firms on their own behalf go directly to the Secretaries of Labor and Commerce rather than to the International Trade Commission. Petitioners are eligible to apply for assistance if imports have "contributed importantly" to "significant" layoffs or declining sales or production. "The term 'contributed importantly' means a cause which is important but not necessarily more important than any other cause." The trade readjustment allowance is increased to 70 percent of the worker's weekly wage, and other benefits in the form of employment services, training allowances, and job search and relocation allowances are provided. Eligible firms may obtain various forms of financial relief and technical assistance. Another change in the program permits entire communities to petition the Secretary of Commerce for public works projects and other forms of assistance when imports or transfer of operations abroad have "contributed importantly" to layoffs or to declining sales or production.

SOME PHILOSOPHICAL DIFFICULTIES

The adjustment assistance program has proved to be an awkward and unpopular attempt at compensating import victims. It is commonly ridiculed by its intended beneficiaries. According to Mr. John E. Mara, adjustment assistance is "no better than flowers for a funeral." It

> might be fine for the fellow who can't do his job because of physical change in himself. But when a man's job is artificially abolished, such as it is when imports put his firm out of business, then I say check imports; restore the injured business. Don't offer the men a sop in the form of another kind of dole.[23]

Even if relocation expenses "were to be absorbed by the program of retraining and other adjustment assistance, nothing can be done about the loss of friends, schools, church, and social relationships that have developed over many years."[24]
What Congressman Burke can't understand

> is with all the people pushing this free trade idea they keep talking about this adjustment assistance and they paint this beautiful picture of what is down the road for the poor fellow who loses his job.

Actually, under this proposal there is no assistance.

Why can't they be honest enough to come out and just don't recommend any assistance, because that is actually what they are doing? Tell people the facts. You are going to lose your job and there is nothing for you at the end of the road. Why hold out this promise to these people when these plants are being phased out?[25]

Exaggeration aside, the Congressman has a point. The adjustment-assistance program does seem to foster a mistaken belief that trade expansion can and should take place without anyone or hardly anyone being harmed.

The very idea of adjustment assistance as an instrument of international trade policy gives rise to questions of consistency with other policy goals. One might ask, for example, why people troubled by changes in trade and trade policy should receive more consideration than people troubled by, say, school busing or rising grain prices. Government constantly makes policy changes that it believes to be morally right or acceptable and that it does not regard as creating a legitimate demand for compensation. The sound presumption in favor of a stable legal framework does not add up to an ethical obstacle to nonunanimous changes in the law.

If one's concern is for the victims of past trade concessions, it is appropriate to ask some questions. Does this concern simply follow from a general humanitarian concern not to inflict or allow avoidable harm of any kind, or does it recognize some special moral or legal claim on the part of such victims? Has making the "concessions" amounted to a unilateral breach of contract? Was the tariff originally offered to business and labor as an inducement to undertake or remain in a work of national importance? The answer to the last question, at least, is typically "no"; instead, industry spokesmen wheedled protection from Congress.

The change in policy in favor of providing adjustment assistance on the basis of injury caused by imports as such rather than injury traceable to past trade concessions reflects the fuzziness of the original concept. As events quickly proved under the 1962 law, workers and firms can be harmed as much by imports caused by changes in tastes and technology as they can by imports caused by tariff cuts. The Tariff Commission's 1969 shift toward greater leniency in adjustment-assistance cases and Congress's action in 1974 to drop any stipulation of a causal link between imports and trade concessions suggest that there was hardly any breach of contract in making those concessions.

If adjustment assistance need not be tied to tariff cuts or other changes in trade policy, why should it be tied to increased imports? During the hearings that preceded the 1974 act, a representative of the American Imported Automobile Dealers Association recommended that "adjustment assistance also be made available for employees in import-dependent industries harmed by decreases in foreign imports due to Executive actions under the safeguard system."[26]

During the same hearings, several free traders and protectionists alike recognized the principle that people harmed by any change in events (policy-related or otherwise) deserved as much consideration as import victims. Thus Secretary of the Treasury George Shultz said that the "basic idea" of the President's trade bill was "not to single out people displaced by imports or firms that are affected by imports for special treatment but rather to look to our procedures for adjustment in general and ask what can be done to make them more effective."[27]

In a discussion with Mrs. Lucy Wilson Benson, President of the League of Women Voters, Congressman Corman asked: "If we are going to have serious dislocations in industry, shouldn't we take care of it no matter what caused the dislocation?"

Mrs. Benson answered:

> Yes, I would think we should have. Obviously it does not do, in a place like Seattle, to shut down several aircraft plants and turn thousands of people out of jobs, . . . but I suspect that the adjustment assistance related to trade may be slightly different from adjustment assistance which might be developed to take care of Government procurement problems such as the aircraft business.[28]

If government has a responsibility to people who lose jobs into which it had lured them in the first place, that is one reason for especial care and selectivity in making its commitments. But this principle is far removed from the argument, which seems to be evolving from the original adjustment assistance idea, that any person harmed by any economic change deserves some kind of compensation. The very relaxation of assistance criteria in the 1974 act shows how difficult it is to confine the compensation principle to actual instances of harm based on broken government promises.

Perhaps assistance really should be generalized. But before we simply "evolve" toward a policy of assisting anyone for any reason, we should consider the consequences. If self-styled victims must prove and not merely complain about injury to receive aid, they will have weak incentives to avoid the actual injury needed to document their claims. Firms will have weakened incentives to reconvert, and workers will have weakened incentives to move or to acquire new skills on their own initiative. Although the harm to be compensated for in the case of tariff cuts or increased imports is relatively small, the costs of a truly generalized adjustment assistance program could be as large as anyone wished to make them. After all, as many import victims have already testified, it really isn't possible to compensate for some of the burdens imposed by economic and political change. Thus a large tax burden could well be anticipated, with its own effects on incentives to work and save.

Perhaps, then, the choice boils down to the familiar one between trying to socialize risk at the expense of opportunity and trying only to provide for monetary stability and the other parts of an overall framework for general prosperity. If that is, indeed, the choice, then "adjustment assistance" turns out to be more contradictory than conducive to a policy of free trade.

NOTES

1. Robert E. Baldwin and John H. Mutti, "Policy Problems in the Adjustment Process (U.S.)," presented at the World Bank Seminar: Industrialization and Trade Policies in the 1970s, October 1972, unpublished, pp. 9-16.

2. Stephen P. Magee, "The Welfare Effects of Restrictions on U.S. Trade," *Brookings Papers on Economic Activity,* 1972, pp. 678-83.

3. 1962 HW&M IV 2114-15 (see Chapter 1, note 9).

4. In *Foreign Economic Policy* (1962), pp. 319, 322. (See Chapter 7, note 42.)

5. 1962 HW&M III 1657.

6. 1962 HW&M II 1257-58.

7. Stephen Enke, in *Foreign Trade Policy* (1958), p. 106. (See Chapter 1, note 5.)

8. 1962 HW&M III 1970.

9. 1962 HW&M III 1976.

10. The Greenville *News,* June 19, 1956, quoted in Fulton Lewis, Jr., *A GATT in Your Ribs* (Washington, D.C.: Fulton Lewis, Jr. Productions [1956]), pp. 10-12. It is not clear, incidentally, why people took the bad news with *mixed* emotions.

11. "Glass Layoffs Sap Life of Arnold and its Workers," *Pittsburgh Press,* entered by John H. Dent, in 1970 HW&M XI, 3147-48.

12. Ibid., 3148-49.

13. 1970 HW&M V 1588 (See Chapter 1, note 1).

14. Union statement included in the Senate Finance Committee Hearings, March 1955, III, 1475.

15. Yale Brozen, address of March 13, 1953, reprinted with slight modifications as "Trade and the Best Interests of the American People," in *Foreign Trade: The Twenty-Eighth Discussion and Debate Manual* (Madison, Wisc.: National University Extension Association, 1954). I, 116.

16. 1970 HW&M VII 2147.

17. J. H. Young, *Canadian Commercial Policy* (Ottawa: Royal Commission on Canada's Economic Prospects, 1957), p. 98.

18. Cf. James M. Buchanan, "Economic Policy, Free Institutions and Democratic Process," *Il Politico,* 1960, no. 2, pp. 265-77, and "Positive Economics, Welfare Economics, and Political Economy," *Journal of Law and Economics,* October 1959, pp. 124-38, especially the last page. The doctrine of unanimous consent is closely related to the voluntary-exchange theory of government discussed above, pp. 83-84.

19. Trade Expansion Act of 1962, sec. 301(b).

20. Baldwin and Mutti, op. cit., p. 19.

21. U. S. International Trade Commission, "Manufactured Granite: Joseph Weiss & Sons, Inc., Brooklyn, N.Y." (Washington: ITC Publication 713, February 1975).

22. Trade Act of 1974, sec. 202(a).

23. 1970 HW&M VII 2071.

24. Abraham Weiss, 1970 HW&M VII 2146.

25. 1973 HW&M V 1505 (see Chapter 1, note 8).

26. Robert M. McElwaine, in 1973 HW&M XI 3390.

27. In 1973 HW&M I 190.

28. 1973 HW&M IX 3007.

This final chapter makes some observations about two topics that can hardly be kept separate: actual steps toward free trade, and tactics of persuasion.

TARIFF BARGAINING

Perhaps the chief question about actual steps concerns the choice between independent national legislation and bargaining with other countries. Many people associate the latter approach with the retaliation and bargaining arguments for tariffs. If foreign countries have import barriers, shouldn't we retaliate in kind? Their barriers harm us as well as themselves, but in general we cannot remedy some trade barriers by erecting others. As Lord Beveridge once quipped, that other countries have bad harbors is no reason for sinking rocks around one's own coasts.

What about trade restrictions for bargaining power? Congressman John Watts asked U.S. trade negotiator Carl Gilbert whether it would strengthen his hand to be given "a list of things" that foreigners could not export to the United States without removing barriers of their own to U.S. trade.

> You wouldn't have to use it, but you could say, "Look, if you are going to do this to us, I have authority, if you can't reach an agreement with me, on reducing some of yours. I am going to put these things on the list that you can't send me."
> That would be just voluntary authority on your part, maybe.[1]

If clever bargaining should succeed, the gain would of course be real; getting rid of foreign trade barriers as well as our own is better than getting rid of ours only. To pass quickly over this point is not to deny its possibly great importance. But what more is there to say about anything so obvious?

Considerations on the other side are more conjectural and involve politics and psychology more than economics. Concern for preserving our bargaining power may lead us to keep tariffs longer than we otherwise would. Trade barriers maintained or increased with a view to future bargaining can hardly help but give at least incidental protection to groups who will press for its indefinite continuation. Preoccupation with bargaining focuses undue attention on whether our negotiators have been tough and vigilant enough. American protectionists often complain that reciprocal trade agreements are not really reciprocal, that the foreigners have outsmarted us, and that even if they do lower some tariffs, their most important trade barriers are the quotas, exchange controls, and discriminations that they maintain. The United States swaps horses for rabbits and sometimes doesn't even get the rabbits. Accurate or not, such charges tend to make us forget that our own tariff cuts, even considered by themselves, are benefits to us and not sacrifices. The usual talk of "reciprocity" and swapping "concessions" almost imagines the negotiating parties saying to each other, "You slit your throat, and I'll slit mine in return." The picture of American businessmen and workers being sacrificed to foreign interests draws support from provisions for "escaping" from "concessions" that turn out to have given away even more than intended. Protectionists can conjure with the image of visionary diplomats selling American industries down the river ridiculously cheap, at best out of ignorance and at worse in furtherance of some socialist plot. Congressman Burke likes to complain about the demise of the "old Yankee trader" and about the "softheaded" trade negotiators who give "something and get nothing back in return."[2] People forget that trade policy is basically a question of *domestic* efficiency and of short-run effects on income distribution *at home,* and not an issue over international frictions that need to be palliated by compromise.

As parts of compromises, a tightening of some trade barriers does not seem peculiar; witness the popularity of international commodity controls and ad hoc "orderly marketing agreements," Nor does it seem peculiar that the pressures of the bargaining process should sometimes make foreigners "voluntarily" restrict some of their exports to us. In some respects trade agreements can actually sanction and dignify protectionism. The idea flourishes that trade liberalization is an international issue to be hesitated and shrewdly negotiated about, something to be carefully measured and reconsidered and sometimes escaped from and reversed. Trade cannot be left free, it seems; it must submit to governmental and international planning.

Especially if free trade would have more symbolic and symptomatic than narrowly economic importance for the United States, there is much to be said for adopting it unilaterally. This step would repudiate the mistaken ideas just mentioned. It would set an example hardly possible under the bargaining approach. But these political and psychological considerations admittedly take us onto shaky ground. If the prospect of concessions from foreigners really is necessary to make Congress and the American public acquiesce in moving toward free trade, perhaps purist objections are idle.

RECIPROCAL TRADE AGREEMENTS AND GATT

The United States has followed the bargaining approach since 1934, when the Trade Agreement Act first gave the President limited power to negotiate agreements not requiring Senate ratification and then to implement them by putting agreed duty cuts into effect. Significantly, the Roosevelt administration sold the program to Congress and the public as an emergency measure to negotiate bigger export markets.

From 1934 to 1947 the United States made only bilateral agreements with other countries. Even then, under the "most favored nation" principle, duty cuts on goods from one country were automatically extended to the same goods coming from all countries, except for a few countries ruled to be discriminating against American exports. To limit these free "concessions," American negotiators usually bargained over tariff cuts on each particular product only with the chief country supplying it to the United States. Sometimes the product was narrowly and cleverly defined so that only our partner in the negotiations could much increase its sales. The agreement of 1939 with the United Kingdom revived a separate classification for bone china, exported almost solely by the English; feldspar china from Japan and continental Europe remained dutiable at the old rates. To limit Japanese competition, the further reductions on chinaware negotiated at Geneva in 1948 introduced "value brackets"; the reduced rates applied only to items of more than a specified value, which came mainly from England and continental Europe and not from Japan. The agreement with Mexico confined the duty cut on sandals to huaraches, almost by definition of Mexican manufacture. Such practices permit observing the letter while evading the spirit of the principle of nondiscrimination.

As the 1948 example shows, this devious practice survived to some extent even under the General Agreement on Tariffs and Trade. GATT was first negotiated by 23 countries at Geneva in 1947. The United States took part under the President's authority to make trade agreements without Senate ratification. Rather amusingly, Congress always carefully specified, in subsequent renewals of the Trade Agreements Act, that its action meant neither approval nor disapproval of GATT. At first, GATT was intended only as a forerunner of a proposed International Trade Organization, whose charter was signed in 1948 but never ratified. GATT carried on, basically and legally a mere agreement but with some features of an international organization, including a secretariat in Geneva and periodic meetings. The General Agreement contains: (1) a code of agreed principles of trade practice, including a ban on quantitative restrictions, but with far-reaching exceptions; and (2) lists of products on which duties have been removed or cut or "bound" against being raised. Members of GATT—87 countries by 1974—account for the great bulk of world trade. (From the start the Agreement has permitted discrimination in trade policy against countries not originally belonging to it, even if they should later join. Japan, which became a full member in 1955, has been the most notable victim of this provision.)

GATT negotiations used to proceed on product-by-product basis, each country's delegation bargaining separately but simultaneously with a number of others and agreed concessions being generalized under the most-favored-nation principle. However, during the sixth or "Kennedy" round of negotiations under GATT, the participating countries agreed on "linear" (equal-percentage) tariff cuts on a broad range of products. The general approach was to reduce tariffs by 50 percent on all goods but for certain itemized exceptions and "product sectors" such as agriculture, steel, and cotton textiles, for which separate bargaining took place. The U.S. derived its authority to participate in the negotiations from the Trade Expansion Act of 1962, which permitted 50 percent reductions of all U.S. tariffs and 100 percent reductions of U.S. tariffs on goods for which the United States and the European Common Market accounted for at least 80 percent of world exports.

In 1973, the United States agreed with 100 other countries to enter into a seventh round of negotiations, and, on January 3, 1975, the "Trade Act of 1974" became law. It allows the President five years to negotiate trade agreements providing for (1) the reduction of tariffs by as much as 60 percent of their rates effective January 1, 1975 ("nuisance" rates of less than 5 percent can be reduced to zero); (2) "the harmonization, reduction, or elimination" of nontariff trade barriers; and (3) "the prohibition of or limitations on the imposition of such barriers (or other distortions)."

The Trade Act calls for negotiations on a "product sector" basis, intended in the words of the Senate finance committee to guarantee

> equivalent competitive opportunities among the developed
> countries of the world in various definable sectors. The requirement
> for achieving equivalence of competitive opportunities within
> sectors does not require equal tariff and nontariff barriers for each

narrowly defined product within a sector, but overall equal
competitive opportunities within a sector. The Committee feels
that appropriate product sectors would include, among others,
such industries as steel, aluminum, electronics, chemicals and
electrical machinery.... [3]

THE RESULTS OF U.S. BARGAINING

GATT and earlier agreements have significantly lowered American
tariffs. Most of the deliberate cuts had already been made by about 1951 or
1952; apparently the limited authority remaining under the Trade
Agreements Act, together with the spirit of the then newly added "peril-
point" and "escape" clauses, inhibited American negotiators. Protectionists
sometimes complain about the extent of duty cuts by citing statistics such
as these: in 1930, customs collections reached a peak of about 45 percent of
the value of dutiable imports; on the average over the period 1929-38, customs
collections amounted to 41.9 percent of the value of dutiable imports and to
16.9 percent of the value of duty-free and dutiable imports together. In
1971, however, these ratios were down to 9.2 and 6.1 percent respectively.
According to one estimate, the average U.S. tariff has fallen to 72 percent
below what it was in 1934.[4]

If we really have come as close to free trade as such figures supposedly
imply, yet have prospered as we have, why not take the one small remaining
step and set the world a dramatic example? Actually, figures of the kind
cited may exaggerate our tariff cuts. The ratio of customs collections to
import values is a poor measure of the extent of protection. Suppose, as an
extreme example, that all goods except duty-free raw materials were subject
to a 1,000 percent tariff that completely blocked imports. Customs
collections amounting to zero percent of total imports would then mean
quite the opposite of free trade. The average restrictiveness of tariff walls
is even harder to estimate and compare than their heights, since
restrictiveness depends on the price-sensitivity of demands for imports.[5]*

Although comparisons of trade barriers between countries are notori-
ously tricky and of doubtful meaning, it may be instructive to cite some of the

---

*Apart from this, even the *effective rates* of duty are likely to exceed the
ordinary published rates. An import duty of x percent gives more than x
percent protection to use of domestic labor and other productive factors in a
protected industry when the industry uses some foreign materials imported
duty-free or at a duty of less than x percent. See above, pp. 62-66.

STRATEGY OF FREE TRADE

estimates arrived at by the International Trade Commission in its study of U.S. trade barriers. We can note, for example, that the post-Kennedy-round average tariff on dutiable industrial products (effective January 1, 1972, the date by which all tariff cuts agreed to during the Kennedy Round were to have been made) is, by one calculation, 12.1 percent for the United States, 15.2 percent for Canada, 11.2 percent for Japan, 7.5 percent for the European Common Market (consisting, for these calculations, of only the original Six: France, Belgium, Luxembourg, the Netherlands, West Germany, and Italy—Britain, Denmark, and Ireland joined later), and 10.5 percent for Britain. Calculated only on *finished* industrial products subject to duty, the percentages are higher: 13.8 for the United States, 16.1 for Canada, 11.8 for Japan, 8.1 for the Common Market, and 12.1 for Britain. The United States imposes relatively high tariffs on certain product sectors, for example, an 18.4 percent duty on textiles and a 19.5 percent duty on a sector called "professional, scientific and controlling instruments, photographic apparatus, clocks and watches."[6]*

Although nontariff trade barriers are, by most calculations more important than tariffs (compare the calculations by Magee, above, p. 62), they are even more difficult to compare. The International Trade Commission provided one comparison on the basis of 1970-1971 data and for 15 quantitative restrictions, including import quotas. The Commission divided world trade into 1,318 product categories and calculated the "number" (the raw number weighted by the assumed restrictiveness of each restriction) of restrictions imposed by each of 17 countries (including the United States, Canada, Japan, and the nine Common Market countries) in each category. Altogether 3,358 such restrictions were counted for the 17 countries. Of the group, the United States ranked 7th in the number of product categories subject to at least one restriction and seventh in the number of restrictions. (The Commission counted 148 product categories and 190 restrictions for the United States. Altogether 26.2 percent of world trade falls into the product categories subject to these restrictions). Another ranking that combined these data and weighted them by total imports of the major trading countries showed the United States to be third in order of restrictiveness.[7]

---

*One really needs detailed knowledge of commodities and their prices to estimate the percentage equivalents of duties expressed as so many cents per unit or as a combination of cents per unit and percentage of value. Browsing through the tariff schedules is worthwhile to get an idea of the fantastically complicated way in which commodities are classified and duties expressed.

A TIMID APPROACH

These figures suggest that the trade-agreements program has not achieved anything close to free trade. That program has proved a timid one, intended more to secure better access to markets for U.S. products (obtained by offering concessions so carefully chosen as to have only a limited impact) than to achieve a more efficient use of American resources. For most of the period since 1934 American negotiators hunted for duties they could offer to cut without markedly increasing competitive imports. Duties on nail clippers, cheap knife blades and handles, and low-priced electric meters, for example, remained above 100 percent even after being cut in half. (As time went on, less and less room remained for thus meaninglessly "squeezing the water out of the tariff.") In his original proposal to Congress in 1934, President Roosevelt promised that "no sound and important American interest will be injuriously disturbed." President Truman did not even limit his assurances to "sound and important" interests; he promised that "domestic producers would be safeguarded in the process of expanding trade" and that the program would not be used "in such a way as to endanger or trade out segments of the American industry, American agriculture, or American labor."[8] President Eisenhower said that no American industry will be placed in jeopardy. Although the Kennedy and subsequent administrations conceded that further trade liberalization would cause some harm, that idea has not won general acceptance. The Senate Finance Committee has been quite explicit about the "import relief" provisions of the Trade Act of 1974:

> If the choice is between (1) allowing an industry to collapse and thereby creating greater unemployment, larger Federal or state unemployment compensation payments, reduced tax revenues, and all the other costs to the economy associated with high unemployment, *or* (2) temporarily protecting that industry from excessive imports at some marginal costs to the consumer, then the Committee feels that the President should adopt the latter course and protect the industry and the jobs associated with that industry.[9]

This rule, literally applied, would reverse past trade "concessions," block new ones, and force the President to protect those very domestic industries which are, by virtue of their vulnerability to imports, the least comparatively efficient.

The "escape clause" described in the preceding chapter is symptomatic; and its evolution reflects increasing Congressional concern as opportunities for merely removing excess protection came closer to being used up, so that further concessions would have to be really meaningful. Opinions differ on just how restrictive the old escape clause concept was. Under the Trade Expansion Act of 1962 affirmative findings were made in only four cases: pianos, sheet glass, certain ceramic tableware, and certain ball bearings. The expanded scope for "import relief" under the Trade Act of 1974, however, portends more such findings in the future.

THE REGIONAL APPROACH

One fashionable variant of the agreements approach to free trade is the formation of customs unions or free-trade areas of limited membership. Apparently inspired as much by political as by economic ideas, the European Common Market does impress believers in a capitalist economy as, on the whole, a welcome development. It represents a further departure from protectionist thinking than seemed at all likely as recently as two or three decades ago. In its first few years, its members achieved higher rates of growth of total production and of trade among themselves than were typical in the rest of the world. (This favorable contrast was probably due, however, more to the continuation of already prevailing European trends, and possibly to optimistic attitudes among businessmen, than to gains in efficiency due directly to tariff cuts.)

Still, the Common Market by no means envisages complete free trade. In moving toward a uniform external tariff, for example, its members having the lowest tariffs were originally expected to *raise* their duties on imports from nonmember countries. Economic theory points to the possibility— though hardly a strong probability—that diversion of trade away from the outside world will outweigh the benefits of trade creation within a customs union. (Recall the example of the discriminatory duty cut in the section on "Taxes and Tariffs" of Chapter 12.) Discrimination against outsiders, particularly against underdeveloped countries that stand to lose markets for their agricultural and mineral exports, may be objectionable on similar grounds.

Another thing tempering the enthusiasm of some observers is the naive infatuation that contributes so much to the fashionableness of the regional approach. If regionalism turns out to be a genuine *approach* to free trade, however, and not a permanent stopping point, purist objections are pointless. If a road takes us where we want to go, we need not worry if some of its early stretches temporarily take us farther away from our destination in straight-line distance. The regional approach may actually have a dynamism of its own if discrimination against countries left outside one customs union presses some of them to form a new union of their own in self-defense and if separate unions eventually merge. Even sheer fad has self-reinforcing features that free-traders might as well take advantage of while the opportunity lasts.

UNILATERAL APPROACHES

Abstractly considered, international agreements could achieve either a sudden or a gradual and either an across-the-board or a selective movement to free trade. In practice, though, the approach through agreements is likely to be piecemeal, selective, gradual, and uncertain. By adopting free trade independently, instead, the United States could show the whole world that it sees tariff removal not as a self-inflicted injury to be carefully measured and paid for but as a direct benefit to itself. This dramatic example might do more for the cause of worldwide free trade than years of negotiations. It would avoid putting the stamp of approval on the protectionist ideas that show up in the inevitable exceptions and reservations and escape clauses of international agreements.

Unilateral action would let us make the transition as we think best. Several considerations are relevant. First, the more narrowly defined the product area on which duties are cut, the more concentrated are the losses and the smaller the broad gains from the cuts. The selective, piecemeal approach gives protectionists the chance to exploit the principle that the squeaking wheel gets the most grease. Particularly if carried out at somebody's administrative discretion, this approach involves power to help or harm particular industries and firms, power possibly subject to political abuse. An across-the-board approach, in contrast, lets each person gain in all of his economic roles except that of being especially connected with a deprotected industry or activity. Furthermore, businessmen would probably be more willing to make adjustments when they knew that instead of having been deliberately selected for early sacrifice, they were simply adjusting along with everyone else to a pervasive if mild economic change. Across-the-board liberalization could be made a matter of principle and avoid the unprincipled wrangling of a piecemeal product-by-product approach.

A related question is whether to adopt free trade in one single law or in a series of laws. The one-law approach would avoid the pains of long-drawn-out indecision and uncertainty, yet need not mean putting free trade into effect at one swoop. Some persuasive arguments can be made for a quick once-and-for-all change: pull the decayed tooth suddenly instead of chipping it out gradually. On the other hand, much can be said for a slow but sure transition, giving interests deprived of protection time for almost painless adjustments. An almost decisive advantage, apparently, is that this would largely sidestep the thorny issue of governmental adjustment assistance. One of several approaches of this kind would be a law, passed once and for all, that introduced complete free trade over a specified time period. Such a law might well junk the Buy-American rules on one definite date and dismantle import quotas and other nontariff barriers over the same period that tariffs were being lowered. It might cut all import duties steadily toward zero, perhaps by 1 or 2 percent a month from initial levels. The more frequent and slight the cuts, the less concentrated the impact on anybody would be and the less incentive merchants would have to postpone imports as the time for each new cut in duties drew near and then stage a stampede of importing immediately afterwards. In fact, cutting tariffs each *day* would not be complicated. The duty payable on each shipment imported could first be figured in dollars and cents exactly as under present tariff rates and regulations and then multiplied by a percentage set slightly lower each day according to a calendar published in advance. A drop in this multiplier by 1/50 of 1 percentage point each day would bring complete free trade in 13 years and 8½ months.

CAMPAIGNING FOR FREE TRADE

Removing tariffs and other trade barriers in some such way seems economically sound and administratively easy, even if politically bizarre. If we ever do arrive at free trade, it probably will have been after an untidy mixture of bargaining and unilateralism, broadness and selectivity, suddenness and gradualness, and progress and backsliding. But should this realistic recognition deter free-traders from advocating whatever they think best and influencing policy as much as they can?

This question leads into some thoughts about the propaganda tactics of free-traders. The core of a free-trade campaign must be economic education. Protectionist fallacies must be exposed often enough and simply enough to win a foothold for understanding outside of academic circles. It is not beyond hope that several hundred thousand or even several million Americans can come to understand the logic of the price system, the gains from trade, and comparative advantage. Eventually they will see that the clash of interests in tariff matters is not between Americans and foreigners but between each particular group of producers on the one hand and the rest of the American people on the other. They will see the importance of free trade not merely for the United States but also for its trading partners in the underdeveloped world, and not merely for direct material benefit but especially as a demonstration of the logic of a market economy. It is unnecessary for a majority of voters to understand the issues in detail. If understanding spreads widely among newspapermen, businessmen and labor leaders, politicians, and others who enjoy influence, such men will carry other voters along with them.

THE APPEAL TO AUTHORITY

Only a minority will care to follow economic reasoning for themselves and check its validity. In appealing to the others, then, how legitimately can free-trade propaganda use the argument from authority? In the past, few economists would have objected. As a recent Nobel laureate in economics has observed, the nineteenth-century economist would first have explained how specialization along lines of comparative advantage promotes efficient use of resources and would then have concluded without hesitation "that the case for free trade was established. The modern economist, on the other hand, is much more nervous about this next step." Changes in circumstances and economic thinking alike have called the free-trade principle into question. Economists no longer accept free trade, even as an ideal, in the way they used to. "Economics has not lost authority, but the preponderance of economic opinion is no longer so certainly as it was on the Free Trade side."[10]

Nevertheless, enough present-day economists have declared themselves personally in favor of complete free trade, with qualifications no more serious than our own, that singling out a few for quotation here hardly seems worth while. Perhaps surprisingly, though, statements favoring free trade are extremely rare in textbooks of international economics. Practically all the texts canvassed avoid a clear-cut position. Quite a few authors straightforwardly analyze the gains from trade, show that each of the leading protectionist arguments is either wrong or of very limited applicability, clearly imply that the freer trade is, the better, drop hints of personal preference for freer trade, but stop short of flatly declaring for *free* trade. This seems odd, since few if any textbooks actually say—though reasons are conceivable why they might—that their arguments for further trade liberalization become less valid according to how closely policy has already moved towards free trade.

How much pause should this state of affairs give to free-traders? Their avowed allies, while numerous, seem to be in the minority among economists nowadays, although outright protectionists are even fewer. The average economist probably recognizes that some of the sophisticated "theoretical-curiosity" arguments can be valid in principle, and he does not want dogmatically to rule out any chance that one might occasionally apply in practice. In his authoritative survey, John R. Hicks finds that analysis of the following topics has done most to undermine the simplicity of the old free-trade position: (1) divergence between private and social benefits and costs, due to such things as monopoly and externalities; (2) terms-of-trade manipulation; (3) balance-of-payments trouble occurring at the same time that expansionary domestic policy is needed to cure or prevent recession and unemployment; and (4) uncertainty about how economic development takes place and a willingness to see diversified experimentation by countries striving for development.[11]* To this list one might reasonably add (5) defense and (6) adjustment difficulties.

Hicks considers the free-trade argument "as valid as ever"; only "the exceptions have grown up and, in the minds of many, have overshadowed the positive argument." Many familiar exceptions received too little attention in the past but should not receive too much now. Hicks confesses that he still inclines towards free trade himself and still sees "an ideal, not in principle unattainable, in which those who prize the inheritance of Adam Smith can still believe, with open eyes and honest minds."[12]

Professor Gottfried Haberler makes much the same point about exceptions to the free-trade rule. Confidence that they are negligible has given way in some very able minds to

almost the opposite conviction: the exceptions have become the rule and vice versa. . . . By feeding unrealistic, exaggerated factual assumptions (concerning external economies, rigidities, etc). and perverse value judgments into the theoretical machine, unwise, pernicious, and perverse policy conclusions can be deduced from a valid theory by logically valid procedures.[13]

Haberler deplores this misuse of classical theory to justify protectionist policies. He goes on to list several reasons why free trade is still the best general policy: (1) Workable competition does prevail, despite exaggerated emphasis on monopoly. (2) Many of the monopolies and rigidities that do exist and many artificialities of government policy are bolstered by protectionism and would wither under free trade. (3) Arguments for

---

*Of point 3, Hicks significantly says that unless we "go right over to a system of flexible exchange rates," the case is strong for import restriction to permit expansion without balance-of-payments trouble. "It is this, more than anything else, which has undermined the intellectual foundations of Free Trade." (Hicks, op. cit., pp. 52-53.)

protection are often contradictory, making rational protectionist policy virtually impossible. (4) Experience demonstrates a far wider gulf between ideal and actual government economic planning than between ideal and actual operation of the market.[14]

Related to concern with theoretical exceptions is another reason why outright support of free trade is a minority position these days. Their training makes economists alert to see that relevant choices are often not between all and nothing, not between only one thing and only another. Rather, they are choices at the margin, choices of whether to have a little more of one thing at the sacrifice of a little of another. A loose analogy with this principle of marginalism causes some discomfort about an all-or-nothing choice between extreme protectionism and complete free trade. The presumption seems to run in favor of some middle position. So many different tariff schedules and kinds of trade control can be devised to choose from that if some are demonstrably wrong, others, anyway, may be right. Complete free trade smacks of laissez-faire doctrine; yet laissez-faire is only one of innumerable conceivable policy patterns and would be best only by extreme coincidence. To many, the doctrine stems from a callously comfortable belief that things will work themselves out for the best if left alone. Or it stems from some sort of superstitious trust in the magical efficiency of a price system. In contrast with mysticism and ivory-tower dogmatism, a hesitation to condemn tariffs completely and a willingness to consider each case on its own merits may appear more factual-minded and realistic. For reasons previously explained in comments on the second-best theories, these slogans hardly justify sympathy for protectionism, but they do indicate psychological reasons for hesitating to endorse free trade completely.

These remarks may seem to carry too far into the realm of psychoanalysis. In mentioning people's motives, though, we are not now concerned with how valid what they say is but with how significant their failure to take a clear-cut position is. Another motive for reticence may simply be that the free-trade case is "old hat" and tiresome; it is a more challenging mental exercise, and more fun, to play around with imaginary policy applications of theoretical gadgetry. For some purposes, "It is better to be bright than right." Still another motive may be the feeling that advocating any policy is unscientific and out of place in scholarly contexts, since value judgments would have to enter in. Some writers may be reacting to exaggerated presentations of the free-trade case in the past. Or an author may expect a free-trade conclusion to have more impact if the reader draws it himself from the analysis presented instead of finding it thrust on him prefabricated; reasons are more important than the author's personal opinion. A final bit of explanation may be self-restraint akin to what judges traditionally used to practice in not making any more sweeping a decision and creating any more law than the case at hand demanded. Similarly, economists may think, as long as free trade is not a politically live issue, why bring it up? Why not stick to advice that people are asking for or are receptive to—advice about *freer* trade.

ADVICE TO FREE-TRADERS

Lacking such restraint, we cannot resist giving free-traders some advice about what kinds of propaganda to use. First, they should avoid overstatement that draws ridicule or easy rebuttal. They shouldn't describe mere tariff policy as more crucial or the free-trade case as more overwhelming than either really is. There is no need to make American tariff policy a scapegoat for the world's economic troubles, or to make tariff reduction the cornerstone of a dream castle. Selling an illusion is out of place.* Representative Dent showed how easy it is to ridicule overstatements. He was referring to a State Department pamphlet on the *ABC's of Foreign Trade,* which details the many shortages that would develop if the United States stopped trading (which no one proposes):

> Does anyone believe that if we fail to pass H. R. 9900 we would be put in the position that this book puts us in by saying that when you wake up, you start down for breakfast, there is plenty of food but you will not be able to have your breakfast cocoa nor your tea and you cannot buy chocolate or bananas or tapioca or Brazilian cashew nuts. I know we would all die tomorrow if we did not have cashew nuts.[15]

Similarly, it is important to avoid suggesting that all concessions to protectionism, even in theory, are signs of ignorance. As Professor Viner said, it may not be bad advocacy to put some emphasis on the fragments of virtue in the opposition's arguments. Ignoring them or not giving them full weight is not going to work in the long run in winning public support.[16]

Second, free-traders should avoid an air of smug do-goodery. They should avoid implying that the United States has been the leading sinner in protectionism. Actually, American trade policy, especially since its

---

*Samuel Lubell uses words like these in criticizing propaganda for free of freer trade. See his *The Revolution in World Trade* (New York: Harper, 1955), especially p. 124.

change of direction from 1934 on, bears very slight responsibility for the world's troubles. Too much emphasis on our alleged responsibilities as a world leader takes attention away from the broad range of economic policies that serve our own self-interest and of which free international trade is mainly just a test and symbol.

Third, it is important to avoid undue emphasis on the world-politics aspect of trade policy, to the relative neglect of other aspects. The "trade in order to keep Japan on our side argument" is troublesome because it is only part of the story.

> In thus focusing on political considerations, we tend to agree with the proposition that trade is a kind of avoidable evil. We seem to say that we provide access to our market, reluctantly, as one of the prices for sustaining our political position in the world. Trade becomes another kind of foreign economic aid, closely related to the tensions of the cold war. If those tensions ever were relaxed, presumably we would consider it reasonable and desirable to reduce or abandon some parts of our foreign commerce.[17]

Fourth, it is wise to avoid linking the case for free trade too closely with a particular method of getting there. Free trade itself need not be discredited by the disadvantages of a particular approach to it. The international-negotiations approach, for example, may work. It may be politically more feasible than other approaches. Riding a fad may be wise opportunism. Still, overemphasis on international conferences and agreements and organizations reeks faintly of false internationalism (as compared with the genuine though unplanned internationalism of the years before 1914). It has an odor of "scientism"—a passion for doing things conspicuously, a vague feeling that results somehow don't "count" unless they have been specifically planned and arranged for and unless some definite party or organization or agreement gets credit for them. This passion for spurious tidiness links with failure to understand the coordination and orderliness that emerge spontaneously in a market economy.

The negotiations approach tends to sprinkle holy water on exceptions to the principle of freedom of trade. Protectionists can easily make fun of GATT: 66 words for its rule against quantitative trade restrictions, 3,500 words for the exceptions; GATT has us all living in legalized sin. Why bother getting agreement on the big print if the fine print takes it away? What justifies making concessions that seem to recognize the validity of protectionism in numerous cases, especially if the narrow material benefits of free trade are only a minor consideration in the minds of its supporters anyway? Why sacrifice the principle when the principle is the main thing in the first place?

Zeal for negotiations lets protectionists conjure up visions of impractical tea-sipping diplomats in striped pants bargaining away industries in deals with shrewd foreigners. Protectionists can complain about the secrecy of negotiations and the disproportionate voting power of small countries. The negotiations approach, especially when linked with domestic adjustment assistance, lets protectionists raise issues of unconstitutional delegation of authority, of excessive administrative discretion, and of scandalous executive immunity from judicial review. And some of these complaints may well be justified. In short, this method of moving toward freer trade, instead of limiting the scope of politics, as a free market is supposed to do, broadens it. While free-trade-minded politicians may find it expedient and necessary to form an alliance with emotional internationalists, free-traders should avoid infatuation with their approach, with gadgetry, and with minor political triumphs.

Our fifth warning is against opportunistically grasping at anything newsworthy to decorate the free-trade case with a veneer of topicality. Too much intermixture of illusions to current events, such as particular international negotiations and bills in Congress, will have the disadvantages mentioned near the beginning of Chapter Seven. The vogue of building the case for a more liberal trade policy around a core of references to the European Common Market is a case in point. In unintentionally linking the case for freer trade with particular historical circumstances, it tends to draw attention away from what is valid in the case for free markets generally.

POLITICAL "REALISM"

Our final and perhaps most important warning is against misguided practicality or political "realism." All too many people have metaphysical notions about historical "trends." For reasons too mysterious to specify, free trade is out of the question as a practical possibility for today's world. For example, in a committee hearing Senator Flanders asked Professor Don D. Humphrey whether, in a peaceful world, he would think of free trade as the ultimate good? Humphrey replied:

"I could only say I believe, Senator, what I have, that as long as I can see the expansion of trade as being mutually beneficial I think we all will be better for it, but I can't foresee the conditions under which completely free trade might be realized today."[18]

Note the hedging. To say that we will all be better for what is mutually beneficial is a tautology. As for what the witness could or could not foresee, the question asked for a recommendation, not a prophecy. And as for what might be realized today, the question was concerned, rather, with what the witness thought of as an *ultimate* good.

In another example, Mr. Walter Sterling Surrey of the U.S. Chamber of Commerce had the following exchange with Congressman Wilbur Mills, then chairman of the House Ways and Means Committee:

> Mr. Surrey. Obviously, the chamber and the chairman are on the same side of the fence. Obviously, we both want an operable free trade system.
>
> The Chairman. Freer trade. I don't think we could survive free trade.
>
> Mr. Surrey. We never achieve the ultimate.
>
> The Chairman. No.[19]

Congressman John Duncan led a witness from the League of Women Voters into the same line of thinking:

> Mr. Duncan. Don't you think that trade, to be free, also must be fair?
>
> Mrs. Benson. Yes, I do....
>
> Mr. Duncan. Would you think free trade across the board would be desirable?
>
> Mrs. Benson. Well, "free trade" I should clarify.
>
> Mr. Duncan. I think we have been exploring too much through the years. We have been talking about that so long that now we find ourselves in trouble.
>
> Mrs. Benson. The League of Women Voters is not in favor of free trade open with no qualifications, with no restrictions, with no governing rules of the game, as it were. We are in favor of liberal trade and in favor of multilateral negotiations and reciprocity. We believe very strongly that reciprocity means just exactly what it says—"You trade with us on this and we will trade with you on that" and so forth. These negotiations, of course, take an awfully long time to bring about and they are not easy and frequently are not successful.[20]

People who make knowing remarks like these get a reputation for being practical, reasonable, and realistic. Yet pursuit of such a reputation leads to muddy thinking. The British economist Sir Dennis Robertson has warned us not to mind whether or not the "temper of the age" makes some policy "politically impossible:" "Let us get the analysis right...." In a similar vein, Professor Albert Rees has decried trimming by economists turned amateur politicians: "Unless thinking people try to decide what the best policies are, and then try to influence actual policy in the appropriate direction, there is no point in discussing policy issues at all."[21]

Professor Clarence Philbrook has keenly dissected the "realistic" practice of compromising between giving the policy advice one really thinks best and giving the advice one thinks stands the best chance of being accepted. In balancing desirability against acceptability, what weight does the advisor give to each? How can he judge acceptability, anyway? The merits of a proposed policy can have great strength in overcoming its initial unacceptability. In the long run, what people think about economic issues depends largely on what beliefs economists either actively promote or passively allow to pass unchallenged. The true mission of expert advisors is the very opposite of adjusting to popular prejudice and misunderstanding. There is such a thing as planting "seeds of thought." Truth has an appeal in its own right. Furthermore, "realism" would become nonsense if all advisors tried to practice it. Each would be trying to adjust his advice to what he thought everyone else's would be; everyone would be trying to jump on everyone else's bandwagon.

"Realism" involves actively or passively concealing truth. It undermines scientific integrity. The "realist" gets his reputation for practicality and reasonableness by contrast with and at the expense of other advisors who view their responsibilities more conscientiously. By his political trimming, the "realist" strengthens a state of general opinion in which the policies he truly but secretly thinks best appear all the more extreme and unrealistic. He thereby unjustly casts the relatively few experts who do speak forthrightly all the more completely into the role of ivory-tower dreamers. He gets the chance to appear realistic only to the extent that other persons are honest; he takes special privilege for himself. In Philbrook's words, his behavior "rests upon an ethical atomism" barred by the principle "that a precept is unacceptable for one man unless it would have an acceptable outcome when followed by all." How, then, can a scholar's "immediate influence... upon practical affairs be deemed a matter of greater concern than the desirability of the direction of such influence as he does wield?" "Only one type of serious defense of a policy is open to an economist or anyone else: he must maintain that the policy is good."[22]

These remarks do not condemn *refraining* from policy advice and sticking to positive analysis. Nor do they condemn an advisor's answering a question about what policy he would consider second-best if his first-best policy were explicitly ruled out of consideration. He can quite honestly and honorably give advice on improving the administration of the customs service, the structure of tariff schedules, or the conduct of trade negotiations, for example, provided he avoids appearing to endorse what he considers bad and provided he explicitly states his immediate concern only with lessening the harm done by a basically harmful line of policy. This obligation follows from the obligation to be clear and not take refuge in a deceptive ambiguity.

It is probably true, though incidental, that outright advocacy of what one believes in will be more effective in the end than studied ambiguity or hedging. "Half a truth is not half so strong as a whole truth, and to minimize such a principle as that of free trade in the hope of disarming opposition, is to lessen its power of securing support in far greater degree than to lessen the antagonism it must encounter. A principle that in its purity will be grasped by the popular mind loses its power when befogged by concessions and enervated by compromises."[23] Failure to declare flatly for complete free trade seems like a tacit admission that it is harmful after all. People who call only for freer trade seem to be saying, "Don't get us wrong. We don't want to leap into the dreadful abyss of free trade; we just want to cavort closer to the brink." Others then take care to keep a good safe distance away. Besides, questions of a little less protection here, a little more there, do not pose a clear issue. It is not possible concretely to specify a rational stopping point between protection as it exists today and free trade. To allow exceptions to free trade (other, perhaps, than as national security requires) is to open the door to logrolling and a false consensus in support of protection. Free trade, on the other hand, is a discussable issue. As a matter of principle, it gives the legislator a reason for not helping his constituents get special privileges at the expense of almost everyone else.

Practical politicians are not always to be blamed for making tactical compromises; their job is rather different from that of expert advisors.* One should distinguish clearly, however, between the goal one is aiming at and the makeshift one accepts for a while as better than nothing. Error cannot be outwitted: it must be beaten head-on. As Professor Haberler writes in ending his book on *The Theory of International Trade*, the only way out is

> to fight the spirit of Protection, to spread far and wide correct ideas about international trade, and to confront the organised forces of sectional interests which support Protection with a powerful organisation drawn from those who suffer from it, that is, from the vast majority of the people of the world.[24]

---

*As Henry George wrote, "the zeal of the propagandist needs to be supplemented by the skill of the politician. While the one need not fear to arouse opposition, the other should seek to minimize resistance." (*Protection or Free Trade,* cited on p. 341.)

NOTES

1. 1970 HW&M I 143 (see Chapter 1, note 1).

2. 1970 HW&M II 651.

3. *Trade Reform Act of 1974,* Report of the Committee on Finance U.S. Congress, Senate, 93d Cong. 62d Sess., 1974, p. 79.

4. U.S. Tariff Commission, *Trade Barriers,* Chapter III, pp. 80-81; Chapter I, p. 7.

5. See Ibid., Chapter IV, pp. 12-13.

6. Ibid., pp. 27, 38, 47.

7. Ibid., Chapter VII, pp. 160-68.

8. Leland B. Yeager, *Free Trade: America's Opportunity* (New York: Schalkenbach Foundation, 1954), p. 76.

9. *Trade Reform Act of 1974,* Report of the Committee on Finance, p. 125.

10. John R. Hicks, "Free Trade and Modern Economics," in *Essays in World Economics* (Oxford: Clarendon Press, 1959), pp. 41-43.

11. Ibid., pp. 46, 52-53, 55-56, 65.

12. Ibid., pp. 42, 65.

13. Gottfried Haberler, "The Relevance of the Classical Theory under Modern Conditions," *American Economic Review,* May 1954, pp. 550-551.

14. Ibid., pp. 550-51.

15. 1962 HW&M V 2865 (see Chapter 1, note 9).

16. Jacob Viner, in *Foreign Economic Policy* (1962), p. 25.

17. Philip H. Trezise, Deputy Assistant Secretary of State for Economic Affairs, speech of January 25, 1962, reprinted in 1962 HW&M V 2841-42.

18. In *Foreign Economic Policy,* hearing before a subcommittee of the Committee on the Economic Report (Washington, D.C.: Government Printing Office, 1955), p. 337.

19. 1970 HW&M IV 1055-56 (see Chapter 1, note 1).

20. 1973 HW&M IX 3006 (see Chapter 1, note 8).

21. Dennis Robertson, "A Revolutionist's Handbook," *Quarterly Journal of Economics,* February 1950, p. 13, and Albert Rees, "Wages and Inflation" (mimeographed technical paper for the American Assembly, Graduate School of Business, Columbia University, undated but around 1951), p. 21.

22. Clarence E. Philbrook, " 'Realism' in Policy Espousal," *American Economic Review,* December 1953, pp. 846-59.

23. Henry George, *Protection or Free Trade,* (New York: Doubleday, Page, 1905), p. 337.

24. Gottfried von Haberler, *The Theory of International Trade,* trans. Alfred Stonier and Frederic Benham (London: Hodge, 1936), p. 393.

SUBJECT INDEX

absolute advantage, 47-48, 52
absolute disadvantage, 47
acreage-reduction system, 220
adjustment assistance, 260-63, 283
adjustment costs of trade liberalization, 249-51, 279
administered pricing, 34, 75, 80
administrative uncertainties, 8
advertising, 9, 17, 29, 31-33
aggregation bias of dead loss, estimates, 57, 65-66
allocation of scarce resources, 17-21
allocative harm from: quadrupling of oil prices, 152; quotas, 61-62, 72-73; monopoly, 26-28, 72-73; tariffs, 54-67, 72-73
altruism, 132-36
American Selling Price, 7, 51
antidumping rules, 8, 125-30
antitrust law, 5, 31, 33
"artificial costs" argument for protection, 185-86
ASP (see, American Selling Price)
average cost, 17, 229
average product of labor, 165-66

balance of payments: argument for protection, 99, 100-03, 105; balancing processes, 93-98, 179, 227; choices concerning, 107; crisis in, 100-01, 181, 223-24, 227; deficits in, 89-90, 91-93, 98, 102, 106, 159; definition of, 90-91; future of, 105-07; inflation and, 100-03; petrodollars and, 103-05; policies, 97-99; protectionism and, 89-90; surplus in, 91-93, 98, 102
balance of trade, definition of, 102
balanced growth, 238
border tax adjustments, 9
bounty (see, subsidy)
Brannan Plan, 155
Bretton Woods system, 89 (see also, fixed exchange rates)
Burke-Hartke proposals, 2, 124, 173-74, 177
Buy-American rules, 7-8, 188, 277

capital controls, 89, 99-100

capital exports, 177-80
capitalism, 3, 81
capital-market imperfections, 234
capital movements, 89-107
central bank: intervention, 98-99, 107, 223; transactions, 91, 100-01
Central Intelligence Agency, 177
central planning, 17, 21-24, 217, 237-39 (see also, economic systems)
cheap-foreign-goods, 139
cheap-foreign-labor argument for protection, 97, 123, 131-41, 162, 166, 175, 255
cheap labor, 50, 138, 226
cheapness, 15-16, 50, 52, 141
CIA (see, Central Intelligence Agency)
citizens' sovereignty, 22, 84
cold-war tactics and strategy, 116n, 155
commodity agreements, 71
Communism, 149
comparative advantage, principle of, 47-50, 52, 137-44, 179, 226, 228, 237, 240
compensation principle, 260, 264, 265
competition, 15-18, 53, 108; fair, 125, 142; unfair, 120-31, 141, 144; workable, 279
concentration in business, 29, 33, 79-80
confiscation (see, expropriation)
constructed value, 127
consumers' sovereignty, 21-23, 84
consumption, essentiality or non-essentiality of, 9, 31-33, 38, 72, 86, 159-62, 241
consumption cost, 55-56, 64, 65, 151, 181, 216, 232; bias in estimating, 60-61; of quotas, 61
consumption gain from trade, 41-44
corporation income tax, 178
countervailing duty, 8, 130-31
Court of Customs and Patent Appeals, 6, 127
Customs Court, 127
customs procedures, 6-7

dead loss: from trade restrictions, 54-67; from oil price rise, 151-52; from a revenue tariff, 187; from a terms-of-trade tariff, 195
defense argument for protection, 116, 117, 147-51, 155-57, 171, 279, 286

291

LELAND B. YEAGER is Paul Goodloe McIntire Professor of Economics at the University of Virginia. He has served as Visiting Professor at Southern Methodist University and the University of California, Los Angeles, and has taught as a regular faculty member at Texas A & M University and the University of Maryland. He received his A.B. from Oberlin College and his M.A. and Ph.D. from Columbia University. He was President of the Southern Economic Association, 1974-75.

Professor Yeager has written on price theory, monetary theory and history, international trade and finance, and social philosophy. He is the author of *International Monetary Relations*.

DAVID G. TUERCK is Director, Center for Research on Advertising, American Enterprise Institute for Public Policy Research, Washington, D.C. He was Associate Professor of Economics, California State College, Bakersfield, and subsequently, Director of Research, Center for International Business during his work on this book.

In addition to *Trade Policy and the Price System,* also with Leland Yeager, he has written several articles in international economics, public finance, and human capital and is editor, with Patrick M. Boarman, of *World Monetary Disorder.* He has been a consultant to the Continental Illinois National Bank and has served on the faculty of the University of Illinois at Chicago Circle.

Dr. Tuerck received his A.B. and A.M. degrees from the George Washington University and his Ph.D. from the University of Virginia.

AMERICAN LABOR AND THE MULTINATIONAL CORPORATION
edited by Duane Kujawa

ECONOMIC INTEGRATION AND THE LAW OF GATT
Pierre Lortie

THE GATT SYSTEM AND WORLD TRADE DIPLOMACY
Robert E. Hudec

GATT PLUS—A PROPOSAL FOR TRADE REFORM: With the Text
of the General Agreement

Atlantic Council of the
United States

INTERNATIONAL LABOR AND THE MULTINATIONAL
ENTERPRISE

edited by Duane Kujawa

MULTINATIONAL CORPORATIONS AND GOVERNMENT: Business-
Government Relations in an International Context

edited by Patrick M. Boarman
and Hans Schollhammer

WORLD MONETARY DISORDER: National Policies vs. International
Imperatives

edited by Patrick M. Boarman
and David G. Tuerck